REAL WORLD

Print Production

with Adobe® Creative Cloud®

INDUSTRIAL-STRENGTH PRODUCTION TECHNIQUES

CLAUDIA McCUE

ADOBE
PRESS

REAL WORLD PRINT PRODUCTION WITH ADOBE CREATIVE CLOUD
Claudia McCue

Copyright © 2014 by Claudia McCue

For the latest on Adobe Press books, go to www.adobepress.com
This Adobe Press book is published by Peachpit
To report errors, please send a note to errata@peachpit.com
Peachpit is a division of Pearson Education

Project Editor: Susan Rimerman
Production Editor: Maureen Forys, Happenstance Type-O-Rama
Copy Editor: Kelly Kordes Anton
Technical Editor: Chad Chelius
Proofreader: Suki Gear
Compositor: Craig Woods, Happenstance Type-O-Rama
Indexer: James Minkin
Cover Design: Charlene Charles Will
Cover Illustration: Alicia Buelow

ISBN-10 0-321-97032-2
ISBN-13 978-032197032-9

9 8 7 6 5 4 3 2 1

Table of Contents

Introduction

Much has changed in the realm of printing since the original edition of this book. Film has been almost totally abandoned in favor of direct-to-plate imaging, and the quality of digital printing processes rivals that of traditional offset. Updating the book has been a bit like time travel, as I deleted sections devoted to processes that have fallen by the wayside and expanded portions that described new-at-the-time techniques that are now commonplace.

I'm not a designer—I'm a printing geek. I spent half my life in prepress, troubleshooting, fixing jobs, and meeting impossible deadlines. I still love printing. I love the heavy rhythm of presses, the smell of the chemicals, the beehive bustle of a pressroom. I love to see paper roll in one end of the press and printed sheets fly out the other end. I hope I can pass some of this printing love on to you.

Who Should Read This Book

If you are a designer or a production artist who would like a better understanding of the pitfalls you encounter when using Adobe Creative Cloud software, you'll find lots of pointers in this book to help you avoid problems. Almost all software provides options that are tempting to choose but are dangerous under some circumstances. It's good to know which buttons *not* to push—and why.

Photoshop, Illustrator, and InDesign form a powerful ecosystem. Consequently, choices you make in Photoshop can limit your options when you place an image in InDesign. Options you choose in InDesign can affect the quality of the PDF you create. And so on. You need an aerial view of the programs' capabilities so you can anticipate the outcome. It would help if you were psychic, too, but that's another book entirely.

I believe that the more designers undertstand about the physical requirements of the printing process, the more easily they can avoid problems. This book can explain why your printer sometimes asks you to modify your designs for print. Better yet, you can beat them to it, and they will compliment you on how well-prepared your jobs always are.

If you are an in-house designer or marketing department member, you may have been thrown into the deep end, suddenly given the responsibility of preparing work for print. This book may help you understand the mysterious new world of print.

If you are a prepress production operator, you'll find many reminders of subtle problems that can lurk in graphics or page layouts. If you're new to printing, you'll find beneficial insights into what's happening on the other side of the pressroom door. And if you're looking for a gentle way to educate clients who keep submitting nightmare jobs, well, a book always makes a nice gift, doesn't it?

For purchasing this book, you are also entitled to bonus Chapter 14, "Print Production Resources." To download, register your book at peachpit.com/register. Create an account if you don't have one (it's free!). Then add this isbn: 0321970322. Look for the content on the "My Registered Products" page and click "Access Bonus Content." If you purchased an ebook, bonus Chapter 14 is already included at the end.

What This Book Is Not

If you're in the market for a hot-tips-and-tricks book, this isn't it. It's not a guide for stunning special effects (unless you consider it a special effect to get your job to print as expected). And, although this book demonstrates how to do some useful things in the Adobe Creative Cloud programs, it isn't strictly a how-to book either. In fact, there's quite a bit of how-*not*-to.

Are there any prerequisites for using this book? Only two, really. First, you should have basic proficiency with your computer and operating system, as well as the basics of InDesign, Illustrator, and Photoshop. The other requirement is arguably more important: You should have a healthy curiosity about the printing process and a desire to build problem-free files.

About the Author

I was a chemistry major. Really. But I had a knack for illustration, and I took some college art classes for extra credit. One of my instructors (Michael Parkes, who has since become a well-known fine artist in Europe) suggested that I change my career path from chemistry to commercial art. I thought, "Well, I'll try it for a while," and took a job at a printing plant that summer. A funny thing happened: I fell in love with printing and never went back to the lab. (Thanks, Michael.) Printing turned out to be the perfect environment for someone who held the dual titles of Class Clown and Science Student of the Year.

NOTE You know you've been in printing a long time if:

- Your grocery list has hanging indents.

- Your driver's license lists your eye color as PANTONE 5757.

- Your shoe size is 6½ plus ⅛-inch bleed.

- You refer to painting your house as a two-color job.

- You decide to write a book called *Real World Print Production with Adobe Creative Cloud*.

As a prepress production person, I always enjoyed troubleshooting, discovering new techniques, and sharing those discoveries with coworkers. I started in conventional paste-up and then moved into film stripping. (It's not what you think. See the glossary in Chapter 1, "Life Cycle of a Print Job.") And I was extremely fortunate (or cursed) to be one of the very early operators of color electronic prepress systems in the United States, so I've been pushing pixels around for a *long* time. Then, because it could perform the same magic as a Scitex or Crosfield system (minus the million-dollar price tag), Adobe Photoshop lured me to desktop computers.

I always believed in educating customers so they wouldn't be intimidated by the mysteries of printing. Not surprisingly, that led to my second career as a trainer, consultant, writer, and presenter at industry conferences.

Acknowledgments

I'm passing on to you some of the Basic Printing Truths imparted to me by a number of fine old printing curmudgeons. Count yourself truly lucky if you're befriended by a craftsman like Rick Duncan, who came up through the ranks, learned how to do everything the old-fashioned way, and was always patient with a kid asking too many questions.

I'm part of an informal fraternity of graphic arts aficionados. While we each have our specialties, our common bond is the love of learning and sharing new tricks. David Blatner, Scott Citron, Sandee "Vector Babe" Cohen, Anne-Marie Concepción, Bob Levine, and Mike Rankin are my InDesign brethren (and sistren), going back to the days when we were considered page-layout rebels. Mordy Golding's passion for Illustrator is contagious, and he shares my devotion to enlightening designers in the mysteries of print.

It's priceless to have friends on the inside at Adobe Systems: Dov Isaacs and Lonn Lorenz have been generous with their dry humor and no-nonsense advice on PostScript and PDF for years. And Noha Edell has long provided inspirational support and encouragement. PDF Sage Leonard Rosenthol has frequently enlightened me on arcane Acrobat mysteries.

I'm pleased to have the opportunity to update this book for Creative Cloud; it's sort of like reincarnation. It's truly gratifying that the first two editions have been used as textbooks in some schools. Thanks to Kelly Kordes Anton for policing my commas and technical editor Chad Chelius for ensuring that I wasn't spreading any myths. Thanks to Suki Gear, Craig Woods, and Maureen Forys for their proofreading, composition, and production work, and James Minkin for crafting the index.

Now go out there and make me proud!

Life Cycle of a Print Job

1

Most consumers don't wonder about the origins of all those catalogs and ads in their mailboxes. They don't think about the design process, and certainly give no thought to those poor guys on third shift in the printing plant trying to troubleshoot a problem job. They're not concerned with the mechanical process of printing. All they think is, "Wow! That really looks good—and it's on sale! I should buy this!" As far as they're concerned, somebody makes pretty pictures on a computer, then somebody else presses a button, then—poof!—there's a printed piece in their hands.

As a designer or production artist, you should know what happens when you're finished with your part of the process. The more you know, the more you can do to prevent problems—and missed deadlines—later in the life cycle of your job.

First, a little history. This is the "you kids don't know how good you have it" part. Why, we didn't even have pixels...

NOTE: See the glossary at the end of this chapter for more detailed explanations of some common printing terms, both modern and historical, used in this chapter and throughout the book. Terms that are italicized in this chapter's text are explained in the glossary, which also includes additional terms you may find helpful.

The Olden Days

In the early 1980s (probably before some of you were born), the responsibilities in the graphic arts professions were rather clearly defined, and there wasn't much overlap of skills or responsibility. Designers might know a bit about prepress and printing endeavors, but they usually weren't required to perform any work typical of those operations. Design was a more hands-on process involving more hand drawing and pen-and-ink work. Production artists created page layouts by gluing down photo prints with wax or rubber cement to a piece of thick illustration board, creating a *mechanical* (short for mechanical artwork). We did type corrections with X-Acto® knives and rubber cement, sometimes going home at the end of a long day with words glued to our elbows and the occasional consonant stuck in our hair. Who knows—maybe that was the inspiration for refrigerator magnet poetry.

The design and print process moved at a slower pace than it does today, largely out of necessity. It's certainly not that we were more patient in those days—it's just that all that handwork took time. There was more specialization. Dedicated typesetters generated text using phototypesetting equipment (after the demise of lead-based hot type), trade shops were specialized graphics houses, which employed cameramen to create color separations and shoot line shots of mechanicals, and dot etchers performed color corrections by etching film with acid solutions to change the size of the dots.

Film strippers combined line shots and color separation films from the camera to create final page film. Page proofs were created by exposing the final composed page films onto photosensitive materials. Color Key proofs consisted of individual color overlays, one for each printing ink. Matchprint proofs consisted of color layers laminated to printing stock. And Cromalin proofs were made by dusting pigment onto a sticky image. Sounds primitive now, perhaps, but we were high tech in our day! Now, digital proofs may use the same brand names, but they're created in a very different manner. And, like many brand names, the term "color key" is now sometimes used as a generic term referring to color proofs.

Proofs and film were given to the printer, where imposition took place (although some trade shops also did imposition and shipped plate-ready films). Bluelines (single-color proofs that actually weren't always blue) were exposed from the imposed flats and then folded up to check the mechanics of the page contents and imposition. Plates were burned from the imposed flats, then mounted on the press. Using the page proofs from the trade shop, pressmen adjusted ink coverage on the press during the process of getting the press up to speed and the ink behavior optimal—referred to as makeready. Then, when everything was up to speed, the customer might be asked to attend a press check to assure that everything looked good. Some of these processes, such as Cromalin proofing, no longer take place. Some have morphed into digital versions. Imposed bluelines, for example, have largely been replaced by output from large-format inkjet printers. Press makeready has been streamlined by technological advances. Press checks, on the other hand, are much the same as they have always been.

In those (relatively) ancient times, the workflow looked something like **Figure 1.1**. There were variations, of course. Some design houses had in-house typesetting and photography, and some trade shops supplied finished plates to printers. Some printers had in-house designers as well as prepress departments to perform trade shop functions. And then, as now, some printers used outside firms to perform specialty finishing such as emboss-ing, foil stamping, and die cutting.

The introduction of electronic scanners and color electronic prepress systems (CEPS) revolutionized the art of color separation. What had been a nuanced and specialized undertaking involving masking, tricky exposures, and chemical baths became accessible to a wider range of graphic arts pro-fessionals. Old instincts for camera work and dot etching were channeled into scanning and onscreen color correction. It was a wonderful new world. And our hands healed up as a result.

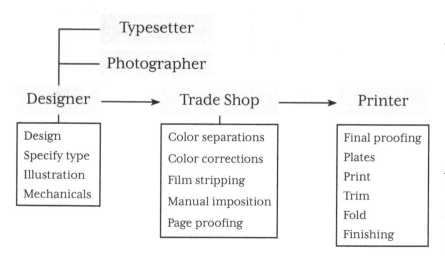

Figure 1.1 *Historically, functions were divided between trades and profes-sions that specialized in an individual aspect of graphic arts and printing. Designers designed, trade shops assem-bled all the pieces, and print-ers printed and performed finishing. Typesetters and photographers were usually independent providers. The advent of desktop publish-ing changed this ecosystem radically.*

Brave New World: Desktop Publishing

With the appearance of the first Apple® desktop units, computers were no longer quite so foreign and mysterious to The Rest of Us. In 1985, the advent of page-layout programs such as Ready, Set, Go!® and Aldus PageMaker® made the computer a replacement for X-Acto knives and hot wax applicators.

Adobe's PostScript® page-description language brought laser printers to life and turned them into viable output devices for camera-ready art. Soon, what had been the sole province of specialized craftsmen became a public playing field. The good news? Anyone with a computer, a page-layout program, and an Apple LaserWriter® could now do much of the work involved in publishing. Tasks that had traditionally been performed in trade shops were accomplished by desktop computer users.

Page-layout applications began to replace the separate jobs of setting type, creating mechanicals, and stripping film. Adobe Photoshop became the most widespread tool for retouching and color correction, seriously eroding the market for the million-dollar, high-end CEPS. New desktop publishers leap-frogged the former apprentice-to-journeyman training of printing craftsmen and had to hit the ground running. And while the capabilities of electronic systems accelerated the pace in the industry and redistributed the tasks, it also redistributed the responsibilities. The distribution of labor began to look more like **Table 1.1**.

While these innovations democratized the world of design and print, they also put powerful tools in the hands of users who often had no understanding of the requirements of print. The process of self-education could be an expensive one—and that's still true today.

Every click of the mouse when you're creating content has repercussions far down the line. Your choice of colors, the dimensions of your document, the program you use—all of these have an impact on the success of the job when that enormous printing press cranks up.

No pressure, right?

Before we tackle some of the requirements of printing and the behavior of some of your favorite design programs, we'll take a look at what happens to your job when it leaves your hands.

	Designer	Photographer	Printer	Other
Design	●		○	
Illustration	○			○
Page layout	●		○	
Photography	○	○	○	
Scanning	○	○	○	
Color correction	○	○	○	
Retouching	○	○	○	
Imposition			●	
Page proofing			●	
Final proofing			●	
Burn plates			●	
Print			●	
Finishing (fold/trim/bind)			●	○
Die cutting			○	○
Embossing			○	○
Foil stamping			○	○

● = Primary vendor   ○ = Possible vendors

Table 1.1 *Who does what? Since the advent of desktop publishing put professional-level tools in the hands of everyone, the design and production tasks are no longer so strictly defined. While it's unlikely that a designer would also be the pressman on a job, designers and photographers now take on tasks that were only performed by niche specialists in the past.*

Job Submission

Your method of submitting files will depend on your print service provider's requirements. Chapter 8, "Job Submission," is devoted to these issues, including some helpful checklists to aid you if your print service provider doesn't provide a similar guide.

Scenic Tour of a Typical Printing Plant

Depending on the size and structure of your print service provider, some of the functions described in this section might be combined. For example, in some companies, job planning might be done by a dedicated planner, customer service representatives, or an estimator. And some prepress departments make no distinction between preflight (looking for potential job problems) and production—they just watch for problems as they prepare a job for later prepress functions. The departments are described in the approximate order in which they handle your job. **Figure 1.2** provides an aerial view of a fictional printing company to give you a general idea of job flow.

The flow of a job in a given printing company is governed by the company's capabilities and the type of work it performs. For example, a small printing company that specializes in business collateral such as letterheads, business cards, and envelopes is not likely to have binding equipment such as saddle stitchers or custom inline inkjet heads for on-press personalization or address printing.

Sales

Typically, the print salesperson will be your first contact and will set things in motion for you by initiating your job's entry into the printing plant's workflow. At this early point in the life of the job, it's important to discuss any concerns and expectations you have about the job. Learn as much as you can about the processes that will be used in manufacturing your job. If your job will require any special stock such as vellum or heavy cover stock, discuss this with the salesperson. Also discuss any special finishing treatments that will be used, such as embossing or die cutting. The salesperson

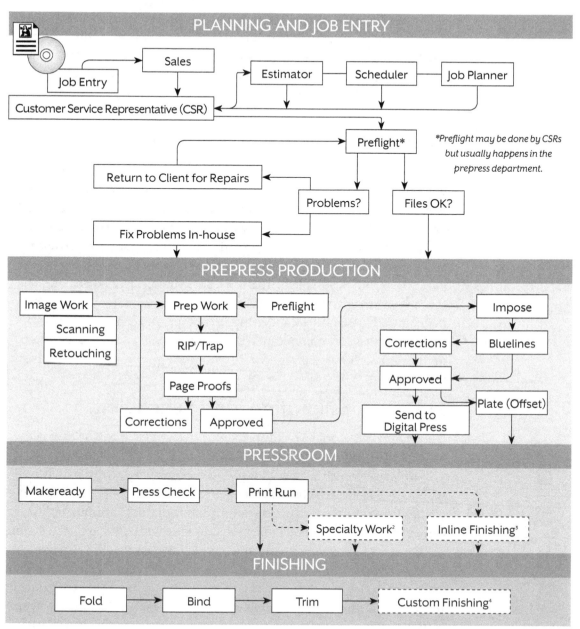

PLANNING AND JOB ENTRY

Job Entry → Sales

Sales → Customer Service Representative (CSR)

Estimator — Scheduler — Job Planner

Estimator, Scheduler, Job Planner → Customer Service Representative (CSR)

Preflight*

*Preflight may be done by CSRs but usually happens in the prepress department.

Return to Client for Repairs ← Problems?

Files OK?

Fix Problems In-house ← Problems?

PREPRESS PRODUCTION

Image Work
- Scanning
- Retouching

Image Work → Prep Work ← Preflight

Prep Work → RIP[1]/Trap → Page Proofs

Page Proofs → Corrections / Approved

Impose → Bluelines → Corrections → Approved

Approved → Send to Digital Press

Approved → Plate (Offset)

PRESSROOM

Makeready → Press Check → Print Run

Print Run ⇢ Specialty Work[2]

Print Run ⇢ Inline Finishing[3]

FINISHING

Fold → Bind → Trim → Custom Finishing[4]

[1] RIP = Raster Image Processor. See glossary at the end of this chapter for full definition.
[2] Specialty press work includes add-ons such as inline personalization, varnishing, and fragrance application.
[3] Inline finishing includes on-press trimming and folding.
[4] Custom finishing includes die cutting, embossing, foil stamping, and hand assembly.

Figure 1.2 *Job flow in a typical printing company. Your mileage may vary. Some printers divide departments differently, and some use external suppliers for operations such as custom finishing. Dashed lines indicate functions that may not be performed by all print service providers.*

will probably be the person who provides you with an estimate of job costs and gives you an idea of the timeline of the job's trip through the printing plant. Initially, the salesperson may be your primary contact, but your job will probably be assigned to a customer service representative (CSR) early in the life of the job.

Customer Service Representative

After you submit your job files, the CSR is likely to become your prime contact point throughout the remainder of the job. If the production staff has any questions about how job issues should be handled, they'll ask the CSR to call or email you for the answer. If you need to send corrected or updated files, you may be asked to contact the CSR rather than the salesperson, because the CSR is closer to the action and more likely to know the current status of your job in the workflow. A skilled, proactive CSR is your best friend and often has the foresight to help you anticipate and prevent problems. Ideally, the CSR is fluent in both design-speak and printing concepts and can act as a translator to keep the lines of communication open between you and production staff for the duration of the job.

Planning, Estimating, and Scheduling

Once your job is accepted by the print service provider, it will be assigned a job number and identifying name, such as *123456 Smithco Annual Report*. This information will become part of a printed job ticket, which will travel with the job materials. The job ticket will be affixed to a physical job jacket containing job materials such as your digital media, inkjet comps, or laser comps you supplied, and other pertinent pieces that are accumulated during the life of the job. In some environments, digital job tickets are also used. Eventually, the job jacket may contain intermediate proofs, instructions for correction cycles, and approved final proofs to be used as a reference during the press run. The attached job ticket serves as a job identifier and job information reference as the materials travel through the printing plant. Some printing plants use bar codes on their job tickets to aid in job tracking, but many rely on plant employees to note a job's process by making entries in computer-based tracking systems.

Job ticketing conventions vary among printing companies, but the job ticket will contain vital information about the job's requirements and specifications, including information such as:

- Job number (a unique identifier assigned at the print service provider)

- Client contact information

- Internal contacts (salesperson, CSR)

- Intended press

- Inks, including specially mixed inks

- Due dates (final print, as well as intermediate events such as page proofs and bluelines)

- Line screen

- Custom handling required, such as special folding, embossing, or other finishing operations

Planners establish the basic flow of your job, including its timeline. The timeline identifies when each segment of the job will take place and how the print service provider can wedge your job into the total schedule of jobs occurring at the same time. They may also plan how jobs will run on press to take advantage of available time—for example, your job may be combined with another client's similar job to run simultaneously and save on the time and materials devoted to makeready.

Like air traffic controllers, *schedulers* track all the jobs running through a printing plant at any given time. They have to ensure that all the plant's equipment is kept humming and that deadlines are met. As they juggle all the live jobs in the plant, they have to take into consideration any jobs whose progress hits a snag. They're constantly rearranging indicators on large scheduling boards, which resemble huge bulletin boards or whiteboards with all jobs represented by identifying tickets or labels.

Estimators determine job costs, including labor, paper, ink, and proofing materials, as well as press time and bindery time. In some plants, estimating and planning tasks are combined. Once the estimating and planning groundwork is laid, the job is often subjected to a preflight process. In some printing plants, preflight is performed by CSRs. In most plants, however, preflight is done in the prepress department.

Preflight

On its way to prepress production, your job will usually be run through a preflight process to check for problems with setup and content. Don't take it personally. It's better to find problems early in the job rather than later when deadlines loom. For files from programs such as Adobe Illustrator® or InDesign®, many prepress departments use dedicated preflight software such as FlightCheck® from Markzware. Some departments rely on dedicated preflight operators to manually check files for problems, and some combine FlightCheck with manual checks geared toward the printer's particular workflow. To preflight submitted PDF files, many print service providers use PDF-specific software such as Enfocus PitStop or the print production tools in Adobe Acrobat® Professional. However preflight is performed, when problems are found, you may be asked whether you'd like to fix the problems yourself or incur a charge for letting the printer fix them. Common problems include issues such as lack of sufficient bleed, overset text, incorrect or extraneous spot colors, or wrong document size.

Preflight personnel are also often responsible for organizing job files into a standard folder hierarchy used by the printing plant.

Prepress

These days, many prepress departments refer to themselves as electronic prepress departments, a holdover from earlier days when the computer-based activities were a parallel process, and manual prepress activities such as film stripping still encompassed much of the work. But now you'd be hard-pressed to find extensive stripping capabilities in all but the smallest shops. As long as plates were still being exposed manually from large film flats, strippers would be called upon to make last-minute corrections by taping out or grafting in replacement film pieces. But with the overwhelming move to computer-to-plate (CTP), dedicated film strippers and their light tables are increasingly rare.

Production

Even if there are no true errors in the way the file is built, it's possible that prepress production operators may still need to tweak your job to get it ready for other parts of the workflow, such as raster image processing (RIPping), trapping, and imposition.

For example, if your job contains large solid areas of black, the prepress production operator may replace the single black ink with a rich-black mix such as C60-M40-Y40-K100 to facilitate a good outcome on an offset press. Gradients created in Illustrator or InDesign are sometimes replaced with Photoshop gradients to prevent a banded appearance in output. Such alterations are for the purposes of improving print quality on the chosen press and are not usually charged to the customer.

Digital Photography

As digital photography has widely supplanted film photography, it's likely that most of your photographs will be submitted as digital images, whether you shot the images, hired a photographer, or used stock photography. Initially, many of these images are supplied as RGB files; some printers prefer that images be in CMYK when they receive your job, unless they are using a color-managed workflow that fully supports RGB images. For more information on converting RGB images to CMYK, see Chapter 4, "Preparing Raster Images." Don't assume you need to convert your RGB images, though—digital presses handle RGB content well, and you may even get richer color with RGB images. Ask the printer what you should submit.

Scanning

If you're using artwork such as drawings, paintings, or photographic prints as artwork, the artwork will have to be scanned. Whether scanning is performed by you, the print service provider, or someone else, you should expect to see random proofs—raw, individual proofs of the artwork before the images are placed into the layout—so that you can determine at an early stage whether color correction or retouching will be necessary. Even the best scan may not be able to initially capture your intent for the image because of the limitations inherent in the scanning process and the inherent difficulty of reproducing some colors in the standard CMYK printing inks. Color correction can compensate for some of these issues, but be prepared for the limitations of CMYK (see Chapter 2, "Ink on Paper," for more on these issues). Early random proofs will prepare you for the appearance of images in the final printed piece.

Image Work

If you're not comfortable with creating clipping paths or performing other image manipulations such as retouching, color correction, or compositing, specialists in the prepress department will do those things. Many prepress operators are accomplished Photoshop users with a good eye for color and knowledge of what works best in the printing environment.

Raster Image Processor (RIP)

Believe it or not, "We RIPped your file" is good news. At its most basic, a RIP interprets the incoming page-description (PostScript or PDF) information and converts that data to a literal bitmap image that instructs the marking engine of the output device how to image the plates or—in the case of toner-based printers—the electrostatic drum (**Figure 1.3**). The RIP governing a large-format inkjet printer controls how ink is laid down on paper. Many RIPs also perform other operations, such as trapping.

Figure 1.3 *A raster image processor (RIP) is a dedicated computer running special-ized software that converts PostScript or PDF files into bitmapped information used by an imaging device such as a platesetter, digital press, or inkjet printer. Since each manufacturer's RIP consists of proprietary hardware and software, capabilities differ among vendors.*

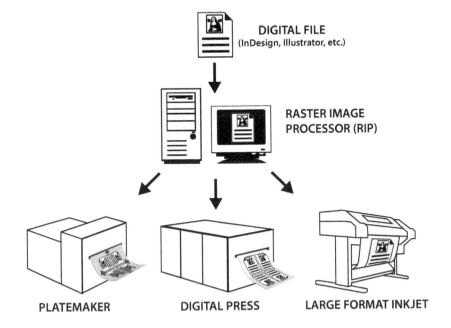

In some workflows, individual pages are processed by the RIP and then combined in imposition software. In other workflows, PDF or PostScript files for individual pages are imposed, and the imposed file is processed by the RIP.

PostScript is actually a programming language that is used to describe and define pages so that output devices know how to image those pages. PDF files contain information that's much like PostScript (and in fact shares many of the concepts of PostScript). But PDFs can also contain information, such as transparency, which goes beyond the capabilities of the PostScript language. Some RIPs take in PDFs but internally convert them to PostScript for further processing. Whereas RIPs have traditionally feasted on PostScript, most manufacturers' RIPs now handle native PDF files.

The Adobe PDF Print Engine

PostScript has given us many years of fine imaging service since its initial release in 1984, but it has its limits: For example, it doesn't support live, unflattened transparency. The Adobe PDF Print Engine, currently at version 3, is not a software product that end users purchase and install: It's used by vendors in their RIP products. Workflows from Kodak, Heidelberg, AGFA, Océ, Xerox, and other manufacturers incorporate the PDF Print Engine. RIPs using the PDF Print Engine haven't dropped support for PostScript; they've added support for the expanded capabilities of PDFs.

Trapping

It's necessary to compensate for slight errors in the alignment of the printing inks as they're laid down sequentially on press. Trapping provides a combination of colors at the edges of abutting color areas to camouflage any slippage. See Chapter 2, "Ink on Paper," for an in-depth description of trapping and why it's necessary. Trapping requirements vary according to printing conditions, and it's best left to prepress professionals. Whereas in the past trapping was accomplished within originating applications such as Illustrator or with dedicated trapping software, the majority of trapping now takes place at the RIP.

NOTE The Adobe PDF Print Engine provides support for JDF job ticketing schemes and variable data printing (VDP) as well as faster and more streamlined processing of files. What does this mean to you? It can translate to faster processing, more reliable output, and difficulty imaging jobs containing transparency, such as drop shadows applied to objects.

Imposition

Using the job information provided by planners, imposition operators combine individual pages in the proper pagination for plating. In some companies, separate groups handle prepress operations (such as preflight) and plating functions (such as imposition). This allows specialized operators to perform plate-related tasks while general prepress operators continue to do preflight and production. For a more detailed description of imposition, see Chapter 3, "Binding and Finishing."

Proofing

Several different rounds—and several different kinds—of proofing may occur in the life of a job:

- Random proofs of images early in the job help determine whether color correction or retouching is needed, especially for color-critical work such as product catalogs.

- Desktop printer output may be used for internal checks of the content of pages after preflight and before proceeding to prepress production.

- Color or single-color proofs (often called bluelines) after prepress production are used for customer markup or approval before proceeding to imposition and output to plates. This type of proof is intended for checking mechanical content, looking for typos, and finding incorrectly placed images.

- Online soft proofs are onscreen proofs (usually PDF-based). Soft proofs are faster than waiting for a proof to print, but unless your monitor is fully calibrated, it is difficult to judge color. It may also be a challenge to judge pagination issues such as crossovers.

- Color proofs of finished pages are used as guides for color matching on press. The proofs may be single page proofs, proofs of reader spreads, or proofs of multiple pages in their final imposed position. These proofs are viewed under controlled conditions in a viewing booth, which is painted a neutral gray and uses special lights for a standardized environment. The color temperature (5000–6500° K) is intended to mimic daylight. (The K stands for Kelvin, a thermodynamic temperature scale.) You may be asked to sign these proofs to indicate that you approve of the color and the content of the pages. This is often referred to as a contract proof, because it constitutes a contract between you and the printer. Your approval of the proof implies that you're satisfied with the appearance of the proof. The printer is then expected to match the appearance of the contract proof on the press.

- Blueline folded comps, created after imposition, are used on press and in the bindery to check page position and content.

Corrections

Printer alterations are sometimes the result of mistakes that are made during production, but they can also be voluntary changes performed by the printer to ensure satisfactory printing under the required press or bindery conditions. For example, if there are large, solid color areas in a single ink, the printer may elect to print that area with two separate applications of the same ink to achieve a uniform appearance on press. Since this is elective, such an alteration is not chargeable to the customer.

Artist alterations (AAs), also called customer alterations, are alterations requested by the designer or the designer's client. AAs include such changes as text changes, replacing images, or moving content. Charges vary depending on the complexity of the change and the stage in the job at which the change is requested. For example, adding a comma at the preflight stage might be a freebie, whereas adding it after the job is on the press might require stopping the press, correcting the affected page, resending it through the RIP, retrapping, reimposing, and burning a new plate (or more if the comma affects multiple colors). The new plate (or plates) must be mounted on press and the makeready process repeated. The expense of labor, materials, and lost press time could be considerable. Once the job is pulled off press, you've lost your slot in the production cycle and, depending on how busy the presses are, you may wait a day or more for another opportunity to run your job.

Creating Plates

In the earlier days of electronic desktop publishing, film was output for individual pages and then taped down in flats on large, clear carrier sheets in the proper printing position. (A flat is just that: a flat carrier sheet with one or more pieces of film in final position.) These imposed flats were used to expose printing plates with powerful light sources. Because intermediate films were stripped and combined to create the page films, and then the page films were used to expose the plates (or to create huge, composite single films for each plate), some tiny details could be eroded by the multiple generations of exposures. Any errors in aligning the individual pieces would affect the quality on press.

The introduction of computer-to-plate (CTP) revolutionized this process. In a CTP workflow, the imposition is digitally created, and then the printing plate is directly exposed in a large imaging device, using no intermediate film. The photosensitive coating on the imaged plate is chemically developed much like photographic film and baked, if necessary, to harden the image for printing. This usually takes place in an inline unit attached to the exposure unit, so a finished plate emerges ready for mounting on the press. Think of the photosensitive plate coating as being a bit tender while it's still fresh. The plate is heated to stabilize the imaged coating so it will be able to stand up to the rigors of being used on the printing press.

The elimination of intermediate films reduces opportunities for error and considerably improves the process. There's less chance for loss of detail and, understandably, some cost and time savings.

A variation of this concept is on-press imaging, which is most commonly used on smaller-format presses. Unexposed plates are then mounted on the press, and imaging units on the press expose the plates in position. This approach can reduce makeready time because plates are already in position on the press when they're exposed, eliminating handling and possible issues with registration.

Pressroom

The printing process that will be used on your job will have some bearing on how your job must be prepared, so the choice of printing process is one more important topic in your initial conversations with a print service provider. Offset printing is probably the process that you envision when someone says "printing press," and it's the printing method you will probably encounter most frequently. But there are other printing methods, and the choice of printing process is dictated by the end product. Gravure is often used for long print runs typical of catalogs and magazines. Flexography is used for flexible packaging such as wrappers, foil bags, and labels. Letterpress printing is most often used for artistic applications these days, such as invitations or special publications. You may think of screen printing as only for clothing, such as T-shirts, but it's also capable of producing fine-art pieces, and often used to print on irregular surfaces such as cans, bottles, and other containers.

In offset printing, preparation in the pressroom includes adjusting the ink coverage, varying the pressure of the ink-bearing plates and the transfer blankets, and adjusting the paper-feeding mechanisms. Much of this process is facilitated by on-press technology, but the pressmen's instincts are indispensable for fine-tuning the mechanics. The term *makeready* refers to the process of getting the press up to speed and the ink behavior optimal. The press crew will be using approved contract proofs to guide them in setup. The color and content of the printed piece should match what the client has approved. Once everything is behaving as it should, you may be asked to attend a press check to approve the results, especially if there are special treatments that are difficult to simulate with a contract proof, such as custom-mixed inks or specialty stock.

Other specialty work that may take place in the pressroom includes personalization, such as addressing, as well as on-press finishing that might include perforation and scoring. In addition, coatings, such as varnishes, may be applied during the press run. Even fragrances and adhesives may be applied with inline units attached to the press.

Digital Printing

Increasingly, digital printing is used for short-run printing jobs, such as brochures, product literature, mailings, and small-circulation magazines. The ability to utilize variable data with digital printing opens up some interesting possibilities for marketing with printed pieces containing content fully customized for individual recipients. Output from high-end digital presses such as the Xerox iGen and HP Indigo rivals the quality of conventional offset presses. Please don't think of these presses as giant copiers: They're most certainly not. Their rich color, short runs, quick turnaround, and sophisticated inline finishing solutions can put full-color printing within reach of more designers. The setup and makeready are faster on digital presses, and there's no need for drying before finishing. Digital presses are not limited to short runs; they're just more affordable for smaller jobs that would be prohibitively expensive if run on large conventional offset presses.

Finishing

There's some overlap between the pressroom and a dedicated bindery, because some finishing functions, such as scoring or perforation, could take place either on press or in the bindery. Traditionally, operations such as trimming, folding, stitching, and die cutting are done in the finishing department or bindery.

Trimming

Large, heavy-duty trimming equipment is used to cut printed sheets to final size or to cut apart ganged content such as business cards. In some cases, trimming may take place before binding, although some pieces are bound first. For example, a business-reply card would be trimmed to the correct size before being bound into a publication. But the signatures of a book would be trimmed after being bound together in the final book configuration, ensuring that exterior page edges are cleanly aligned.

Folding

Simple folding may be performed inline as the printed sheet comes off the press, or it may be done in the bindery. More complex folding, such as pocket folders or packaging, requires dedicated folding equipment. More complicated folding operations may require handwork to finish the job, which adds to the cost of the job.

Stitching

When a piece requires stitching, thread may be used to anchor the pages of a signature for subsequent binding into a larger, finished book. But wire is often used for stitching smaller-page-count projects, such as magazines. In this process, the gathered pages are fed into stitching heads that feed, bend, and cut the wire simultaneously, resulting in a stapled piece. You'll often hear the term saddle stitching, which refers to the way a group of pages is held—as if draped over a saddle—while it is stitched.

Die Cutting

A *die* is a shaped metal cutter that is used to trim the edge of a printed piece in a special shape or to punch a shaped hole through the piece. The tabs on the edges of dividers are a simple example of die cutting. Many companies have standing dies for tab creation and can supply you with a template for creating your artwork so that it fits their existing dies. This avoids the cost of creating a custom die.

In a more complex example, a packaging piece may require that the printed sheet be scored and die cut to the final configuration for folding, creating all the interlocking panels that fold up to create the final box. If you're creating artwork for packaging, it's important to work closely with the print service provider and the die creator to ensure that your artwork is correct. Special handling is required at the intersections of panels to avoid artwork falling onto the wrong panel. Many printing companies do not create custom dies in-house, so be prepared for the cost and time involved in creating them. While the design of a custom die can be computerized, the assembly of the die itself still requires the knowledge of skilled craftspeople. For more information on die cutting, see Chapter 3, "Binding and Finishing."

Binding

Binding comprises many forms of assembly, from stitching to bookbinding. The most common forms of binding are saddle stitching (see the previous section on stitching) and perfect binding, in which multiple signatures are combined into a bundle, anchored with an adhesive, and then bound with tape or paper binding to hold them together with a flat spine.

Additional binding methods include coil binding, comb binding, and wire binding. Some binding methods may require that you avoid placing artwork in a specified margin so that it clears the punching or binding area. Consult with the print service provider early in the job to determine what the practical page area will be when binding is taken into consideration. For more information on binding methods, see Chapter 3, "Binding and Finishing."

Gluing

Binding methods such as perfect binding require gluing to keep all the pages together. But gluing is also an integral part of the manufacturing process for pocket folders and packaging. Because glue should be applied to a clean, ink-free substrate, artwork for the job needs to provide clean areas for glue application. Consult with the print service provider as you create your files so you'll know where glue needs to be applied. The printer may have to modify your artwork to accommodate gluing.

Fulfillment and Shipping

Some printing companies provide services beyond the production of printed pieces. Many offer mailing and fulfillment services, or they partner with other companies to provide such services. Fulfillment is especially useful for product literature and other pieces with a relatively long life span, such as product manuals, pocket folders, and presentation binders. Rather than requiring the customer to store boxes or stacks of printed materials, the printer keeps the inventory and ships it as needed.

Printers that specialize in mailers, such as catalogs, often offer mailing as part of the job cost and process. This may include variable data addressing (whether on-press or offline) as well as the actual mailing.

Glossary of Printing Terms

This glossary is by no means a comprehensive record of printing terms. But it may come in handy during your conversations with a print service provider. Some terms are now being reused to describe more modern printing processes (for example, "camera-ready art," in a world with very few remaining stat cameras).

1C: A one-color job is a project that is printed with only one ink (such as the black-only text of a book). Also written 1/C and 1-C.

2C: A two-color job prints with two inks. While this is frequently a combination of a spot color and black, it can be any two inks. Also written 2/C and 2-C. You may have guessed that **3C** would be a three-color job.

4C: A job printing with four inks, usually the four process inks—cyan, magenta, yellow, and black (CMYK).

2/1: Two-over-one. A job printed with two inks on one side and one ink on the other.

4/1: Four-over-one. A job printed with four inks (usually CMYK) on one side, and one ink (usually black) on the other.

Aqueous coating: A water-based coating applied over the entire printed area, usually by the last printing unit on a press. Aqueous coatings protect the printed ink and may enhance the appearance of the piece. For example, a pocket folder may benefit from the ability of aqueous coating to prevent scuffing as the pocket folder is repeatedly handled.

Artist alterations: Changes requested by a designer after the job has been submitted to the printer. Simple changes early in the job (such as correcting misspellings) may incur little or no charge, but a change once the job is on press would be extremely expensive.

Baseline: An imaginary line at the base of a row of text. All text sits on the baseline; descenders such as the lowercase *y* extend below the baseline.

Bindery: Sometimes also called a finishing department, the bindery performs trimming, folding, gluing, and stitching for finished pieces.

Blanket: An intermediate, rubber blanket used in offset printing to transfer the printing ink to the paper surface. The inked printing plate transfers ink to the blanket, which then applies the ink to the paper. The use of the intermediate blanket is the reason the printing process is called offset printing.

Blueline: Before digital processes, a single-color proof made by exposing photosensitive paper to a strong light source through film (usually a multipage, imposed layout for plate). Bluelines are used for proofreading, checking for scratches in film, and correct pagination of the flat. In a computer-to-plate (CTP) environment, since no plate film is necessary, bluelines are often output on large-format inkjet printers. And they're not necessarily blue anymore.

Bump plate: A second impression of a color, to strengthen the appearance on paper. Often used for large area coverage and for color enhancement of product imaging and fine art prints.

C1s (C-one-s): Paper coated on one side only.

C2s (C-two-s): Paper coated on both sides.

Cameraman: In the days before scanners, cameramen used masking and exposure techniques to create film color separations on large cameras. Transparencies, color prints, or original artwork were mounted on a large plate and then photographed through color filters to generate the films for the printing inks.

Camera-ready art: Ink drawings for illustrations, logos, or finished mechanicals ready to be photographed by the cameraman. The line shots of the clean, camera-ready artwork were used as the starting point for film stripping. Even though this process is obsolete, the term is still sometimes used to describe finished, ready-to-print art.

Case binding: Bookbinding process in which multiple signatures are sewn together. Then, glue is applied to the spine edge of the combined signatures, and a hard cover is pressed into place.

CEPS (color electronic prepress system): A specialized computer system for retouching and assembly of images. Marketed by Scitex, Crosfield, Linotype-Hell, and Dainippon Screen, they often cost in excess of a million dollars. Largely rendered obsolete by the advent of Photoshop and the affordability of the Mac.

Chase: A frame that contains the metal printing components used in a letterpress printing press.

Coil binding: Also called spiral binding. Pages are punched (usually at the left or top edge), and then a single coil (spiral) of plastic or wire is threaded through the punched holes to anchor the pages together. Coil binding is useful for presentations and workbooks because pages lie flat when the finished piece is opened. One disadvantage is that there is no printable spine.

Color break: How color should be used in various areas of a page. In the days of physical mechanicals, colored markers were used to mark a tissue paper overlay so that film strippers would know how to apply color to type, rules, and boxes. Since the underlying mechanical artwork consisted of only black-and-white contents (to facilitate the shooting of line shots), an indication of color break was necessary. For example, headlines might be circled and marked to print as M100–Y100, and quick sweeps of a blue marker, accompanied by a written instruction, might be used to indicate that all boxes on the page should print with a mix of C50–Y15. It was sort of like coloring books for adults. The term color break is still sometimes used in discussions of page-layout contents.

Color cast: An unwanted color shift in an image, such as an overall pink tint to a scene that should be all grays and whites.

Color management: Calibrating and profiling devices to ensure color consistency among monitors, printers, proofing systems, and printing presses.

Color separations: In the conventional days, an individual sheet of film was created for each printing ink to be used in reproducing artwork. In four-color designs, four pieces of film were used one each for cyan, magenta, yellow, and black. For a duotone image, two films would be generated, one for each ink (usually black plus a spot color but not always). For tritones, three pieces of film would be generated, and so on. Color separations were formerly created by cameramen until the introduction of scanners. Now, even though film is rarely output, the term separation is still used to refer to the division of color images and graphics into the printing inks.

Color temperature: A standardized measure of the value of a light source to control viewing conditions. Think of a piece of iron being heated in a furnace. As its temperature increases, the color given off by the piece of iron goes from dull red to bright red, followed by orange, and so on. The

Kelvin temperature scale is used, under which water freezes at 273K (the abbreviation for Kelvin), and all molecular motion stops at 0K. This is, no doubt, more than you care to know. But, for reference, it may be helpful to know that a household tungsten bulb measures about 2700–2800K, and average sunlight is approximately 5000K. The sun at high noon measures between 6000–6500K. For many years, the graphic arts industry was standardized on 5000K viewing conditions, often referred to as D50 lighting. But in recent years there has been a move toward the brighter, 6500K (D65) standard.

Comb binding: A binding method in which pages are punched, and then a comb-like piece of curved plastic is inserted (usually at the left or top edge). The teeth of the curved comb (hence the name) curl into the punched holes, and the curvature of the insert draws it closed. Comb binding allows the finished piece to open flat, which makes it suitable for textbooks and workbooks. Since the exterior of the bound piece is solid, the spine can be imprinted, although this isn't frequently done.

Comp: Short for comprehensive. A representation of the final printed piece, usually printed on a desktop printer and manually assembled to show a client (or the print service provider) how the finished piece should look. Comps are helpful for checking pagination and for planning complicated pieces such as those involving inserts, tabs, or custom trimming. Also sometimes called mockup.

Continuous tone: A smooth transition from one color to another, such as the variations of color in a color photograph. While the emulsion of a photographic print can replicate continuous tones, printing presses cannot. Instead, the printing process approximates a variety of colors by using halftone dots (see Chapter 2, "Ink on Paper," for more information on halftones).

Contract proof: A proof intended to represent the appearance of the final printed piece. Contract proofs are used for color and content matching on press. Traditionally, they are made by exposing proofing materials through final film, but now they are usually generated digitally from the same information used to generate plates. Signing a contract proof constitutes an agreement between printer and client. The client's signature indicates that the proof shows correct color and final content. The printer is obliged to match the proof on press.

Converter: A manufacturing facility that makes products such as envelopes, folding cartons, and displays.

Creep: The tendency of inner pages of a book (or large signature) to push outward, pushing the edges of inner pages beyond the edges of outer pages. Compensation is performed during imposition to minimize unwanted cropping of page content.

Cromalin®: A product of DuPont™, the Cromalin proofing system originally provided analog (film-based) proofing, but now the same name is used for digital proofing solutions.

CTP (computer-to-plate): Direct imaging of a printing plate from digital information. CTP replaces previous methods of generating intermediate film and exposing plates. The imposition is digitally created, and then the printing plate is directly exposed in a large imaging device using no intermediate film, then baked briefly to harden the surface.

Cure: To dry or harden an ink or other applied material. Heat, pressure, air, or ultraviolet light may be used, depending on the material and the substrate to which it is applied. The purpose of curing is to minimize smearing or scuffing of the printed piece.

Custom-mixed inks: While the variety of ink recipes available from PANTONE®, Toyo Ink, and other firms provide a huge rainbow of colors from which to choose, it is sometimes necessary to mix a custom color to get exactly the right shade. There's more involved than "a cup of this and a cup of that," since what's important is the appearance and behavior of the ink on the final printing surface under press conditions. To ensure realistic expectations, the printer should provide an ink draw-down, which is a thin film of the custom ink applied to paper (ideally, the actual printing stock) to simulate the appearance of the ink when printed.

Die (cutting): Blade-like pieces of metal mounted in a wooden platform, used to cut out shaped printed pieces, such as pocket folders or packaging.

Die (embossing): Sculpted metal pieces, used with heat and pressure to mold paper for artistic embellishment. Usually there is a positive and negative version of the shape to be embossed.

Die cutting: Using pressure and shaped metal dies to cut a printed piece in an interesting shape. Die cutting is sometimes done by the printer and sometimes done by outside specialty companies that subcontract with the printer.

Digital camera: Filmless photography, thanks to tiny photosensitive circuitry. Images can be downloaded directly to a computer and used immediately in design. Maybe you should soften those wrinkles first, though.

Digital press: While this term usually refers to plateless, toner-based printing devices, it may also refer to presses that enable on-press imaging of conventional plates. The output of high-end, toner-based presses rivals the appearance of offset printing while enabling functions such as the customization of each piece using variable data.

Dot etcher: A skilled craftsperson who performed color corrections by delicately etching color-separation films in mild acid baths. The acid eroded the edges of halftone dots, which would alter the diameter and thus the amount of ink that the resulting printing plate would hold. Etching a positive film would lighten color, and etching a negative film would increase color. To prevent etching in some areas of the film, the dot etcher would paint on a varnish-like protective mask. After etching, the mask would be removed with a solvent. While this may seem primitive compared to the ease with which we now make color corrections in Photoshop, the concepts are the same. In fact, many dot etchers were quick to adopt Photoshop and excelled at using the program to perform color corrections. Imagine how relieved they were to go home without acid burns in their clothes! Dot etching, alas, is completely extinct.

Dot gain: The tendency of ink to spread when applied to a substrate, resulting in a perceived darkening of the printed image. Touch a fine-point pen to a paper towel and you'll get the idea. Dot gain is an unavoidable physical occurrence, but plate imaging and press controls can mitigate it. Contract proofs should approximate the results of dot gain so that the printed piece isn't a surprise.

Duotone: Rendering an image in two colors of ink (usually black and a spot color). Tritones use three inks, and quadtones use four inks (usually three spot colors and black). Used to achieve a special visual effect, or to provide more interesting rendering of images in two-color or three-color jobs.

Embossing/debossing: Using pressure and shaped dies to press paper into a three-dimensional relief. Embossing raises the surface on the finished side; debossing indents the surface on the finished side. When used in an unprinted area, this is referred to as blind embossing.

Estimator: A knowledgeable and important part of the printing plant's front line, an estimator is responsible for estimating the time, labor, paper, ink, and other materials that will be required to complete a printing job.

Fake duotone: Usually, printing a black-and-white halftone over a color tint to add a bit of color to a grayscale image.

Film stripper: A nearly extinct breed of trained crafts people who used tape, photographic masks, and darkroom techniques to combine type and images for final film. In some ways, the film stripper was the equivalent of a production artist of today, although the job title made for some very awkward moments during introductions. "You're a stripper?!" This would be followed by a brief explanation to your date's parents, during which you attempted to condense the printing process into a few compelling sentences.

Finishing: The manufacturing processes that take place after the job leaves the printing press. Finishing can include such processes as folding, binding, trimming, die cutting, embossing, and foil stamping.

Flat: Pieces of film taped to plastic carrier sheets for subsequent exposure. Film strippers taped the component parts of a page to flats and then exposed them in a certain order through masks to create a finished film for the individual printing inks. Platemakers taped down films for pages in the correct position as part of very large imposed flats. Because of computer-to-plate technology, these processes are no longer used. Instead, pages are created in page-layout programs, and imposition software positions the pages in the correct orientation for directly exposing plates.

Flexography: A printing process that uses fast-drying inks and plastic, rubber, or photopolymer plates with raised image areas carrying the ink. Flexographic printing transfers the ink directly to the printing surface rather than using an intermediate blanket as in offset printing. Flexo printing, as it is usually called, is often used for printing flexible substrates such as plastic sheeting or thin packaging foils. While flexography may have previously been regarded as inappropriate for higher quality work, that's no longer the case. Improvements in inks and plate materials have greatly expanded the capabilities of flexography.

Foil stamping: Using pressure and heat to transfer a special, film-backed sheet of color (often metallic or iridescent) to printed paper. Hot foil stamping uses a die to transfer a shaped design to paper and can be combined with embossing for elegant effects. An alternative method, cold foil stamping, is applied on press.

Folding dummy: A blank sheet of paper folded in the configuration that will be used in finishing the job. Pages are numbered to indicate the correct imposed page position. A folding dummy may be made by the planning department or by imposition operators and is used to check for correct folding and imposition.

Folio: A sheet of paper folded in half; for example, the outside and inside pages of a four-page brochure. *Folio* is also used to refer to page numbers.

FPO (for position only): Placeholder content used in the early stages of design. FPO images are later replaced by final, high-resolution images.

Ganged: Business cards or other similar pieces may be ganged together for simultaneous printing and then separated when the printed sheet is trimmed apart. Ganging saves time, material, and labor.

Grain: The predominant direction of fibers in paper, which can determine the direction in which folding is best performed.

Gravure printing: A specialized printing method using engraved metal cylinders. Chrome-plated gravure cylinders are capable of extended printing runs, making gravure appropriate for catalog, publication, and packaging applications. After printing, the chrome plating can be stripped off and replaced so the cylinder can be reused.

Gripper edge: The edge of a sheet of paper used to pull the paper through the press. Sometimes called feeding edge and leading edge.

Halftone: Since it's not possible to print millions of colors in a continuous-tone fashion, the predominant printing processes approximate a wide range of colors by using cyan, magenta, yellow, and black inks (usually) printed with halftone dots of varying diameters. (See Chapter 2, "Ink on Paper," for a more detailed description.)

Hot type: A method of creating type with a raised printing surface by injecting molten metal into a shaped form called a matrix. Usually a combination of lead, tin, and other metals, the molten metal filled the mold and cooled to form the printing surface, called a slug. A slug might be just a single word, portions of a page, or an entire page. This process is also the source of the term leading (pronounced *ledding*). Thin strips of lead were placed between lines of text as shims to provide space between the lines. The concepts and terms remain, although we no longer have to pour hot lead.

Imagesetter: A digitally driven device for imaging film. A raster image processor (RIP) converts incoming PostScript or PDF information to very high-resolution bitmaps that guide the imagesetter's marking engine to expose the film with a laser or light-emitting diodes.

Imposition: Placing individual pages of a multipage document in the correct position for final printing.

Job jacket: A large plastic or cardboard carrier containing materials for a job. Usually open on one side like a big, flapless envelope, the job jacket allows the job materials to travel together throughout a printing plant. A job jacket might contain your original digital media and hard copy, as well as any proofs and necessary paperwork pertaining to the job. Usually an identifying job ticket is affixed to the job jacket to identify it and serve as a job information reference.

Job ticket: Usually attached to the job jacket, a job ticket contains important information about a printing job, such as the job number, the customer name, contact information for key personnel, the number of inks used, the press to be used, and important dates in the job's timeline.

Knock out: In printing, an area where no ink prints. For example, white text knocks out of an area of black ink, leaving unprinted paper. The term is also used to refer to creating a silhouette of a portion of an image, as in knocking out an object so that its background disappears.

Laminate: To coat a printed piece with a clear film by using heat, pressure, and adhesive. Laminates are used to protect printed pieces from abrasion and other wear and tear.

Leading: The amount of space between the baseline of one line of text and the baseline of the following line of text, usually expressed in points. Pronounced *ledding*.

Letterpress printing: Printing from a raised plate or collection of printing components that are held together in a chase. The pressure of letterpress printing creates a slight indentation, especially in heavy stock. It is a slow, mechanical, hand-intensive process, but creates unique pieces. Used by Gutenberg to print his famous Bibles, letterpress was once the standard printing process before offset printing began to replace it in the 1950s. Now it is used mainly for invitations, announcements, and fine-art printing.

Linen tester: A small, rectangular, folding magnifier used to check artwork, proofs, or printed pieces. It's called a linen tester because of its origins in the fabric industry.

Line shots: In the old manual days, a camera shot of black-and-white, hard-edged artwork such as type or line drawings. High-contrast film eliminated shades of gray, thereby producing a sharp image with no soft edges. The digital equivalent would be line-art scans.

Lithography: A printing process based on the mutual repulsion of water and oil. Oil-based ink adheres to areas of a lithographic printing plate that are not moistened by water.

Loupe: A small, folding magnifying glass that is used to examine small details in artwork, on a proof, or on a printed piece. A loupe folds into itself horizontally, whereas a linen tester pops up vertically.

Lowercase: Uncapitalized text such as a, b, c, d, and so on. As compared to uppercase (capitalized) text such as A, B, C, D. Originally, the term referred to the physical location of the wooden case containing the uncapitalized letters that were made of molded lead.

Makeready: The process of getting a printing press up to operating conditions. Makeready includes adjusting ink feed, paper tension, and blanket pressure. Also used to refer to the waste material produced during this process, then recycled.

Matchprint: Originally a film-based proofing system marketed by 3M, the Matchprint proofing system became a product marketed by 3M's spin-off company, Imation. Ultimately, Kodak Polychrome Graphics purchased Imation, and now Matchprint is a digital high-quality inkjet system.

Mechanical: In the days of manual artwork creation, a mechanical consisted of hand-inked artwork and black-and-white photo prints that were affixed to heavy artboard with adhesive wax or rubber cement. Line shots of the mechanical were used by film strippers as the starting point for creating film for printing. Now, the term is still sometimes used to describe a finished page-layout file.

Mechanical color: The process of cutting complicated, stencil-like masks for color break. Since each distinct color mix in a page required a separate mask, the process was exacting and time consuming. Fine knives were used to cut shapes in a red (Rubylith® brand from the Ulano® Corporation) or amber (Amberlith® brand also from Ulano) varnish-like coating on a thick, clear plastic backing. Once the masking shape was cut, sections of the coating were lifted and peeled off to reveal the clear plastic. Since the amber or red mask was opaque to the light used to expose the film, film strippers used these masks in the darkroom to create the final page films.

Moiré: An undesirable interference pattern created between inks of different angles, especially when printing images containing patterns of their own, such as photographs of textile or clothing.

Offset printing: Offset printing is based on lithographic principles, which take advantage of the repellent properties of oil and water. The imaged area attracts oil-based inks, whereas the nonimaged area attracts water. On each revolution of the press, a thin film of fountain solution (a water-based dampening agent) is applied to the plate, followed by a film of ink, which only adheres to areas not coated with water. The ink image is transferred to a blanket, which then transfers the ink to the paper. The use of an intermediate blanket is the reason the process is called offset printing.

OPI (open prepress interface): A method developed originally by the Aldus Corporation (but also implemented by other vendors) that allows the use of low-resolution (and thus smaller) images in creating a page layout. These low-resolution images represent the original high-resolution images but take up less hard drive (or server) space and print more quickly. They contain PostScript comments that identify their high-resolution replacements. During final imaging, a server- or RIP-based process replaces the low-resolution image with the high-resolution image. OPI is used less often with today's faster networks and larger storage devices, but it is still implemented in workflows that deal with high volumes of images, such as catalog production. Pronounced "oh-pea-eye," not "opey."

Overprint: To print text or artwork over an image or color tint (for example, black text over a background image); also called surprint.

Page proof: A proof of an individual page, which is usually created to obtain customer approval of color and content at a fairly early stage in the job.

Pagination: Placing page files in the correct printing order during imposition for trimming and binding.

PDF: Portable Document Format. A format originated by Adobe Systems to contain artwork and text in a form that is faithful to the original work, which can be viewed and printed by anyone with the free Adobe Reader or a third-party PDF viewer.

Perfect binding: Combines multiple signatures into a bundle, anchors them with an adhesive, and then applies a tape or paper binding to hold them together for a flat spine. The paper binding may also be a printed cover that allows a title and other information to be printed on the spine.

Personalization: A data-driven method of inserting a recipient's name or other personal information during printing. In offset print environments, this is usually done via press-mounted inkjet units, although processes such as addressing may be performed during later stages in the bindery. As data-driven processes become more sophisticated, and the inkjet units faster and more refined, it is becoming possible to personalize with more than just a few lines of type—even custom images can be applied.

Pica: A unit of measurement. There are six picas in an inch. A pica is equal to 12 points.

Planner: A printing company specialist who establishes which press will be used to print a job, how the job will be imposed for the press, and what finishing processes should be scheduled to complete the job. Planners may also be involved in job scheduling. In many printing plants, estimating and planning may overlap or may even be performed by the same person.

Platesetter: An output device that uses a laser or light-emitting diodes (LEDs) to expose the photosensitive surface of a printing plate by using digital information.

Point: A unit of measurement. There are 72 points in an inch. Text size, leading, baseline grids, and the thickness of rules and strokes are almost always specified in points. Some designers specify everything in points and picas, but many are accustomed to specifying page sizes and the dimensions of objects in inches, and they only use points when referring to text size and rule thickness.

PostScript: A programming language used to describe the contents of a page so that an imaging device such as a laser printer, an imagesetter, or a platesetter can produce output. Developed by Adobe Systems, PostScript was the major driving force in the birth of desktop publishing. Since its advent in 1985, PostScript has gone through several revisions. The current version of PostScript is Level 3.

Preflight: Inspecting job files at an early stage of the job to find content errors that might prevent the file from printing as the customer intends. While there are dedicated software programs such as FlightCheck from Markzware, some print service providers rely on skilled preflight operators to examine files. Designers can also preflight their outgoing jobs as a check before submitting the job for print. This allows problems to be fixed before incurring repair charges from the print service provider.

Prepress: All the preparatory work that takes place before actual printing. Prepress includes preflight, production work to correct or modify files for printing, proofing, trapping, imposition, and plating. It may also include scanning, retouching, and color correction.

Press check: Once makeready is complete and the printing press is in an optimal running state, the client is asked to approve the printed output for content and color. This is often necessary when custom inks or tricky substrates are involved—components that may be difficult to represent faithfully with proofing. Since printing companies often operate 24 hours a day, you may find yourself invited to a press check in the middle of the night. Wear comfortable shoes.

Press proof: While current proofing methods are adequate for simulating actual printed pieces under most circumstances, special add-ons such as custom inks or applied varnishes may present challenges. For exacting jobs, such as complex promotional pieces or annual reports, it may be necessary to perform a small press run to determine if everything looks as expected. While this adds considerably to job cost, it may be worthwhile on a high-profile job to ensure that the finished piece meets expectations.

Printer alterations: Changes made to a job by the printer, to ensure successful print, such as creating a rich black build to use instead of only black ink in a large area of coverage. The costs of printer alterations are not charged to the client.

Printer's spreads: The printing position of pages on the press, determined by the imposition requirements of the job. While pages two and three face each other in a printed eight-page brochure, they don't print together.

Instead, page two prints next to page seven, and page three prints next to page six. When the pages are bound together, they are read in the correct order. See Chapter 3, "Binding and Finishing," for more information about the process of imposition.

Process colors: The four basic printing inks—cyan, magenta, yellow, and black, also referred to as CMYK.

Proof: A simulation of the final printed piece, used to check the content of the job. Necessary corrections should be marked on the proof, and the marked-up proof should be compared to the next round of proofs to ensure that the requested changes have been made. Signing a proof indicates that you consider everything to be correct in the proof.

Resolution: In images, the number of pixels per inch (or per centimeter in metric systems). In devices (such as laser printers or platesetters), the number of dots per inch (or per centimeter) that the device is capable of imaging.

Registration: The alignment of all inks printed on a press. Since each color is applied by an individual unit on press, there is some possibility of the successive colors not aligning. While modern presses have sophisticated controls for maintaining proper registration, mechanical or environmental problems may cause slight misregistration, as can stretching or deformation of the paper itself during the printing process. A multicolor fringe at the edge of color areas is a symptom of misregistration.

RIP (raster image processor): A specialized computer that uses a combination of proprietary software and hardware to translate PostScript or PDF input to a very high-resolution bitmap image that drives the marking engine of an output device, such as an imagesetter, platesetter, or desktop printer.

ROOM (RIP once, output many): The practice of processing a page in a RIP, and then using that same information from the RIP to generate proofs, film (if necessary), and plates rather than reprocessing the original digital information through different RIPs for different output. Using the same data for multiple outputs ensures that no processing errors creep in. Using one vendor's RIP for proofing output and a different vendor's RIP for platesetting can result in a proof that does not represent what will be on the plate. This can lead to surprises on press. Surprise is not necessarily a positive thing in printing.

Saddle stitch: Binding multiple pages together with staple-like metal stitches. Often used for magazines and catalogs. See Chapter 3, "Binding and Finishing," for more information about saddle stitching.

Scanner: A device for converting reflective artwork, photographic prints, transparencies, or film negatives to digital information. Early scanners were large, expensive devices with daunting controls that required careful mounting of artwork on large, heavy clear drums. But with advances in optics and software, they have been largely replaced by flatbed scanners, and prices have plummeted accordingly.

Scatter proof: A preliminary color proof of images and other artwork, used to determine if color correction and retouching will be necessary before the job is printed.

Scheduler: A printing-company specialist who determines when each portion of a job occurs (barring errors or other problems). The scheduler must consider how long each process takes and must factor in the effects of other existing jobs, staffing resources, and the required final deadline for the job.

Score: To press a groove into paper or board for easier folding. This ensures a smooth, predictable bend while lessening the chance that the paper or board will tear when folded.

Screen angle: The angle along which the halftone dots of a color are positioned. In a multicolor job, each ink prints at a different screen angle, to minimize the interference pattern called moiré.

Screen printing: A printing method in which a finely woven stretched screen carries a hand-cut or photographically exposed mask. The mask acts as a stencil, and ink is squeezed through the mesh of the screen in open areas of the mask onto the intended substrate. While you may associate screen printing only with apparel printing (such as T-shirts), it's also used for spot application of scratch-off coverings for game pieces, scratch-and-sniff areas, and printing on irregular surfaces such as molded pieces.

Screen ruling: The number of halftone dots per inch (or per centimeter). Since the pattern is square, the vertical measure of rows of dots is expressed as *lines per inch*. For example, 150 lpi (lines per inch) indicates 150 dots per linear inch (both vertically and horizontally). The more dots per inch, the more detail that can be rendered in print. Fine line screens (200 lpi or higher) are used on higher-quality jobs, on coated paper. For uncoated paper, such as newsprint, lower screen rulings are used (usually 85–100 lpi).

Sheetfed press: An offset press that takes in single sheets of paper from a stack rather than a roll. Typical sheetfed press paper sizes are around 20 by 28 inches or 30 by 40 inches, although there are larger-format (and smaller-format) presses as well.

Signature: A printed sheet folded one or more times to create a single section of a multisection piece. Pages are imposed in the correct position so that when the sheet is folded, trimmed, and bound, the pages will be in the proper reading order. (For more on imposition and signatures, see Chapter 3, "Binding and Finishing.")

Silhouette: To eliminate the background surrounding the important element in an image. This may be done by erasing the background or (more commonly) by creating a mask or path that allows the element to display without the background. Also called knockout, dropout, blockout, silo, or KO, depending on your locale and your local printer's particular slang.

Spiral binding: see coil binding.

Spot color: A specially prepared ink used to image colors that fall outside the range of process colors, including fluorescent and metallic colors.

Stat camera: A large camera used to photograph drawn artwork and mechanicals, producing high-contrast negatives used in film stripping.

Stochastic screening: A method of placing ink dots in a seemingly random pattern rather than using conventional halftone screen patterns. Stochastic screening can eliminate moiré patterns and create smoother appearing flesh-tones. You can look at the output of any inkjet printer (even that one next to your computer) under a magnifying glass and see what a stochastic pattern looks like.

TAC (total area coverage): The maximum amount of ink that can be printed in a given area, determined by the stock and the type of press. For example, newsprint usually tolerates a maximum of about 240%, coated paper running on a sheetfed press could support up to 320% or more. The percentage is determined by adding up the amounts of each color of ink in the area; for example, a color build of C100–M100–Y60–K60 is 320%.

Trade shop: A print service provider that works for other printing providers and performs services such as scanning, retouching, and other prepress services. Some trade shops also provide printing and finishing services.

Transparency: A transparent, positive color image such as a 35 mm slide. Larger formats include 4 by 5 inches and 8 by 10 inches, but the advent of digital photography has made the use of transparencies (and the need to scan them) somewhat less common.

Trap: To create overlapping areas of common color in order to minimize gaps during slight misregistration on press. Trapping is usually performed at the RIP stage, although it's also possible to create traps manually in many applications. (See Chapter 2, "Ink on Paper," for a more detailed explanation of trapping issues.)

Typesetter: The definition and responsibilities of a typesetter changed with technological advances. Typesetters no longer handle tiny molded lead characters locked in a chase (container). Currently, typesetter usually refers to a specialist who uses page-layout tools to set type with an emphasis on readability and style in long documents.

UPC (universal product code): A machine-readable identifier that consists of two components—a bar code and human-readable numbers. The first six digits identify the product's manufacturer, and the remaining digits identify the product itself and provide a check digit used by the code reader to determine if the code has been read correctly. It's not difficult to generate UPC artwork with special barcode fonts or dedicated software, but you must be mindful of requirements such as minimum size, location, and color of the code itself. It's important that busy backgrounds or dark colors don't interfere with the legibility of the UPC, which is why it's often placed in a white rectangle. You'll have to plan for this when you're creating artwork for publication covers or books, as well as packaging.

UV (ultraviolet) coating: A clear coating that is applied on press, then cured by passing under UV lamps. UV coating provides more protection than varnish or aqueous coatings.

Uppercase: Capitalized letters, such as A, B, C. As compared to lowercase text, such as a, b, c, d. Originally, the term referred to the physical location of the wooden case containing the uncapitalized letters, which were made of molded lead. Capitals were kept in an upper case, hence the name.

Varnish: A coating applied overall to protect a printed piece, or over selected parts of the sheet (spot varnish) to enhance the design.

VDP (variable data printing): At its most basic, VDP can be the personalization of a printed piece by inserting the recipient's name and address: "Dear [your name here]." While this can be accomplished by using press-mounted inkjet heads with acceptable results, the increased use of fully digital presses opens the way for more extensive customization. Since each impression on a toner-based digital press is unique anyway, a database-driven process can insert custom text—even images—to narrowly target the printed piece to the recipient's demographic or buying history. While variable data printing is more expensive because of the programming and planning involved (as well as the cost of demographic information and mailing lists), the response rate from such targeted mailings is substantially higher than for generic mass mailings.

Vertical camera: See stat camera.

Viewing booth: A cubicle-like area that provides a controlled viewing environment for judging color. Although a printed piece will be viewed by recipients under a variety of lighting conditions from fluorescent or tungsten to daylight, it's important during production to have standardized lighting and surrounding surfaces so that everyone from designer to retoucher to pressman is viewing proofs and printed materials in a common environment. To prevent any influence from the surroundings, the surfaces of a viewing booth are painted a neutral, medium gray, using matte paint to avoid reflections. To ensure consistent lighting, fluorescent bulbs of a specified color temperature are used. Originally, D50 (5000K) bulbs were used, but there has been a move in recent years to D65 (6500K).

Web press: A roll-fed printing press. Trimming to individual sheets may take place at the end of the press on an inline unit called a sheeter, or the printed web may be rolled up onto a takeup reel for offline trimming. The size of the web press dictates the width of the paper roll it accepts.

Wire binding: Similar to comb binding, but wire binding uses wire that is bent into tooth-like prongs.

Ink on Paper

2

The craft of printing is a combination of art and science that has been developed and refined over hundreds of years. Because printing is a complicated mechanical undertaking, numerous variables affect the printing process. Such factors include the type of press, the direction of the grain in the paper as it goes through the press, the kind of ink being used, and the prevailing temperature and humidity during the press run. Stand by a thundering offset press that is running at full speed, watch the paper race through the printing units, and consider the tons of machinery churning out your job. You'll wonder how it ever works at all—it's an impressive feat. A skilled pressman is an artisan who can work miracles, but there are still some physical limitations to what can be achieved with ink on paper. It's a long trip from what you see on your monitor to the printed paper that flies out of the press.

Fundamentals of Black-and-White Printing

The *black* in black-and-white printing is black ink. The *white* is the paper. When you hear a print job referred to as a two-color job, that means that two colors of ink will be required to print it. That may seem obvious, but I can recall a befuddled print salesman who submitted a job marked as "2-color job." We couldn't see any objects in the file that would generate a second

TIP In the South, where I live, there are subtle nuances to some sayings. For example, if your brother breaks his leg, you sympathize by saying "Bless your heart." If he broke his leg while trying to fly off the roof with homemade wings, you say, "Bless your little heart," which is a nice way of saying "You idiot."

color, so we asked him to clarify. "Of course it's two colors!," he snapped. *"Black* and *white!"* Bless his little heart.

Printing a single ink on paper is somewhat simpler than printing a four-color job (see "Fundamentals of Color Printing," later in this chapter), but the same rules apply. A black-and-white photograph displayed on your monitor is made of a continuous range of 256 levels of gray, but a printing press doesn't print hundreds of shades of black ink. Instead, a single color of ink is printed in tiny dots called halftone dots, which simulate the shades of gray by varying the diameter of the dots (**Figure 2.1**). It's a convincing illusion because, unless your eyesight is very good, the individual dots are not apparent. An image printed by this method is commonly called a halftone.

Figure 2.1 *A black-and-white image looks smooth on your monitor. But it's actually printed with thousands of tiny halftone dots (right).*

Screen ruling (also called screen frequency) is the measure of halftone-dot frequency (**Figure 2.2**), usually expressed in lines per inch (lpi). Typical screen rulings range from 65–85 lpi (used in newspapers) to 133–150 lpi (often used in magazines and books).

Screen ruling:
Lines per inch (lpi)

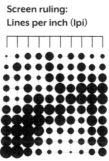

Figure 2.3 *Screen ruling is measured in lines per inch (lpi).*

Some high-end magazines and art books are printed at even higher line screens—up to 200 or 300 lpi. The higher the screen ruling, the more faithfully images can be rendered, because finer detail can be maintained. So why wouldn't everything be printed at 300 lpi? Because printing conditions impose certain limitations. The coarse stock used for newspapers simply won't support fine line screens. Ink sinks into the absorbent stock and spreads, which is a phenomenon called dot gain. Try drawing small dots on a paper towel with a fine permanent marker and you'll get an idea of the effect. The screen ruling is determined by the print service provider, based on the type of paper being used in the job.

To better camouflage the rows of dots, they are printed at time-honored angles. For example, the dots in a black-and-white halftone image are usually printed at a 45 degree angle (**Figure 2.3**). You don't have to create the halftone dots or figure out the appropriate angle for them. Those attributes are determined by the print service provider. The halftone dots don't come into being until the job is processed by the raster image processor (RIP).

Figure 2.3 *Screen angle: 45°*

If screen angles and screen frequency are the print service provider's problem, why should designers and production artists even care about such issues? Because it's helpful to have realistic expectations of the printed outcome, and both screen angle and screen ruling have an impact on printed work. Highly patterned image content, such as woven fabric, can result in an unpleasant visual effect, called a moiré, when the patterns imposed by image resolution, line screen, and screen angle combine to generate the final product.

Scanning at very high resolutions may help in some instances, but it will also produce large image files. Blurring the troublesome content may help but is sometimes undesirable ("I thought this was a tweed jacket. It looks like velveteen."). Changing the screen ruling or screen angles may reduce moiré in one part of the image but increase the effect in another area.

DPI, LPI, PPI, TLA

Because the acronyms for various forms of resolution are often used interchangeably, it's easy to get confused.

dpi (dots per inch): Used to describe the resolution of an imaging device such as a desktop printer, an imagesetter, or a platesetter. The typical desktop printer's resolution ranges from 600 to 1200 dpi, while the resolution of an imagesetter or platesetter is usually 2400 dpi or higher.

lpi (lines per inch): Describes the frequency of halftone dots, measured along a row of dots (see Figure 2.2).

ppi (pixels per inch): Describes image resolution. For most printing applications, image resolution should be 250–300 ppi. The rule of thumb is that image resolution should be 1.5 to 2 times the printing screen ruling, but the common convention is to save images at 300 ppi.

tla (three-letter acronym)

Fundamentals of Color Printing

While a printed color image may appear to contain thousands of individual colors, it usually consists of just four inks, referred to as process colors: cyan, magenta, yellow, and black (CMYK). The process inks are transparent, so when they are combined on paper, they produce other colors (**Figure 2.4**). Thus, cyan plus yellow makes green. Cyan plus magenta makes violet. Yellow plus magenta makes red, and combining yellow, magenta and cyan makes an unattractive muddy brown. That's still a fairly small box of crayons. How can you make all the colors you need?

Figure 2.4 *The four process inks combine to create much more than just four colors.*

In traditional offset printing, the illusion of so many colors is the result of varying sizes of halftone dots, which allow different amounts of the four process colors to interact in a given area. Other printing methods use different ruses to fool the eye into seeing more than four colors, but the concept is the same: Use varying amounts of CMYK to approximate a wide range of colors (**Figure 2.5**).

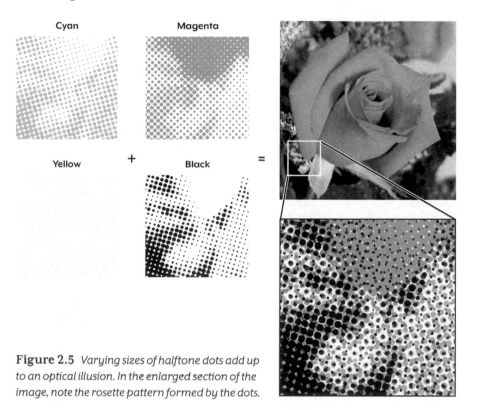

Figure 2.5 *Varying sizes of halftone dots add up to an optical illusion. In the enlarged section of the image, note the rosette pattern formed by the dots.*

It's important to avoid unsightly patterns, called moiré (**Figure 2.6**). To see the moiré effect, put one piece of window screen on top of another, and then rotate one piece of screen (and be thinking of an excuse for cutting up the kitchen screen). It's a challenge to eliminate an obvious pattern.

Figure 2.6 *Incorrect intervals between screen angles can result in a distracting moiré. This can also be caused by a combination of screen angles and image content such as woven fabric.*

To combat moiré patterns, there are time-honored intervals of 30 degrees between the angles of the inks to create the desired rosette pattern (**Figure 2.7**). Yellow, being the lightest, is 15 degrees off from one of the other colors.

Figure 2.7 *Optimal screen angles add up to form a rosette pattern. Yes, it's a pattern, but it's usually not noticeable.*

Screen angle preferences vary between print service providers and may sometimes be chosen to accommodate job content (**Table 2.1**).

Table 2.1 *To minimize patterns, screen angles are traditionally 30 degrees apart (for example, 45 degrees and 75 degrees). Angles are chosen to minimize interference with the other colors when all inks are combined in the printed piece. Print shops and RIP manufacturers may utilize custom angles.*

Screen Angle Combinations

C 75°	M 15°	Y 0°	K 45°
C 15°	M 45°	Y 0°	K 75°
C 105°	M 75°	Y 90°	K 15°

Solving the Moiré Problem: Stochastic Screening

One solution for moiré is to eliminate screen angles entirely by using a printing method without the conventional grid of regularly spaced dots. Stochastic screening, also called *FM* (frequency modulation) screening, uses a seemingly random distribution of very small dots (**Figures 2.8** and **2.9**). If you have an inkjet printer, you have a stochastic output device right on your desk. Look at an inkjet print through a magnifying loupe and you'll see how the scattered arrangement of tiny dots creates an image.

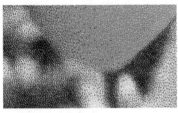

Figure 2.8 *Stochastic screening*   **Figure 2.9** *Stochastic screening, enlarged*

After its first appearance in the 1980s, stochastic screening failed to gain much acceptance due to limitations in plating and proofing systems of the time. But it is experiencing a resurgence in the printing industry, thanks to the advent of CTP, as well as increased implementation of digital (rather than film-based) proofing systems.

Stochastic screening offers some advantages over conventional halftones:

- Reduced chance of moiré—since there are no angles, there is almost no chance for an interference pattern to be created.
- Ability to use lower-resolution images.
- Ability to print images containing more than four ink colors without screen angle issues.
- Retention of smaller details in images.
- Reduced ink usage.
- Misregistration on-press is less obvious.
- Smoother rendition of skin tones.

(continues on next page)

But stochastic screening has not replaced the old-fashioned halftone dot. In fact, it's used only in a minority of printing. There are some challenges to using FM screening:

- The need for extreme cleanliness in plating: Dust may be bigger than a stochastic dot.
- Modifications to RIPs can be expensive ($15,000–$25,000).
- Slightly increased RIP processing time.
- On-press dot gain is higher than with conventional screening.
- The possibility of visible graininess in large highlight areas.

Consult your print service provider to determine whether stochastic screening is something they offer and whether it might be appropriate for your job. There may be increased job cost because of special handling.

Screen Values: Recipes for Color

When you need to describe a combination of cyan, magenta, yellow, and black that will print a particular color, such as the dusky blue in **Figure 2.10**, the recipe is written in this format: C=75 M=50 Y=25 K=0. Think of halftone dots as occupying a square grid, each in its own square of the grid. The numbers signify a percentage of the area of the square that will be filled. If the square is full, it's 100 percent. If half the area of the square is filled, it's 50 percent, and so on.

Figure 2.10 *Dusty blue: 75 percent cyan, 50 percent magenta, and 25 percent yellow.*

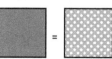 =

Limitations of CMYK

While an extensive range of colors can be rendered with various combinations of cyan, magenta, yellow, and black inks, there's still a limit to what CMYK can create. The human eye can see a huge range of colors—larger than even the large gamut of a computer monitor. But the total gamut of the process inks is considerably smaller than the human eye can see, or even the range that the monitor can display. Consequently, images that are quite vibrant on your monitor may print disappointingly dull. It's not because your print service provider is incompetent. It's because of the limitations of the printing-ink spectrum. In **Figure 2.11**, the large, colorful toe is an approximation of the range of colors perceived by the human eye. The solid triangular line corresponds to the range of colors that can be displayed on an RGB (red-green-blue) computer monitor. The much smaller dotted shape indicates the approximate gamut of CMYK inks. Note that the CMYK blob, while rather constricted, does not fall entirely within the RGB gamut. Some colors—bright yellows and cyan shades—fall outside the range that can be displayed faithfully on a monitor. Even a finely calibrated and color-managed monitor has its limitations.

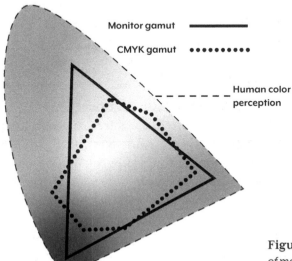

Figure 2.11 *A rough comparison of monitor and CMYK gamut to the range of visible light.*

This is not intended to plunge you into despondency over the limitations of the printing process. If your expectations are realistic, you can be prepared for the limitations of CMYK. And, equally importantly, you'll know when you need to step outside the world of cyan, magenta, yellow, and black to get what you want.

Why CMYK—Not CMYB?

It's easy to imagine that B might be mistaken for blue and thus confused with cyan. But where does the K come from? One theory holds that the K is from *key*, referring to black being printed first, so other colors can be aligned to its registration marks. Another notion is that the K is lifted from the end of the word black. Whatever the true origin of the mysterious K in the acronym, it's here to stay.

Spot Colors

A spot color is used when it is necessary to print colors that fall outside the range of CMYK inks. While it's obvious that inks such as fluorescent colors and metallics can't be faithfully imitated by process colors, some rather common colors fall outside the CMYK universe, such as bright orange and navy blue. That's why we need spot colors.

You're probably familiar with the Color Formula Guides from PANTONE® Inc. The terms *spot color* and PANTONE are often used interchangeably in the United States, although that's not strictly correct. The PANTONE PLUS SERIES FORMULA GUIDE is a recipe book for printers, providing ink-mixing formulas for more than 1,600 standard colors, many of which cannot be accurately rendered in process colors. While the name PANTONE has become synonymous with spot color, there are other spot-color resources, such as the Toyo Color Finder from Toyo Ink, and the DIC guide from Dainippon Ink and Chemicals, Inc. (used predominantly in Japan). And there are PANTONE swatchbooks that don't depict spot colors, such as the PANTONE PLUS SERIES CMYK Guide, which contains only colors created by combinations of cyan, magenta, yellow, and black, and the COLOR BRIDGE guides, which show spot colors next to the nearest CMYK equivalents.

While adding a spot color to a four-color job will increase the cost of printing because of the need to purchase additional ink, create another plate, and increase press setup time, it ensures that important colors will print as desired. If the printer has only a four-color press, the fifth color will necessitate a second run through the press, which will require more cleanup and further makeready time. But using a spot color can also eliminate problems caused by slight misregistration on press. Consider a job containing elements in a burgundy color consisting of a process color build of C=10 M=100 Y=35 K=50. Even the most conscientious pressman can find it challenging to keep fine elements such as small type and narrow rules in register across a large press sheet. It can also be difficult to keep the balance of four inks consistent from one part of the paper to another or from one press sheet to another in a long, multipage job. Any variation will result in color shifts, which would be especially noticeable in facing pages. Replacing the process build with a single ink, such as PANTONE 209, simplifies both registration and color-consistency issues. The increase in printing costs (as opposed to a four-color job) might be justified by the improved outcome.

New PANTONE PLUS Swatch Libraries

InDesign CC, Illustrator CC, and Photoshop CC use the new PANTONE PLUS libraries. These libraries use Lab color values by default; the CMYK Coated/Uncoated and COLOR BRIDGE Coated/Uncoated libraries provide CMYK values. The numbering system is the same as in previous PANTONE libraries, but 560 new colors were added to the basic guide, and the guides are now arranged chromatically rather than numerically.

The spot-to-CMYK conversion values have also changed, based on improved pigments and computerized press controls. If you attempt to replicate an old job in which a designer picked spot colors but printed the job as process, you may find that picking from the new PANTONE PLUS library and converting to CMYK results in different values. This could be problematic if the new job is intended to match the original work.

Adding to the confusion, you'll find that the built-in spot-to-CMYK conversions in InDesign and Illustrator yield different CMYK values than you'll see displayed in the PANTONE Color Bridge book. My advice? Go with the Adobe conversions; they seem to do a better job of approximating the spot color.

CV, CVC, CVU, M, C, U: Many Acronyms, Just One Ink

It's time to dispel some urban myths about spot-color designations. The terms *coated* and *uncoated* refer to paper, not ink. PANTONE 185C is PANTONE 185U is PANTONE 185M (apologies to Gertrude Stein). The C represents coated paper, and U signifies uncoated stock. These designations are primarily intended to keep you oriented as you view color on your computer monitor. For example, you may notice that a U version of a PANTONE color looks a bit less saturated and a bit darker compared to the C version. It's just an attempt to mimic ink behavior on different stocks. In the past, CVU meant "computer video uncoated," and CVC meant "computer video coated." You may encounter those designations in old files, as well as M for matte (a semi-dull paper surface).

What should you choose? Considering that it's the ink number that's significant (and that your monitor will never be a perfect match to the ultimate printed piece), feel free to just select your swatches from the Coated library and go on with your life.

Approximating Spot Colors with Process

It's a widespread practice to pick colors from a swatchbook, such as the PANTONE PLUS Color Formula Guide, even for jobs that are intended to print as process. Just because everyone does it doesn't mean it's right. (Sorry; I don't mean to sound like your mother.)

The problem with this approach (as with so many things your mother warned you about), is that it can lead to disappointment. Remember that the purpose of spot colors is to render colors that fall outside the range of CMYK, so process approximations of spot colors are often unsatisfactory.

For example, a CMYK conversion of a dark blue such as Reflex Blue loses some luster in the translation. It's unfortunate, but this is as close as a combination of cyan, magenta, yellow, and black can get to the navy blue of the official Brand X logo. As long as you know to expect this color approximation, you aren't shocked by the printed piece (**Figure 2.12**). But the president of Brand X will certainly be disappointed.

Figure 2.12 *The Brand X logo should be Reflex Blue, a navy blue. The CMYK conversion results in an unsightly purple. If you have a PANTONE swatch book, compare to the real Reflex Blue swatch.*

In the interest of realism on process jobs, consider selecting colors from a purely CMYK-based swatchbook instead, such as the TRUMATCH Colorfinder or one of the PANTONE process guides. If you want a single-source swatchbook showing how PANTONE+ spot colors compare to CMYK equivalents, the PANTONE+ Color Bridge™ provides helpful side-by-side swatches.

Press Issues

Although it's a highly developed endeavor, the application of ink to paper on a printing press is still a high-speed, physical process. As such, it's subject to the vagaries of temperature, humidity, and craftsmanship. Factor in cantankerous machinery and it's amazing anything ever gets printed. While you can't run the press, you can anticipate some common problems and build your files to facilitate printing.

Registration

Because printing inks are applied to paper in succession on an offset press, not simultaneously, accurate alignment of the printed inks (referred to as registration) is crucial. While a small amount of misregistration can be easily camouflaged within the natural variation of colors in images, it can be a glaring problem in some special cases. This is most apparent when dissimilar color areas meet with no ink in common. In **Figure 2.13**, the reversed letters of the two-color logo fall apart if it's printed badly out of register. Is it reasonable to expect the pressman to maintain tight register? Of course. Keeping such art in very tight register in two dimensions over a large press sheet can be challenging.

Figure 2.13 *Even slight misregister in a two-color logo can be fairly ugly. (Here, bad register is exaggerated for dramatic effect.)*

Even under the best-controlled press conditions, paper is subject to small amounts of stretching due to the physical stress of traveling through the press. Admittedly, the illustration shows a press sheet that is flagrantly out of register, which indicates two important facts: press conditions are awful, and you need to start looking for a new printing company. However, even under ideal conditions, such art may suffer at least very small shifts, and you should be emotionally prepared. How can you compensate? If you're allowed to do so, print such artwork in shades of a single color. Then, registration isn't an issue (**Figure 2.14**).

Figure 2.14 *One solution to registration challenges: Print the logo in a single color.*

If you're designing a logo or other art element, you should keep this potential issue in mind. If possible, design to minimize the heartbreak of misregistration by ensuring that color areas share at least one common ink; or, better yet, print in a single ink.

Trapping

As you saw in the Brand X logo, if there is misregistration on-press, the result can be unsightly gaps between color areas that don't share a common ink (**Figure 2.15**).

Figure 2.15 *Misregistration can cause gaps between color areas that don't have an ink in common (exaggerated for dramatic effect; no printer is likely to be this far off).*

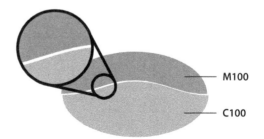

M100

C100

The remedy for this problem is to use trapping, which involves creating a rim of common color between the dissimilar color areas. In **Figure 2.16**, the C100-M100 trap is greatly exaggerated for illustrative purposes. In practice, trap thickness is usually around 0.003 inch and fairly unobtrusive.

Trap thickness may vary depending on prevailing press conditions and the conventions of the print service provider.

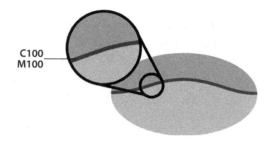

C100
M100

Figure 2.16 *Trapping between two dissimilar colors (here, greatly exaggerated).*

Here's some great news: It's not your problem. Trapping is an arcane pursuit that's best left to the print service provider, who uses specialized trapping software. Some trapping solutions can be complex, such as those involving metallic inks or neighboring gradients. And some trapping decisions depend on the order in which inks will be printed. You kids don't know how good you have it; we old folks had to hand-carve traps, in the snow, barefoot.

In trapping, the darker color defines the edge of objects being trapped to each other, and that determines which objects spread (expand), which objects choke (contract), and which objects remain sharp (unchanged). In **Figure 2.17**, you can see that different approaches to trapping are required for different circumstances.

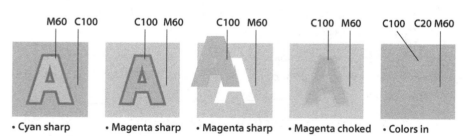

Figure 2.17 *Depending on the color, a shape may be spread (expanded), choked (shrunk inward), or left sharp (neither spread nor choked). The darkest color defines the edge, so lighter colors are spread into darker colors.*

- Cyan sharp
- Magenta spread
- Trap: C100-M60

- Magenta sharp
- Cyan spread
- Trap: C100-M60

- Magenta sharp
- Cyan spread
- Trap: C100-M60

- Magenta choked
- Cyan sharp
- Trap reduction: C50-M30

- Colors in common:
  No trap necessary

The trap line consists of a combination of the adjacent colors, and it is usually not as obvious as it is in the illustration. There's some exaggeration in Figure 2.17, to call attention to the trap itself. However, sometimes it is desirable to subdue the visible trap line, especially when lighter colors combine to create a heavy trap line. The color in the trap area can be reduced from

C100-M60 to C50-M30 to make it less noticeable; this is called trap reduction. In the last version, trapping is unnecessary because the objects have colors in common, so there's unlikely to be an unsightly gap in printing.

Even though trapping is the responsibility of the print service provider, you should keep it in mind as you design. If you feel that trap lines will mar the appearance of your artwork, consider creating artwork with common colors so that trapping is unnecessary. Also, as you examine proofs, you're usually looking for large errors, such as missing elements or incorrect color. But, as you can see, you should also be mindful of the little things, such as traps.

Large Ink Coverage Areas

Moving from tiny traps to the opposite end of the size spectrum, you'll discover that printing large color areas on offset presses presents some problems as well. (You're probably starting to wonder, "Is there *anything* that's easy to print?") Most ink is transparent, not opaque, and its thickness when applied to paper is measured in ten-thousandths of an inch. Consequently, covering a large area with a single spot-color ink can be challenging. Think of painting a wall. It often takes two coats to achieve smooth color coverage. Similarly, one solution is to apply two passes of the ink (called a double hit). But this can increase the cost of the job because it involves an additional unit on the press as well as extra ink. Depending on the ink color, the first instance of the color might be a screen tint (say, 50 percent) rather than a solid to avoid an overly heavy final appearance.

If the job already uses four-color process, a less expensive alternative is to create a process equivalent of the screened underlay described in the previous paragraph, then run a single pass of the spot color on top of it.

Before you take the law into your own hands and start trying to solve these problems on your own, have a conversation with your printer about the issues involved. Don't over-engineer the job in an effort to help. Either seek guidance from the print service provider's prepress department, or leave it to the professionals to handle your job appropriately for their printing conditions. While you may incur some additional cost, these special treatments pay off in a better-looking, more professional finished piece.

Rich Black

You don't have to be running spot colors to have large color areas requiring special treatment. On an offset press, large solid black areas usually need to be beefed up or they will appear weak. The solution is referred to as rich black, but the definition of a rich black varies by print service provider. In some cases, just adding a bit of cyan (40 to 60 percent) is considered sufficient, although this can result in a cool black with a bluish tinge. To avoid a color cast to the rich black area, many printers add a neutral balance of the three other process colors. This author was raised to believe that C=60 M=40 Y=40 K=100 constituted rich black, but your mileage may vary. And your printer may fervently disagree with that recipe; such things vary from shop to shop. As always, consult your printer for guidance.

If artwork or type knocks out of a rich black area (also called reversing out), it will require special handling to keep edges sharp and avoid color fringes (**Figure 2.18**). Once again, press misregistration is the culprit.

Figure 2.18 *Misregistration in a four-color rich black can be ugly. This calls for special handling.*

Remember that, in trapping, the darkest color defines the edge. The case of rich blacks might be considered a sort of reverse trap. You want only one color to define the edge of the type or other white artwork—the black ink. To accomplish this feat, it's necessary to pull back the other colors so that if any misregistration occurs, the other colors don't peek out and create a pink, blue, or yellow halo at the edge of the reversed type.

As you can see in **Figure 2.19**, the white type is knocked out of all four plates of a rich black area. Since the black plate defines the edge of the type, its knockout is sharp (not choked or spread). But the knocked-out type is pulled back in the cyan, magenta, and yellow (hence the bloated appearance). This same approach is used for type or art reversing out of a double-hit spot color.

Figure 2.19 *Special treatment for text reversed out (knocked out) of a four-color black.*

Here comes the familiar, comforting reminder: Setting up this pull-back treatment is the print service provider's responsibility. But it's good for you to be aware of these complexities as you design. All this trapping, knocking out, spreading, and choking (sounds kind of violent, doesn't it?) is part of the daily grind for the print service provider, but you can design in anticipation of these issues. Be mindful of your print service provider's specifications for minimum type size that can be safely reversed out of a multicolor build such as a rich black; even with pull-backs, tiny reversed type can be a challenge to print (and read).

Problem Inks

NOTE There are now substitutes for Reflex Blue that are better-behaved. The imitation Reflex Blue inks print with a very slightly different hue from that of "official" Reflex Blue, but they are not subject to the drying problems and bronzing effects of the genuine article. Talk to your printer about whether an imitation Reflex Blue ink might be advisable for your project. It may cost a bit more, but reducing job complications may be worth the added expense.

By the way, Reflex Blue isn't the only problematic ink; Rhodamine Red, Violet, fluorescent inks, and others can exhibit drying and scuffing problems, as well as color shifts when coated or exposed to UV light.

Inks are a mysterious amalgam of pigment, carriers, solvents, waxes, and extenders. Ink problems can be caused by multiple issues, including inadequate drying time, absorbent stocks, and poor adhesion. But some problems arise from the pigments themselves. Because of its common use and stubborn personality, perhaps the best-known is Reflex Blue, which is a navy blue. Reflex Blue is notorious for scuffing, smearing, oxidizing, and slow drying times. If you use Reflex Blue in your job, be prepared to tack on an extra day or so for additional post-press drying time. Additives can speed up the drying process. Depending on how heavily the color is used in your job, you can also expect slight surcharges for protective coatings (discussed later in this chapter). An aqueous coating, applied on-press, is a common solution. Clear aqueous coatings usually cover the entire printed area, preventing scuffing without changing the color of the piece. UV coatings, though, can be problematic, because the heat may accelerate the bronzing effect and accentuate a resulting purplish color shift.

While Reflex Blue is used in formulating many of the dark blue PANTONE colors, it's most troublesome by itself. It may also contribute somewhat to slower drying times and scuffing to some extent in inks mixed with it, but not as aggressively as when used alone. Drying agents can be added to Reflex Blue ink, and aqueous coatings can reduce oxidizing and scuffing.

Specialty Inks

Metallic and fluorescent inks can add visual interest to a printed piece. Metallic inks, while somewhat expensive, are still less costly than using foil stamping. Foil stamping is a special finishing process involving heat, pressure, and thin sheets of metallic foil. See Chapter 3, "Binding and Finishing," for more information on foil stamping. The problems they pose are once again due to key pigments. Actual aluminum or bronze (zinc/copper) powder provides the basic metallic appearance, while additional pigments introduce other tinges. Metallic inks as accents are not too troublesome, but these inks can mottle over large areas. Unlike most inks, metallic inks are almost opaque, which affects trapping and the order in which the ink is printed. Usually, metallic inks are printed first because of their tendency to adhere poorly to previous inks. While metallic ink will never be as shiny as foil stamping, it's most convincing on coated stock but may almost completely lose its metallic appearance on very absorbent uncoated stock. Varnishing metallic ink will not make it shinier (in fact, even gloss varnish will slightly diminish the metallic appearance), although it will subdue metallic ink's tendency to scuff and flake. If you're creating stationery, be very cautious about using metallic inks. The stress of being passed through a laser or inkjet printer can cause metallic flakes to dislodge and find new homes deep inside the printer.

Because of the metallic content, the inks are also subject to oxidation (especially the bronzes). While varnishing (discussed in the next section) may slow down the process, be prepared for some dulling over time. Also be prepared to consider somewhat extended drying times as part of your job timeline. Your printer will tell you what to expect.

Fluorescent inks can add a vibrant punch, but their pigments have a limited life span, especially if exposed to sunlight for extended periods. Printing a double hit of the ink can enhance its vibrancy, since fluorescent inks tend to be transparent. They are also sensitive to heat, so such inks are not the best choice for stationery that will be run through a laser printer or copier because of the heat involved in fusing.

Custom Mixed Inks

If you just can't find a PANTONE or Toyo swatch to match the color you want, your print service provider can custom-mix an ink that's just right for your job. Expect to pay more for this service since it involves extra labor and may consume extra ink (mixed as insurance for the print service provider). If you anticipate reprinting the job at a later date, tell the print service provider up front so they can retain the recipe for future use. It's not practical to "mix enough for later." Unlike wine, ink does not improve with age.

Coatings and Varnishes

Coatings are applied for two reasons: for special visual effects or to protect ink from scuffing or rubbing off. There are three general categories of coatings in print:

- Aqueous coatings are water-based coatings. They're applied on-press and cover the press sheet uniformly with gloss, matte, satin, or dull finishes. They behave best on coated or matte stocks because the inherent coating on such stocks provides an even surface and consistent absorption. Aqueous coatings can be applied to uncoated stock, but there is the risk of mottling due to the nonuniform surface of uncoated stock. Aqueous coatings actually provide better scuffing protection than varnishes.

- Ultraviolet (UV) coatings are cured by UV light for quick drying. Available in matte, dull, satin, and gloss, they can be applied inline on a specially equipped press.

- Varnishes are applied on-press and are available in the standard assortment of gloss, dull, satin, and matte. There are also special varnishes that impart a textured finish such as a gritty, sand-like feel, a crackled appearance, or a velvet surface. Varnishes are usually applied overall, but special effects can be obtained by using spot varnishes to highlight artwork. Spot-gloss varnishes, for example, can highlight artwork to make it stand out from the page, especially on matte stock. Applying a spot-gloss varnish on a square-cut image is fairly painless, but there's a bit more work involved in spot varnishing silhouetted artwork (**Figure 2.20**). The separate plate used for a spot varnish is created in the way a spot color is created.

Figure 2.20 *Adding a spot varnish can accentuate part of a graphic, but creating the varnish plate requires some work (try to imagine that the last letter is **very** shiny). For a single character such as this, the technique is simple. For a more complex shape, such as a bicycle, the artwork for the varnish must follow the contours of the subject.*

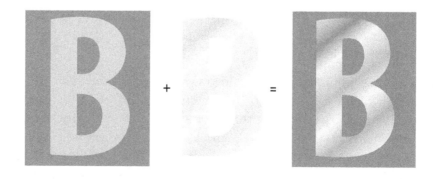

Note that since varnishes and aqueous/UV coatings are sealants, it's necessary to apply the varnish or other coating as the last pass. Pieces requiring gluing (such as pocket folders or packaging) require spot application of such coatings, since gluing and folding take place after varnish or other coatings are applied. Spot application applies the varnish much like an ink, isolating it to certain areas (rather than applying it as an overall coat) so that glued areas are free of ink and varnish. This allows the glue to adhere correctly.

Digital Printing

In their earliest iterations, digital printing devices were not much more than glorified laser printers. The toner-based engines were beefed up to print faster and bigger, but they were still prone to have all the characteristics of laser printers. Color consistency between impressions was quite problematic, innocent environmental influences such as humidity were mortal enemies of registration, and halftone reproduction on high-speed, black-and-white machines was, to be charitable, miserable. While digital printing has always offered advantages, such as relatively affordable short runs and the ability to print variable data, it was initially deemed appropriate only for basic direct mail or text-only pieces because of the superior quality of offset printing. But all of that has changed.

Digital Printing Advantages

The gap between digital and conventional offset printing is closing, and the premium digital print offerings from vendors such as Xeikon, Kodak, Xerox, and HP Indigo rival the appearance of offset printing while still offering the additional appeal of customization and short runs.

Short Runs

Without the need to image and mount plates, toner-based digital printing offers some advantages. The minimum run for a digital job can be 200 or less, rather than 10,000. This can lower the cost threshold for color printing for many jobs.

Variable Data

You've received those compelling personal letters: "Dear [Your Name Here]."
Such customization is the most basic form of variable data publishing (VDP).
Since each impression of a document on a toner-based digital press can
be different, even images can be customized for very targeted direct-mail
pieces. Preparing such a piece requires careful planning, and the VDP software used by the print service provider is rather expensive. However, you
may find the added expense and complexity worthwhile, because it's been
shown that customized direct mail pieces elicit much higher response than
generic mailings. If you have used the mail-merge features available in a
word processing program, or the Data Merge features offered in InDesign,
you have done basic variable data publishing. The complexities of setting up
VDP work are outside the scope of this book.

Digital Printing Issues

While offset printing benefits from at least 100 years of refinement, digital
printing is a relatively recent undertaking. Digital printing offers some solutions, such as reducing the expense of short print runs. But it introduces
new challenges, such as the behavior of toner on paper and paper-size
limitations. Large areas of uniform color can sometimes be problematic on
toner-based systems. For example, a brochure cover that is printed with a
full-bleed build of C100-Y80 may look slightly mottled compared to the same
piece printed on a conventional offset press. For now, it's just one of those
things that you have to anticipate. Design around the limitation by using a
collage of images or smaller areas of color in which any mottling will not be
glaringly apparent (**Figure 2.21**).

Figure 2.21 *A screen build that covers large areas uniformly on a conventional offset press (left) may appear mottled when printed on a toner-based digital press (right).*

Unlike offset printing, most toner-based presses don't require rich blacks. Not only is the dense black nature of toner sufficient for complete coverage, adding three other colors can interfere with the toner's adhesion to paper and may actually make things worse.

Most toner-based printing lacks the inherent shine we're accustomed to seeing in printed pieces, even on coated stock. This is due to the nature of the toners themselves. The HP Indigo presses use a slurry of toner in a carrier (called HP ElectroInk), so their output often more closely resembles traditional offset printing. But all of the toner-based output can be coated either via extra imaging units or through coating stations attached to the press. Stand-alone coating equipment can also be used, but this requires that the printed pieces be moved to a separate coating machine and fed through it.

There are other differences between toner-based printing and conventional offset printing. For example, most digital printing processes do not require trapping because the toner is usually placed onto a carrier, and all colors are transferred to the paper in one impression, which often eliminates misregistration. Many digital presses use stochastic screening rather than conventional halftone dots and angles. These differences contribute to digital printing being a viable alternative to offset.

Registration

On most toner-based digital presses, toner for all four process colors is accumulated on a carrier that is held by the strange miracle of electrostatic force, then deposited as a single transfer to the paper. As a result, registration is somewhat easier to maintain than on offset presses, which apply each color separately from individual inking units. Sophisticated internal monitoring in these modern presses also ensures consistency. These devices demand tight environmental controls. Slight changes in humidity and temperature can play havoc with output, so toner-based digital presses are usually sequestered in specially constructed rooms that are engineered to maintain a constant environment.

Spot Colors on Toner-Based Digital Presses

Currently, spot-color offerings are limited on toner-based digital presses. Although HP Indigo and Xeikon presses do offer additional units for available spot colors (which include several metallics and fluorescents), not every

PANTONE color is available for these presses. However, this limitation is not as dire as it sounds. Even though the primary toner colors are called cyan, magenta, yellow, and black on these devices, the pigments are not identical to those used in offset process colors. In some ways, this is actually good news. The toners are often more vibrant than standard process inks, so they can simulate a wider range of PANTONE colors without resorting to actual spot colors. PANTONE provides digital process chip books certified for the HP Indigo and Xerox digital presses.

Paper Requirements and Limitations

Most digital presses are sheet-fed and have much smaller mouths than their offset brethren, which generally limits their output to approximately tabloid sizes. Roll-fed devices such as the Xeikon presses, however, cut the paper only after printing. And while the imaging width is about 19 inches, the total length of a piece can be banner size.

While there is a wide range of paper certified for toner-based digital presses, stock choice isn't unlimited. Consult your print service provider for samples of supported stock before you get your heart set on a particular paper that is subsequently not deemed appropriate. The complicated paper paths in such devices preclude the use of extremely thin (or extremely heavy) stock. And the high heat of fusing the toner to the substrate can cause curling or waving. In the interior of a digitally printed piece, this may not be so noticeable, but covers may require the extra step of lamination to prevent curling.

Cracking and Flaking

Toner is fused to the surface of paper rather than being partially absorbed as conventional offset ink is. Consequently, it's sitting on top of the paper like a coat of inflexible paint and is prone to cracking during any folding or creasing processes. Consider this as you design for toner-based digital output, and avoid large instances of crossover art if possible. A rule here and there or the occasional line of headline text shouldn't be a problem. But the more toner encrusting the paper along the fold, the uglier the outcome can be.

Resolution and Screen Ruling

For conventional offset presses, platesetters are often used to digitally image plates. Data-driven lasers expose the photosensitive surface of a plate, which is then developed and mounted on a press. Imagesetters (which have largely given way to platesetters) are used to expose film, which is then used to create an image on a printing plate (see Chapter 1, "Life Cycle of a Print Job," for more information on imagesetters and platesetters). Whereas imagesetters and platesetters achieve resolution of 2400–3600 dpi, most toner-based electrostatic systems fall between 600–1200 dpi. Consequently, while these systems are capable of fairly high line screens (150–200 lpi and higher, depending on the vendor), be cautious about using very fine line weights or type that has extremely fine serifs. It's a good idea to ask your print service provider to provide specifications so you know the limitations of their printing process before you go too far in your design.

Your Monitor Is Not Made of Paper

Seems hardly worth mentioning: Your monitor uses transmitted light to display a semblance of your design piece, whereas the final printed job consists of ink on physical paper. When you think of things in those terms, you shouldn't be surprised that the two realities don't look the same. Yet, it's easy to forget the fundamental fact that your monitor is not displaying ink on paper, and it can be tempting to make color decisions based on what you view onscreen. Wouldn't it be great if your monitor could more closely match the printed outcome of your job? Your monitor will never be identical to the printed piece, but it is possible to control your software and your monitor for a much closer match.

A Quick Overview of Color Management

It's a challenge to modify your monitor's display to simulate ink on paper. It involves color management, which is the science of profiling one device (such as a monitor) to match another device (such as a press). Profiling is the process of using specialized (and often expensive) equipment to evaluate devices such as scanners, monitors, proofing systems, and presses to determine the color characteristics of each device. Once these characteristics are known, the information can be used by software such as Adobe Photoshop to display an image onscreen in a way that more realistically represents how the image will appear when it is printed. Implementing color management is not cheap, it's not easy, and it's not for the faint of heart. Color management gets easier as more software incorporates support for it, but it's best left to dedicated color-management consultants to set up a color-managed workflow. Even then, the setup must subsequently be maintained with conscientious calibration of monitors and printers in order to ensure optimal results.

An in-depth exploration of color management is outside the scope of this book. For an excellent—and very readable—resource on color management, I highly recommend that you buy a copy of *Real World Color Management, 2nd Edition* by Bruce Fraser, Chris Murphy, and Fred Bunting (Peachpit Press, 2004), and take it to the beach with you.

Feeling a bit intimidated by the concepts of color management? Don't feel bad—that's normal and appropriate. But here's some good news: Even if you fall short of a fully color-managed workflow, you can still benefit by implementing some simple procedures in the interest of consistency between the color on your monitor and the appearance of ink on paper.

Control Your Environment

- Minimize lighting interference. Subdue the ambient light in your work space, and avoid glare on your monitor screen. Beware of incidental light reflected from brightly colored painted surfaces. Strive for consistency despite the changing light of day, and if you're like most of us, half the night. The ideal solution is to block windows, have a neutral gray room, and install lights that meet the color temperature of sunlight (more about lighting in a bit).

- Subdue that psychedelic monitor background. Vivid surrounding colors complicate color judgments when viewing images. And consider the after-effects of constantly staring at a brightly colored desktop. Your eyes' color receptors grow weary, which affects what you view afterward. For example, stare at a bright green square, then shift to a white piece of paper. You'll see a pinkish cast to the paper. So, dull as it may seem, an old-fashioned gray desktop is your best bet. If that makes you cringe, compromise by using a grayscale image, and tell your friends you're going through an Ansel Adams phase.

- Take off that bright red shirt (*how does she know what I'm wearing?*)— reflected light from your clothing can factor into how you view color on your monitor.

- Calibrate and profile your monitor. For best results, consider using a colorimeter such as the X-Rite i1 Display Pro or ColorMunki Display. These solutions utilize specialized measuring devices and companion software to build custom color profiles for your monitor. Whichever approach you choose, you should allow your monitor to warm up for at least 30 minutes, and set it to display at least "thousands of colors." It's best if your monitor is set to 24-bit color ("millions of colors"). Each utility guides you through appropriate setup, including which settings to use for the contrast and brightness of your monitor.

  Calibration is not a one-time endeavor. CRTs (cathode ray tubes: think of old televisions) were prone to drift over time, but they have been almost completely replaced by more stable flat-screen LCD monitors. An Apple iMac is almost nothing *but* monitor. But even LCD monitors should be calibrated approximately every 200–250 hours. If you are doing color-critical work, keep in mind that monitors have a finite life and eventually must be replaced when they can no longer be kept within reasonable values.

- Treat your desktop printer kindly. Despite the temptation of buying discount paper and inks, you'll find that you get the most predictable printing results by using recommended brand-name paper and ink cartridges. Yes, it's true that printers are cheap because the intention is to get you hooked on ink cartridges. But printer manufacturers put considerable research into creating colorants and substrates that work well together. What you save on off-brand refills and cheap paper will be offset by frustration when your output looks lousy.

- Invoke printer profiles. Even if you can't afford custom profiles for your devices, use the aforementioned monitor profiles and the canned printer profiles that are added when you install a printer, so that at least you'll be in the ballpark. Current versions of most graphics software offer color-management controls that make it fairly easy to plug in canned printer profiles when you print.

Realistic Expectations

If your expensive monitor is freshly calibrated, you've profiled all of your printers, painted your room a neutral gray, and you wear nothing but non-reflective black clothing...well, you're very stylish. But even the best monitor and most expensive desktop printer provide, at best, an approximation of what will happen when your job goes to press. It's important to have a realistic idea of how your job will look, and everything you can do to improve its appearance on your monitor and your in-house output is beneficial. You don't want any surprises late in the game.

Consequently, your final judgment on job appearance should be based on contract proofs created by your print service provider. Over time, you develop a sense of the relationship between what you see on your monitor, what comes out of your desktop color printer, and how a job will eventually print. I suppose you could call it "mental color management." Your honed instincts may prevent disappointment when what you create on your monitor is translated to ink on paper. But you don't write "OK" on your monitor—you write it on the printer's proof.

Viewing Color

Companies such as X-Rite and GTI specialize in color-viewing solutions, and your printer's viewing booth will give you an idea of industry standards. The booth is painted a neutral gray, and may even be in a special color viewing room that is painted neutral gray.

Viewing booths use standardized sources of illumination that are manufactured to tight tolerances in order to produce 5000K light. Why 5000K? You can argue that the recipients of printed pieces will view them under a wide spectrum of lighting conditions, from kitchens to garages to bathrooms and basements, so why does it even matter? The printing industry had to settle on something to serve as a common viewing condition for judging color, and 5000K is meant to approximate direct sunlight.

Having a standardized viewing environment avoids a phenomenon known as *metamerism*, wherein two colors may appear to match under one light source but don't match under different lighting conditions. For example, a sample paint chip and a piece of fabric might appear very close in color under a store's commercial lighting but look very different when viewed in your own living room. Sound familiar?

There's much more to determining the ideal light source than just color temperature; other considerations include spectral power distribution, color rendering index, and lumens (bored yet?).

If you'd like to improve the conditions under which you view color in your office or home, there are suppliers that sell lighting that falls in the desired 5000–6500K color temperature range. Although such lighting solutions are not targeted to the graphic arts industry, they provide better conditions than the tungsten or fluorescent lights in your environment.

To determine if your light source is acceptable for acceptable color viewing, you can use one of the lighting indicator patches available. PANTONE offers lighting indicator patches for both D50 (5000K) and D65 (6500K) conditions (**Figure 2.22**). If the light source falls within the acceptable range, the lighting indicator patch appears to be a uniform color; if not, you will see an obvious difference between two areas of the patch.

TIP For in-home or small office color viewing, consider the solutions available from OttLite (www.ottlite.com). The OttLite 508 Daylight Illumination bulbs fall between 5000–5800K, and are reasonably good for judging color. While the OttLite lamps aren't certified for color viewing, they provide a better viewing condition than the tungsten or fluorescent lights in office and home environments.

Figure 2.22 *PANTONE sells light-sensitive patches in two ranges: D50 (5000K) for traditional color-critical lighting conditions, and D65 (6500K) because many monitors are set to 6500K. A visible difference between the two stripes indicates that the light source is not accurate.*

The Printing Industries of America (www.printing.org/RHEM) offers RHEM lighting indicator patches (**Figure 2.23**). Under 5000K lighting, the patch is a uniform reddish purple. Under a light source that falls outside the approved range, stripes become apparent.

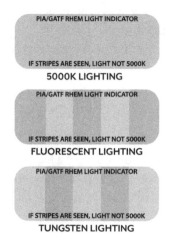

Figure 2.23 *RHEM lighting indicators display one pattern of stripes under tungsten lighting, and another pattern under fluorescent lighting. These adhesive stickers can easily be placed on proofs and artwork and used to judge the lighting conditions.*

What About Your Monitor?

Monitors are usually shipped with a white point set to 9300K (a bright, bluish temperature). If you set the white point of your monitor to 5000K, it will seem reddish and dark by comparison. Consequently, it's a widespread practice to set monitors to 6500K. This may seem inconsistent, given the seemingly sacred 5000K viewing booth lights, but it's a workable compromise.

Contract Proofs

Before a commercial print service provider cranks up a multimillion-dollar press for your job, proofs will be generated to check color and content. Internally, print service providers may use various kinds of proofs to check various aspects of a job. For example, desktop inkjet or laser output is used to check for problem fonts or mechanical issues, large-format prints are used to check imposed pages, and film-based proofs or digital proofs are used for color matching. Whereas in the olden days, print service providers generated film to create proofs, we've moved into the age of direct-to-plate printing, so film output is almost nonexistent. But don't feel that a digital proof is somehow less reliable than a film-based proof. If digital proofs are based on the same data from the RIP that creates plates, they should be reliable for content. However, not all digital proofs show halftones, so you may be unable to check for problems such as moiré. And it may not be possible to generate a digital proof on all paper stocks.

A signed contract proof carries obligations (hence the word contract). The designer's signature says, "This proof accurately reflects my intended design. Match this on press, and I'll be happy." And the print service provider's responsibility is to match the color and mechanical content of the contract proof on press.

In addition to portraying the mechanics of the piece, such as type flow, image crop, and page content, contract proofs are also intended to indicate what the final color should be when the job is on press.

If the printed piece doesn't match the proof you signed, you have a legitimate gripe with the print service provider. If you miss something important on the proof, but the print service provider faithfully matches it, you're at fault. So it behooves you to very carefully inspect a contract proof before signing off on it.

Trimming, Binding, and Finishing

3

Getting ink on paper isn't the whole story. The printed piece must be trimmed to its final size and subjected to any required folding and gluing. Build it the wrong size in the beginning and you'll suffer the slings and arrows of irritated prepress operators who have to perform surgery on your file; layout repairs cost money and time. The mechanical alterations required to mend incorrect page size or configuration can be complex (and expensive). Even if your artwork is perfect, you must keep in mind that trimming, folding, binding, and fancy finishing treatments such as embossing are all physical processes. As a designer, you can't control those physical processes. But if you take those possibilities into account as you prepare artwork and create page layouts, you may be able to minimize adverse effects.

One Size Does Not Fit All

Even if you don't sew, you can nonetheless anticipate the unfortunate results of using a defective pattern. The old adage "measure twice, cut once" applies to any manufacturing process, whether it's sewing, carpentry, or printing.

Building your files without considering the finishing processes (like trimming and binding) can cost you money and delay your job. Consequently, the more you know about folding, trimming, binding, and imposition, the better prepared you'll be to correctly build files. Let's start with two dimensions—width and height—and work our way up to the challenge of designing in three dimensions. Think of it as one of those fun spatial reasoning games that you loved as a child. (Or maybe you didn't. In that case, you'll hate this part of the book.) And all games have rules....

Rule Number One: Build to the Correct Trim Size

If you're creating an odd-sized piece—say, a 5-by-4 inch invitation—don't put it all alone in the middle of a letter-sized page. Instead, create a custom page size that matches the final trim size of your piece. In Adobe InDesign, specify the trim size as you begin the document, along with bleed, if necessary (**Figure 3.1**).

NOTE There's a lot of colorful language in printing, and much of it has to do with the arts of trimming, folding, and binding: creep, dummy, bleed, guillotine, jogging, nipping, perfect, shingle, twist, punch, bust...
I believe some of these were also dance crazes in the 1960s.

Figure 3.1 *To specify a custom page size, enter the correct values in the Width and Height fields as you create a new file in InDesign. Don't forget to click More Options and specify the correct bleed amount.*

If you're using Adobe Illustrator, the Artboard dimensions equal the trim size. For more information on the way Illustrator handles Artboards, see Chapter 11, "Illustrator Production Tips."

Why is this important? Take a simple business card as an example. The print service provider doesn't feed little individual 3.5-by-2 inch pieces of paper through a press to create cards one at a time. Nor does your business card float alone in the middle of a press sheet as in **Figure 3.2**.

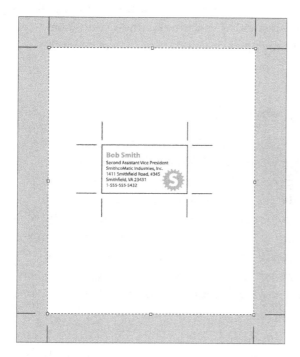

Figure 3.2 *Incorrect: A single business card on an oversized page.*

Instead, multiple copies of the card are printed simultaneously—imposed— for a press sheet, which is subsequently trimmed to final size to yield the individual cards. That's why it's important to supply artwork at the correct trim size (**Figure 3.3**).

Figure 3.3 *Correct: A single business card built to correct trim size: 3.5-by-2 inches.*

If you supply business card art as a lonely card on a letter-sized page, a pre-press operator will have to copy the card art into a new page of the correct size (or change the dimensions of the existing file). In addition to requiring an extra, time-consuming step, this also introduces the possibility of error—not copying some little detail or moving something in the process. **Figure 3.10**, later in this chapter, shows one method of imposing business cards. The imposition used by the printing company might be different, depending on the press and paper used.

Rule Number Two: Provide Bleed

Trimming is the finishing process that chops the printed piece to the final size. Since this is a mechanical process, it helps to have some margin for error during the trimming processes. Consequently, any time there is art-work intended to extend to the edge of the page, it's necessary to provide *bleed*—extra image beyond the edge of the true page size. Commonly, bleed extends 1/8 of an inch (.125 inch or 9 points) beyond the trim line, but your print service provider may request a different bleed value, especially on larger pieces such as posters or pocket folders. As with all issues, it behooves you to check the print service provider's specifications as you begin the job.

However, Rule Number Two does not invalidate Rule Number One, which stipulates that you should build to the correct trim size. Start with the correct trim size, and then add the extra image (or flat color) beyond the trim limits by dragging the edges of the appropriate frames. In InDesign or Illustrator, pull on the handles of image and tint frames to extend them beyond the page edges for sufficient bleed (**Figure 3.4**). You may have to scale up an image to provide adequate bleed (or perform some cloning in Photoshop).

Figure 3.4 *Extending artwork to provide bleed. The document is built to the correct final trim size, and the bleed extends beyond the trim.*

In Illustrator, if artwork extends to the visible Artboard edge, the Artboard is equivalent to the trim for your artwork. You can specify a bleed zone outside the Artboard and invoke that bleed zone when you print the file or save it as a PDF. In Illustrator CC, any artwork extending beyond the bleed zone is retained whether the file is saved as an EPS (Encapsulated PostScript) or native AI file.

Rule Number Three: Stay Away from the Edge

You may have your heart set on that adorable doggie paw-print border, but placing it too close to the edge or fold may result in disappointing results if there's any error in printing, folding, or binding. The closer your artwork is to the trim edge, the smaller the margin (literally) for error, and the more obvious any inaccuracy will be. What to do?

Don't place artwork perilously close to the edges (both internal and external). But, if you just must, make the margin as wide as possible to camouflage any problems. A small trimming error is less obvious against a larger total margin (**Figure 3.5**). Which leads us to Rule Number Four.

Figure 3.5 *In an ideal world, your border prints and trims perfectly. But a slight misalignment during trimming or binding can produce disappointing results (center). The effect is exaggerated for dramatic effect, of course, but you get the idea. A larger margin (right) can make it easier to camouflage a binding error.*

Rule Number Four: Follow the Print Specifications

Your print service provider should provide folding and trimming specifications to guide you as you create your work, including information such as:

- Minimum distance from edges and folds for artwork

- Minimum amount of bleed (usually 1/8 inch)

- Suggested sizes for panels in folded pieces

Folding: High-Speed Origami

Consider something as simple as a three-panel, letter-fold brochure. If all the panels were the same width, the innermost panel would buckle, and the piece would never fold completely flat—the brochure would spring open or the oversized panel would crinkle when forced (**Figure 3.6**). You can demonstrate this for yourself by folding a sheet of paper into approximate thirds, as if you were going to stuff it in an envelope.

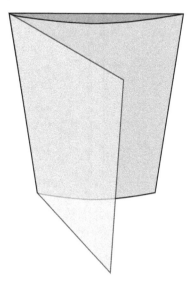

Figure 3.6 *Wrong: A three-panel piece with equal-sized panels. The inner panel buckles, so the piece can't fold properly.*

The solution? Make the fold-in panel narrower (**Figure 3.7**). Sounds simple, but think of the effect on your design: You have to build your design to accommodate the shorter third panel. In the past, the usual approach was to build such a piece as a two-page job—one page for the outside and one for the inside. However, there are now more flexible ways to build such projects, given the ability to create multiple artboards in Illustrator and the ability to have different page sizes within a document in InDesign. We'll take a look at those approaches in Chapter 11, "Illustrator Production Tips," and Chapter 12, "InDesign Production Tips."

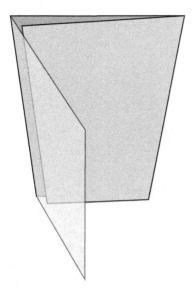

Figure 3.7 *Correct: Three-panel piece folded so the innermost panel is narrower. Now the piece folds flat.*

TIP If you aren't fluent in picas, you may find it frustrating that InDesign uses picas by default. If you prefer to work in inches (or ciceros, or anything else), just go to InDesign > Preferences > Units & Increments (PC: Edit > Preferences > Units & Increments) and change the setting with no document open. Every future new document will use the setting you choose. This won't change existing documents; you'll have to fix them when you open them.

The customary short trim amount is 3/32 inch. So, for example, if the finished flat (open) width is 11 inches, you would build the file with two panels that are 3.6979 inches wide and one panel 3.6042 inches wide. Keep in mind that the inside and outside of the piece are mirrors of each other: The outside of the brochure will need the short trim panel on the left, and the inside of the brochure will need the short trim panel on the right (**Figure 3.8**).

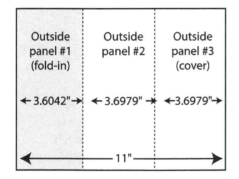
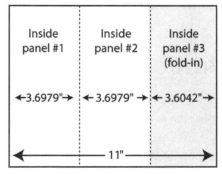

Figure 3.8 *The outside and inside of a trifold brochure, showing where the short-trim fold-in panel falls on each side of the brochure.*

TIP Need a template for a folding project, but don't feel like doing the math? You might want to use www.foldfactory.com. Subscribe to build and download templates in 85 popular styles. You can also learn a lot about folding from the great resources on the site.

Some folding configurations, such as the accordion fold (also sometimes called a Z-fold), don't require short panels (**Figure 3.9**).

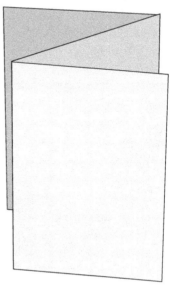

Figure 3.9 *Folding configurations such as the accordion fold don't require a short-trim panel.*

As always, check with the print service provider early in the game to ensure that your artwork meets their requirements. Note that thick paper stock may necessitate even greater short-trim values (that is, even more lopped off that short-trimmed panel) to compensate for the thickness of the folded piece.

Before starting, ask your print service provider what panel sizes they suggest, based on the paper stock to be used on the job and the requirements of their equipment.

In fact, your print service provider may be able to provide you with a standard set of measurements—or even a working template file—to use as the basis for your folding piece.

Imposition

The process of laying out individual pages or other pieces in final printing position is called *imposition*. The size and configuration of an imposition arrangement is dictated by the dimensions and printing orientation of the paper running through the press.

Simple Imposition

As mentioned earlier in this chapter, business cards don't shoot out of the press one by one. Multiple cards are laid out on each sheet, then cut apart. If you've created business cards on a desktop printer, you have some idea of what's involved. It's fun trying to get the edges of your artwork to line up with the perforations on the paper stock, isn't it? Of course, the imposition and trimming capabilities of a commercial printer are much more sophisticated.

When you order business cards, the printer is not going to ask you to send an imposed file (if he does, find another printer). Instead, you will just send artwork for the single card.

But if you'd like some sense of what's involved in imposition, it's pretty straightforward to set up a simple business card (**Figure 3.10**).

Figure 3.10 *Simple, ten-up imposition for homemade business cards. Looks easy enough (dashed lines indicate trim).*

However, if there is artwork that needs to bleed off the edge of the card or fall close to the trim edge, the imposition and trimming process must ensure that, if there are small errors in the process, important artwork is not inadvertently trimmed off.

To avoid awkward edges on pieces with artwork that bleeds or is positioned close to the edge, the prepress operator has to be a bit creative with the multicard layout, arranging the art so that similar sides of the cards print adjacent to each other (**Figure 3.11**). Keep this trick in mind the next time you're printing homemade cards. It may save some paper—and some aggravation.

Figure 3.11 *Artwork that bleeds presents additional challenges during imposition and trimming. Here are two possible solutions to trimming cards with bleed (dashed lines indicate a cut).*

On the left, a double-trim layout (easy to lay out but requires additional cuts).

On the right, a more economical layout requiring fewer cuts.

Nesting

To efficiently print and cut shaped pieces such as packaging and other die-cut pieces, *nested* impositions (**Figure 3.12**) may be used (also called *ganged* impositions). Nested impositions may even include pieces from multiple jobs, arranged to facilitate not only economical use of paper but also to save on ink and to maximize the efficiency of the die-cutting process.

Setting up a nested imposition involves more than just positioning artwork (although that alone can be complex); the arrangement also has to take into consideration ink coverage to ensure predictable imaging.

Imposition software such as PREPS from Kodak (graphics.kodak.com) and packaging solutions such as ArtiosCAD from Esko (www.esko.com) provide powerful options for creating complicated nesting layouts for print.

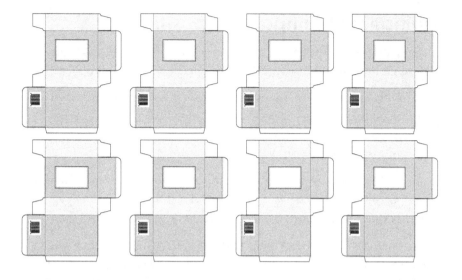

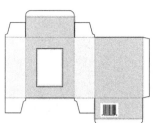

Figure 3.12 *Nesting impositions can increase the efficiency of both printing and die cutting a job. Here, nesting has doubled the number of pieces on a press sheet.*

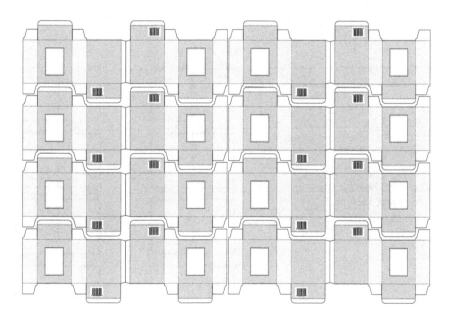

Pagination: Multipage Imposition

Let the spatial reasoning games begin! As you move beyond single pieces like business cards, you will discover that things get a bit more complicated.

When multipage pieces are imposed, the sheet is folded and trimmed to become a group of printed pages, called a *signature*. Depending on the page size, the press capabilities, and the type of binding to be used, a signature could comprise 8, 16, 32, or more pages.

This might be a good time to get a little destructive in the name of science. Buy (or borrow) a weekly news magazine and leaf through it. The pages appear, as you might expect, in *reader's spreads*: 2–3, 4–5, 6–7, and so on.

But pry out the staples at the center of the magazine and note how the pages were printed. For example, in a saddle-stitched 96-page magazine, you'll find that page 96 is printed across from page 1, page 95 is across from page 2, page 94 is across from page 3, and so on. This arrangement is referred to as *printer's spreads* (**Figure 3.13**).

Figure 3.13 *Reader's spreads (left) compared to pages imposed in printer's spreads (right). Pages 4 and 5 face each other in both examples because they make up the center spread of the eight-page piece.*

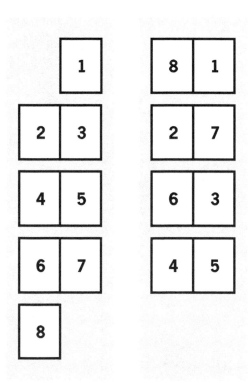

If the spatial reasoning challenge of figuring out which pages should face each other on the final printed sheet frightens you, there is good news: You don't have to build your files in printer's spreads. In fact, you shouldn't. It's better to let the print service provider take care of imposition. Build your facing-page document as two-page reader's spreads. Additionally, don't build your spreads as single pages (that is, don't put pages two and three on one big page).

If your print service provider requests that you supply files already in printer's spreads, you have a right to be concerned. Imposition of pages is a very basic printing service, and a printer who lacks that capability is likely to fall short in other areas. Asking you to perform imposition places additional responsibility on you, and the complexity of imposition increases proportionally with the number of pages in your publication.

Because facing pages don't actually print next to each other (except for the center spread), a number of errors can creep in. Variations in ink coverage across a press sheet may result in colors not matching, and errors in print, trim, and binding can cause crossover elements to be misaligned or mismatched in the finished piece (**Figure 3.14**).

Figure 3.14 *Reader spreads as they appear onscreen (left), compared to printer spreads exhibiting printing and binding problems (right). Color and binding errors are exaggerated for dramatic effect.*

Thanks to sophisticated press controls, the results are rarely this dramatic, but you should take this into consideration as you design. Is there a crucial piece of artwork that needs to span two pages? If so, it will fare best if it's placed on the center spread, where it will print intact. Now that you know that most spreads are not printed together, this may also inspire you to avoid placing photographs so that they extend onto a facing page. Since the pages aren't printed together, even a very slight variation in ink coverage between the pages could become obvious where the two portions of the photograph meet at the center. It might be better to stop the photograph at the inner edge of one page rather than continuing it onto the facing page.

You might consider modifying your design to allow for these issues. Move artwork away from the center fold to avoid crossover issues entirely. That's not cheating; it's *planning.*

Keep in mind that the awful outcome depicted in Figure 3.14 is a dramatic exaggeration of a worst-case scenario. Believe me, the printing and binding process is not this sloppy (if it is, it's time to find a new print service provider). But it gives you some sense of what can go wrong.

To get a feel for how your piece is actually printed, folded, and trimmed, ask your print service provider to give you a *folding dummy* for your job. It's a folded and numbered representation of how your pages will be printed, and it's very helpful as you contemplate the mechanics of your job.

If you're given to origami, you can make your own miniature folding dummy for an eight-page document by following the illustration below. This isn't meant to replace an authentic folding dummy created by your printer. It's just a great way for you to get some sense of what really goes on when your pages are split apart and grafted back together in the finished, imposed piece (**Figure 3.15**).

Figure 3.15 *A simple folding dummy for an eight-page document. Note how the pages are positioned, front and back, and the order in which the folds are performed.*

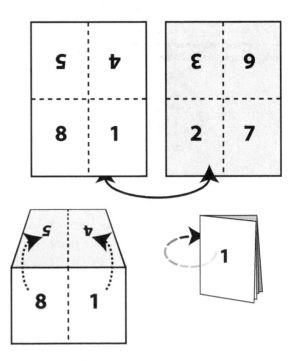

If you're creating a piece that contains a fold-in panel, remember that the fold-in panel will be short-trimmed, and position your art accordingly, allowing for at least a .125 inch reduction in page width on those pages. Build the file as shown in **Figure 3.16**, wherein the dashed lines over pages 6 and 7 indicate the short trim.

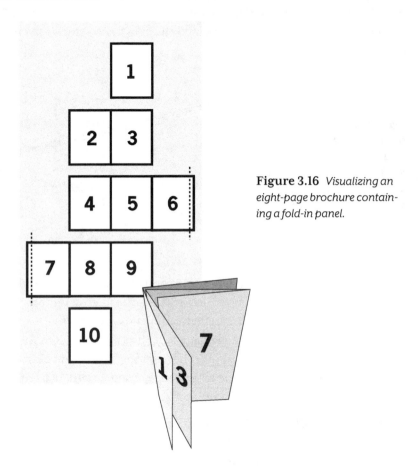

Figure 3.16 *Visualizing an eight-page brochure containing a fold-in panel.*

Note that the page numbers in the illustration are just for identification. You'll have to decide whether to number pages by position in the document or by viewing order. For example, as this piece is opened and unfolded, the pages would actually be viewed in this order: 1, 2, 3, 4, 7, 5, 6, 8, 9, 10. Some designers elect to omit page numbers in such brochures because they must decide between the order of the pages in the page-layout application and the order that the pages are revealed as the reader unfolds the piece. Feel free to claim that page numbers would just detract from your fresh, clean design.

It's not just the width and height you have to worry about when preparing your piece for print. Paper thickness also contributes to the behavior of a finished printed product. To illustrate, stack several sheets of heavy paper, and then fold the stack in the middle. Notice what happens to the edges of the individual pieces of paper—they don't line up because the cumulative paper thickness at the fold drives the innermost pages out (**Figure 3.17**). This is called *page creep*. The more pages (and the heavier the stock), the more pronounced the effect.

Figure 3.17 *Paper thickness causes edges of pages to creep outward during binding. When the finished pages are trimmed, artwork on the inner pages will be closer to the trim edge.*

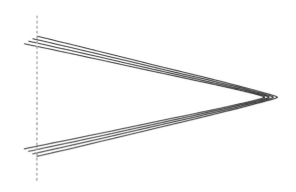

But look at a saddle-stitched publication, such as a weekly magazine: All the pages are nice and even. Why? Because the finished, assembled piece is trimmed after all the pages are stitched together. Of course, this makes for a more attractive magazine, but consider the side effects. On the innermost pages, artwork near the edge of the page should be even closer to the trimmed edge of the page, so the appearance of some elements—such as page numbers or decorative borders—should become inconsistent.

The fix? To maintain a consistent outer margin despite the page creep, the page content must be shifted incrementally to compensate for creep, using an approach known as *shingling* (**Figure 3.18**).

Figure 3.18 *Shingling to compensate for page creep during folding. To keep the external margins consistent throughout the bound piece, page content is moved inward, which results in tighter inner margins (right).*

 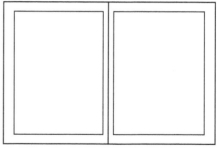

The closer a page is to the center of the magazine, the more content must be moved very slightly inward. While this results in tighter margins at the center, the result is usually less noticeable than margin errors would be on the outside edges of the pages.

The good news is that designers aren't expected to do shingling. It's done by the print service provider as part of the imposition process, which positions individual pages correctly for final printing, trimming, and binding. But you should still be mindful of the process as you design your pages so you can minimize problems. It helps if you design with generous inside margins to compensate, so that moving content inward during shingling won't cause any artwork to be crammed into the spine of the printed and bound piece.

Some binding processes incur shingling more frequently (or to a more pronounced degree) than others. As you might expect, binding a relatively large number of pages, such as those in a weekly magazine, will result in the need for more shingling than binding a publication containing only eight pages.

Perfect binding, which combines multiple small signatures and binds them together with a flat spine, minimizes page creep because of the limited number of pages in a single signature and because the signatures are next to one another as opposed to being nested within each other as in saddle-stitch binding.

Binding Methods

Many ways of combining multiple pages into a single, finished piece are available. At home, we use staples, paper clips, or binder clips to consolidate sheets of paper. The methods used in printing plants, as you might expect, are rather more elaborate. Different binding methods are utilized for different types of publications—saddle stitching for small publications, perfect binding for textbooks, comb binding for cookbooks, to name a few.

Saddle Stitching

Take another look at the magazine that you deconstructed earlier. The staples that anchor the pages at the spine of the magazine are actually created from a spool of wire. For the binding process, the loose sheets (folios) of printed pages that constitute the magazine are draped together over a saddle-like holder (hence the term *saddle stitching*). The stitching wire is fed into position, cut to the correct length for the thickness of the magazine, bent into shape, and then the legs of the staple are driven through the pages. Finally, the legs are bent into the final staple shape (**Figure 3.19**). Of course, this all takes place at high speed, in about the same amount of time it takes you to say the word *magazine*.

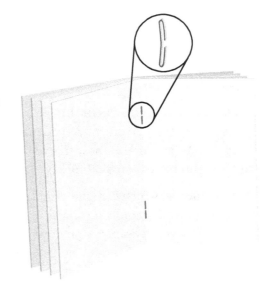

Figure 3.19 *In saddle stitching, wire is fed from a roll and then cut to form staples, which are driven through a sheaf of paper and then crimped.*

Perfect Binding and Case Binding

Perfect binding is used for larger publications such as textbooks (and some high-page–count journals). In perfect binding, creep is not as large an issue as it is with other binding methods, although it can still occur. Whereas magazines might combine about 100 pages in a saddle-stitched issue, when perfect binding is used, pages are gathered in much smaller groups—such as 16-page signatures—which are likely to result in less-pronounced creep. Then, multiple signatures are stacked together, trimmed (or ground off), and then glued together at the spine (**Figure 3.20**). Finally, a cover is added to enclose the pages, which is held in place by glue along the spine. For larger books such as textbooks, the spine is reinforced by adhering a cloth strip to the spine of the gathered signatures before affixing a hard cover. This is called *case binding*.

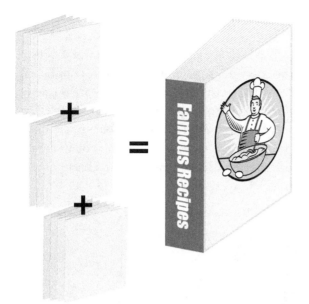

Figure 3.20 *In perfect binding, individual signatures are stitched with thread to keep their pages in place. Then, multiple signatures are gathered together and anchored with adhesive on the common spine. Finally, the cover is glued into position.*

Although the smaller constituent signatures in a perfect-bound book are not subject to the degree of creep that you might see in a magazine, you still have to consider some of the side effects of combining a high number of pages with the relatively stiff spine of a perfect binding. Even in a comparatively slender, perfect-bound magazine of 192 pages, there is pronounced pinching of the pages at the center of the finished magazine, making it difficult to read some text near the interior bound edge. You can compensate for this by using wider inside margins when you build your pages (**Figure 3.21**).

Figure 3.21 *Anticipate the pinch of perfect binding by setting wider inside margins (right).*

Comb Binding

Often used for publications such as cookbooks, textbooks, and workbooks, *comb binding* allows a book to be opened flat. Rectangular holes are punched in the pages of the book, and then the teeth of the plastic comb are pushed through the holes. Because the combs are coil-like and curly, the teeth curve back under a spine-like collar that forms a solid spine for the bound book (**Figure 3.22**). The plastic combs come in a variety of colors and diameters. Comb-bound books usually use heavier stock for the front and back covers, or they use clear plastic sheets as a protective first page.

Figure 3.22 *Comb binding allows books to be opened flat. It's great for cookbooks and workbooks but makes it challenging to add a printed spine.*

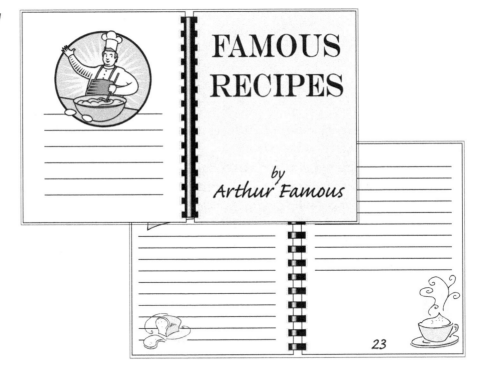

Comb binding has one disadvantage: It's a challenge to put a title or other copy on the spine, although it's possible to apply adhesive labels or even imprint the plastic combs by using silk screening at extra cost.

In preparing artwork for a publication that will be comb bound, you have to provide sufficiently wide inside margins so the punched holes won't impinge on any content. Your print service provider can give you specifications for the safe area.

Most print service providers and many office-supply stores can perform comb binding for you. But if you frequently produce short-run books or other small-quantity publications that require comb binding, you might consider purchasing punching and binding equipment of your own.

Coil Binding

In coil binding, a spiral of wire or plastic is threaded through round holes punched in the book (**Figure 3.23**). As with comb binding, coil binding (also called spiral binding) allows a piece to lie flat when open. However, there's no way to imprint a spine, and you must create a wide inner margin to define the live area as you design the piece so that the artwork in the page will clear the punch holes.

Figure 3.23 *Coil binding is suitable for notebooks, cookbooks, and textbooks. While this binding method allows a book to lie flat when open, there's no way to imprint the nonexistent spine.*

Other Binding Methods

If you're creating textbooks or notebook-like workbooks, you'll encounter other punch-and-bind methods that are similar in configuration to comb and coil binding. *Wire binding* uses tooth-like loops of wire similar in appearance to the teeth of comb binding, but it produces a sturdier binding than the plastic combs. By now, you're probably reciting the mantra, "Use wider inner margins to avoid the punch holes." Hold that thought. It applies to most specialty-binding methods.

For heavy-duty books with constantly changing content, such as a wallpaper sample book, *post binding* may be the most appropriate solution. In this binding method, metal posts are pushed through punched holes in the book and anchored with bolts that thread into the post centers. This method has the advantage of allowing you to add or replace pages, and it's possible to have an exterior cover with an imprinted spine.

Special presentations or other artistic publishing concepts may involve custom binding solutions such as handmade covers or cases and decorative binding devices such as screws or ribbons. Such pieces are usually used in very limited print runs and entail a considerable amount of handwork. Consequently, these undertakings require extremely careful planning.

Moving Beyond Two Dimensions

When you start building more complicated pieces, it's really helpful to create a dummy of some sort, so you can visualize the finished piece. It's easy to think of how the finished piece will look, but you need to consider how the piece will print and fold so you can create it correctly. An anatomically correct dummy will let you visualize both the inside and outside and will shed light on the difficulties of positioning tricky artwork. In fact, the challenge of lining up all that stuff in your head may force you to simplify the geometry of your concept.

Consider a pocket folder (**Figure 3.24**). Folded, its configuration resembles a simple, two-page spread. But take a folder apart so you can see how the pocket and its glue flaps are positioned, and you'll see that the printed piece is rather more complex. Any art falling over the pocket has to be carefully aligned with art on the inside of the piece, and this can present a challenge in design as well as in printing and finishing.

How do you build such a piece? Think of it as having an inside and an outside, and build it as a two-page document. As with all printed pieces, build to trim size. But you also have to think in three dimensions to take into consideration the physical processes of folding and gluing.

Figure 3.24 *The outside of the finished pocket folder looks like this...*

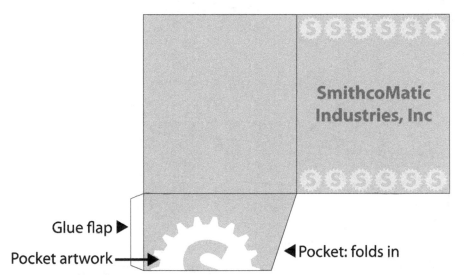

...but it should be created like this. Note that the pocket and glue flap affect the overall dimensions of the piece.

The complex trimming for a piece like a pocket folder requires a shaped cutter called a *die*. If possible, obtain artwork for the finished *die line* to use as the basis of your file as well as a physical example of the final configuration. A die line is a drawing of the open, flat piece, with all the folds and cuts indicated. This will help you determine how the artwork must be positioned on the panels of the pocket folder.

You'll also learn a lot about how your files must be created if you disassemble a printed example of a finished pocket folder. You'll see how the thickness of the heavy stock affects artwork at the folds, and you'll see how you must accommodate gluing requirements in your design.

Most print service providers who specialize in printing pocket folders can provide vector artwork for standard die lines, which you can use as a guide for building your piece. Since the glue area must be blank because glue will not adhere to printed stock, follow the print service provider's guidelines for the size and position of the unprinted area to ensure that no artwork falls within it (**Figure 3.25**).

Figure 3.25 *The inside of the finished pocket folder may look like this...*

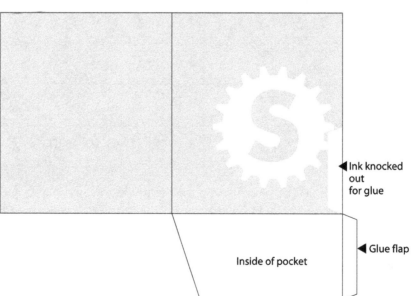

...but it prints like this. Ink must not be applied in areas that will be glued.

Ink knocked out for glue

Glue flap

Inside of pocket

In addition to considering the unfolded size of the folder, you must include the glue flap in the overall size of the piece. In Figure 3.25, the folded size would be 9-by-12 inches, but the actual size of the artwork is 19-by-16 inches to accommodate the 1-inch glue flap and the 4-inch height of the pocket itself (**Figure 3.26**).

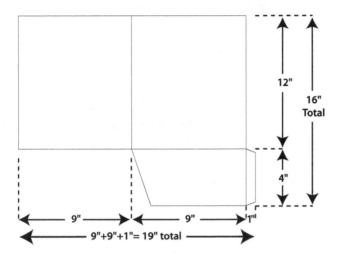

Figure 3.26 *The dimensions of pocket-folder artwork must include the glue flap and the pocket area. It's helpful to take apart a blank or printed example that is made from the cutting die that will be used on your job. This helps you visualize how the artwork should be created.*

Die Cutting

When your design requires specially shaped edges or complicated folding and assembly, special *dies* must be created to score and cut the printed piece. Scoring is the act of pressing an indentation into the stock to facilitate folding the final piece. Die cutting is the process of cutting the printed piece into a custom shape. Packaging and pocket folders are examples of pieces that require both scoring and die cutting. Scoring compresses the stock at fold points to ensure predictable folding, and die cutting creates the shape necessary for the printed piece to become a pocket folder or package. The die consists of steel cutting and scoring edges anchored in a sturdy wooden base. Although much of the design of cutting dies is now assisted with computer-driven manufacturing, there is still considerable handwork and skill involved in making a successful cutting die. Provisions must be made to ensure that cuts are clean and complete, scoring is correct, and excess material is safely removed without clogging the die or damaging the cutting edges.

The cutting die is mounted on a specialized die-cutting press, which uses pressure to score and cut the stock. Most die-cutting devices are platen-based, meaning that the die is a flat surface. But there are also rotary die-cutting presses, which require that the die be affixed to a cylinder. Not all printing companies perform their own die cutting. Some opt instead to contract with companies that specialize in such custom finishing.

If you intend to create a specialized piece for which the printer has no existing die, work closely with their finishing department (or the outside finisher, if that part of the job is being outsourced) to ensure that your artwork is built correctly. They can help you understand finishing issues affecting your job, and their advice can steer you away from problematic designs. It's important that you obtain a die line before you finalize your artwork (**Figure 3.27**). It may be supplied as an EPS or imaged on clear film. Carefully follow the dimensions of the die line as you plan your design and you'll minimize problems during the finishing process.

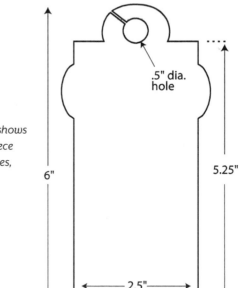

Figure 3.27 *Die-line artwork shows the dimensions of the finished piece and indicates any scores, punches, or perforations.*

Creating correct artwork for a die-cut piece can sometimes require that you create custom bleed areas that consider the irregular trim of the finished piece. Bleed on a die-cut piece is more than just a concentric rind around the trim. A beveled approach is required where colors meet some trim points to minimize the chances of color falling in the wrong place on the finished piece (**Figure 3.28**). Die creation is a combination of art and engineering. Don't embark on creating the art for a piece that will be elaborately die cut without first consulting with your printer's finishing department or finishing supplier. They may have an existing die line that you can use as a basis for designing your piece, which would reduce job cost.

Figure 3.28 *Die-cut pieces like this hang tag may require complicated bleed construction. Note the beveled treatment where two colors meet.*

Embossing

Embossing adds dimension to paper by pressing the paper stock between shaped metal pieces, resulting in a raised surface on the top (reading side) of the paper. Heat and pressure help push the paper into the shape of the embossing dies (**Figure 3.29**).

Figure 3.29 *Heat and pressure combined with a pair of shaped dies (top) are necessary to produce an embossed effect on paper (bottom, shown in cross section).*

Debossing is the same concept, but the shape of the dies creates a convex shape, pushing the surface of the paper down rather than raising it.

There are several variations on the concept of embossing:

- **Blind embossing** is an embossed effect in an unprinted area of the paper, thus creating artwork solely from the shape of the embossing.

- **Registered embossing** is aligned with a printed area already on the paper. While registered embossing heightens the dimensional effect, it requires more precision than blind embossing.

- **Glazed embossing** describes the shine that may appear as part of the embossed effect, especially on dark stock. Sometimes glazing is induced intentionally, although the higher heat often used to produce the effect can lead to scorching, and thus must be applied cautiously.

If you plan to use embossing to enhance your printed piece, consult with the print service provider and any participating outside finishing supplier to ensure that the effect you visualize is possible with the stock you intend to use. Understandably, the stock must have sufficient weight to withstand the embossing process. The pressure and heat used to shape the paper can weaken the paper, especially when attempting to force it into extreme or highly detailed embossing dies. The paper must be flexible enough to accomplish the effect but strong enough to hold up to the deformation. Any texture inherent in the paper must also be taken into consideration as well as any other finishing effects (such as folding or perforation) occurring close to the embossed area.

The embossing dies are based on artwork such as an Illustrator file or raster artwork. As you prepare artwork to be used as the basis for embossing, consult with the finishing experts to ensure that you provide artwork in the appropriate format. It's likely that skilled artists will modify your artwork to create the dies and perform handwork on the metal dies to ensure that the final embossed piece matches expectations. Plan for the extra time and cost involved in creating and refining embossing dies. Something this elaborate can't be hurried, but the results can be stunning.

Foil Stamping

Often used as an accent for book covers and packaging, foil stamping uses a heated, raised metal die to transfer decorative foil from a roll of carrier material onto the underlying paper. The foil may be metallic, colored, or iridescent. Some foils are holographic in nature, creating a rainbow or three-dimensional effect when applied. Some are just clear, adding a sheen and a touch of dimension where they're applied. The best results are achieved on fairly smooth, coated papers, because a pronounced texture may prevent the foil from adhering uniformly. However, a slight texture can offer a nice contrast to the smooth area of the foil application. In addition, foil may not adhere to some coatings, such as some waxy varnishes, so you should use aqueous coatings or nonwaxy varnishes before foil stamping.

As with embossing, artwork must be created to serve as the basis for the foil stamping die, and it's important to consult with knowledgeable specialists as you begin the process. Foil stamping is most effective in reasonably small areas such as type or patterns. It can be difficult to cover large areas successfully with foil stamping. But if you want a realistic metallic effect, foil stamping can accomplish what could never be equaled with metallic inks. And combined with embossing, foil stamping can create some beautiful effects.

Combination foil dies perform two functions—they shape the stock by embossing, and simultaneously apply the foil.

A less expensive approach to foil application is *cold foil*. In this method, a UV-activated adhesive is applied to the paper in the shape of the design. Foil is deposited from a carrier roll and the adhesive is cured as the printed sheet passes under UV lamps. Foil that doesn't adhere to the adhesive is removed. While it doesn't achieve quite the pronounced metallic sheen obtained by using hot foil stamping, cold foil is a good option when large area coverage is needed. Because the adhesive is applied on press like a conventional ink, no expensive stamping die has to be created.

Preparing Raster Images

4

Whether you acquire an image from a scanner, a digital camera, a royalty-free CD with 1,000,000 images, or a stock photography vendor, it's made out of pixels. *Pixel* is shorthand for *picture element*, the smallest unit of information in a digitized image. Even though pictures on your monitor look like smooth transitions of color, zoom in sufficiently and you'll see all the little square pixels that actually make up the image (**Figure 4.1**). While pixels make it possible to do much of what we do in the graphic arts, they're also the cause of some important limitations.

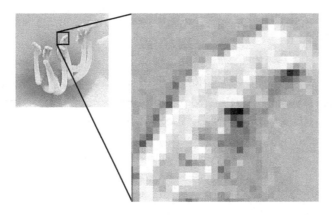

Figure 4.1 *Images are made of pixels. Think of them as tiny mosaic tiles.*

Ancient Times: B.P. (Before Pixels)

In the olden days of graphic arts, enormous cameras were used to photograph artwork such as drawings, reflective photographic prints, transparencies, and painted illustrations. Highly skilled specialists commandeered these monstrosities, some of which occupied entire rooms (the cameras, not the specialists). The use of colored filters, masking, and exposure methods to produce *color separations* (a separate piece of film for each printing ink) was rather arcane and required years of apprenticeship and study to perfect. And since every step required the use of specialized film, there were a lot of trips to a darkroom to develop the results in chemical baths. It all seemed very high-tech at the time (well, compared to cave paintings), but the process was quite time-consuming.

All About Pixels

Film has given way to pixels, and we have gone from dog-eared color photographic prints and moldy 35mm slides to storing our family photos on piles of CDs, and now into the nebulous world of cloud storage. What was once the province of the darkroom became a daylight venture, and the tools of the craftsmen became available to anyone brave enough to wade in.

Scanners

While early scanners still required highly skilled graphic arts professionals to operate them, they greatly sped up the process of capturing artwork for color separations. Early analog models used photomultiplier tubes and a daunting array of knobs and buttons to perform the same job that had been done by the huge cameras. The first scanners were petite only by comparison to their gigantic camera ancestors: Many could easily dwarf a Volkswagen. It was necessary to mount artwork on a heavy, clear plastic drum and then painstakingly ensure that there was no dust or a trapped air bubble to mar the scan. Scanner operators came from the ranks of color-separation cameramen, and their years of finely honed instincts for camera separations translated well to the newer methods. Thus began the move to digital capture and storage of image information, resulting in our devotion to the pixel and the advent of digital retouching.

In the mid-1990s, improvements in the capabilities and simplicity of flatbed scanners, coupled with the widespread usage of Adobe Photoshop, led to a major change in the way color separations were performed. It was no longer necessary to mount artwork on cylindrical drums, and the numerous knobs were replaced with onscreen buttons and dialog boxes. The digital imaging revolution was underway. Suddenly, people who weren't sure what color separation meant were making color separations.

As flatbed scanners have become more automated and less expensive, it's relatively easy even for novices to make a decent scan. But the more you know about what constitutes a good image, the better the chance you can create a great image from the pixels generated by your scanner.

Digital Cameras

Today's scanners capture transparencies, negative film, paintings, and illustrations and express them as pixels. High-end digital cameras now rival—or exceed—the ability of film-based cameras to capture photographic detail. The image captured by the camera is a digital original, so there's no need to scan a print. Of course, the better the camera and the photographer, the better the image. The rapid evolution of digital image capture is such that today's cellphones take pictures with more inherent information than the earliest digital cameras.

While conventional camera film—such as 35mm transparencies—must be scanned to be used on your computer, digital camera images can be downloaded directly to the computer and used immediately. Digital photography also cuts out the middleman. Unlike film images, digital images don't have any grain, although an image photographed in low lighting conditions may tax the resolving capabilities of a digital camera's sensor, resulting in unwanted digital noise.

Consumer point-and-shoot cameras deliver captured images as JPEG, a compressed format. There are degrees of compression, from gentle to aggressive, and you may never notice any visible artifacts betraying the compression. But higher level "prosumer" cameras and professional digital cameras can deliver images in the Camera Raw format, which is subjected to minimal processing by the camera. While you cannot place a Raw file directly into Illustrator or InDesign, Raw images can be opened directly in Photoshop and saved in another format, such as Photoshop PSD.

TIP While you can't place a Camera Raw file directly into Illustrator or InDesign, there is a workaround. In the Camera Raw module within Photoshop, hold down Shift as you click Open (the Open Image button changes to an Open Object button): this will open the image as a Smart Object in Photoshop. Save the image as a PSD, and you can then place it in Illustrator or InDesign while retaining the secret Camera Raw editing ability. Back in Photoshop, just double-click the Smart Object to edit in Camera Raw.

Raw files can be color corrected in the Photoshop Camera Raw environment without losing additional information. For example, an image shot under daylight conditions but with the camera's white balance set to fluorescent lighting can be corrected with one click in the Camera Raw environment without the loss of information that would be incurred by using a Levels or Curves correction in Photoshop.

If you are a point-and-shoot photographer who just wants to capture moments from a quick vacation, you may consider Raw files to be overkill. But for professional photographers, Camera Raw is a powerful and flexible format, often enabling the recovery or enhancement of details and tones that would be lost in a JPEG file.

Imaging Software

Once you have captured pixels, it's likely that you'll feel compelled to modify them. The industry standard imaging application is Adobe Photoshop, and for good reason. Photoshop provides controls for color correction that enable a knowledgeable user to achieve results equal to those of a knob-twisting scanner operator. Its tools surpass the capabilities of the original, million-dollar dedicated systems. If you're just beginning to learn Photoshop, you won't lack for educational resources. You could probably build an addition to your house from the books devoted to exploring Photoshop. You can add Chapter 10, "Photoshop Production Tips," to the pile.

Photoshop is arguably the most versatile and widely accepted application for image manipulation, but there are other applications that perform useful imaging functions as well.

Adobe Photoshop Elements® (Mac/PC) might be regarded as "Photoshop Lite," but it still packs a hefty arsenal of retouching and color-correction tools. The product is geared toward enthusiasts and lacks support for CMYK images.

Adobe Lightroom™ (Mac/PC) is engineered for use by photographers and provides sophisticated tools for organizing and color correcting images.

Apple iPhoto® (Mac only) is geared toward hobbyists, with organizational tools and limited color-correction capabilities. However, it offers no support for CMYK images.

Aperture (Mac only) is targeted to photographers and includes support for Camera Raw files. It provides organizational tools as well as color-correction controls but provides no support for CMYK images.

These are not the only solutions that exist for manipulating images. There are painting programs, such as Painter™ and Paint Shop Pro® (both from Corel®), which let you easily make images resemble watercolors or oil paintings. Imaging tools for consumer and hobbyist photographers increase on a daily basis. However, most of these programs don't offer support for CMYK images, so they're not the best tools if you're preparing images for print.

Let's face it—if you're designing for print, you can't live without Photoshop. When the name of a product becomes a verb — "Please Photoshop that out"— it's a sure sign that the product has become the industry standard.

Resolution and Image Fidelity

The resolution of an image is generally measured in pixels per inch (ppi) unless you speak metric, in which case it's expressed in pixels per millimeter. Determining the proper resolution for Web images is simple: 72 ppi at final size. But there are strongly held (and hotly debated) beliefs regarding the appropriate image resolution for printing. Some hold that 150 percent of the final screen ruling value is sufficient, and some believe twice the final ruling is preferable, largely because it's easier to calculate the resolution. For example, an image that will be printed at 150 line screen should have a resolution of 300 ppi. In the past, when typical hard drives held 80 MB, networks were glacially slow, and RIPs choked on 15 MB PostScript files, it was important to trim off every little bit of fat, so we agonized over resolution. But now, with hard drives measured in hundreds of gigabytes, and RIPs with much more robust digestive tracts, we can afford the luxury of a few extra pixels. That said, there's rarely an advantage to exceeding 300 ppi, except in some cases for higher line screens such as 175 lpi printing. So put away the calculator. For most circumstances, 300 ppi at final size is adequate and provides a bit of elbow room if you have to slightly reduce or enlarge an image.

But you do have some leeway, depending on the nature of the image and how it will be used. For example, a gauzy, soft-focus shot of a sunset that will be used as a ghosted background accent in a magazine can be used at 200 ppi with no problem. A highly detailed close-up image of an important piece of antique jewelry in a 175 lpi art book should be at 300–350 ppi. At the other end of the spectrum, an image for use in an 85 lpi newspaper can be 130–170 ppi, because much of the information in a 300 ppi image would be lost when printed in the coarse newspaper screen ruling. Consider the determination of appropriate resolution to be an equation based on image content and the final printing line screen rather than an absolute number.

Scaling Up

When enlarging or reducing an image, don't be afraid to *slightly* reduce or enlarge an image. But be aware that when an image is scanned or captured by a digital camera, it contains a fixed number of pixels. When you enlarge an image, you're attempting to generate missing information in a process called interpolation; the result is never as good as a proper-sized original scan. And the more drastic the transformation, the less satisfying the outcome (**Figure 4.2**).

Figure 4.2 *You can't truly make something from nothing. Notice the loss of detail in the scaled-up version (D) versus the original (A).*

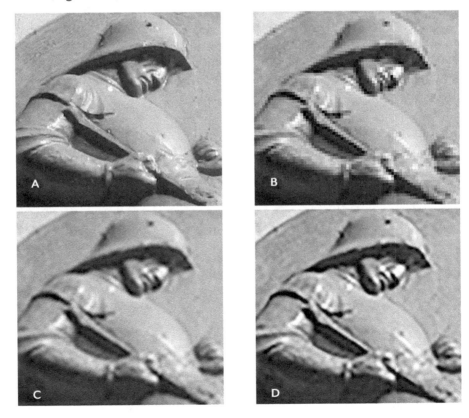

Because of the limitations imposed by resolution, it's helpful if you can anticipate how the image will be used and control photography or scanning accordingly. For typical image content, you can probably scale up to 120–125 percent. If the image is background content without much detail, such as a soft-focus landscape, you have more leeway and can probably get away with scaling up to 150–200 percent. Conversely, if you need to maintain very small details, you may be limited to a maximum of 120 percent.

Photoshop CC introduced a new method that does a better job of scaling up images and upsampling them to higher resolutions—Preserve Details. While the results won't be equal to a higher resolution original image, it's a definite improvement over earlier methods (**Figure 4.3**).

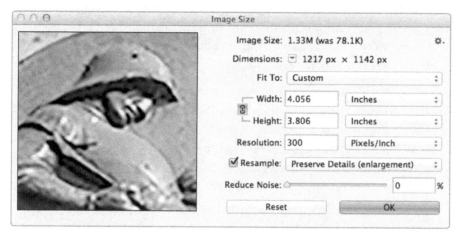

Figure 4.3 *If you have to scale up an image, or artificially increase its resolution, be sure to choose the Preserve Details option in the Photoshop CC Image Size dialog box. Tip: If you select "Automatic," Photoshop CC chooses the best method for resampling.*

Scaling Down

Scaling down an image also involves interpolation. While the loss of data may not be quite so obvious when you reduce the size of an image, there can be some softening of detail. For best results, choose the Automatic option in the Image Size dialog box in Photoshop CC; it applies some sharpening to camouflage the reduction in detail. While it's acceptable to scale images in InDesign, if you find it necessary to scale an image below 75 percent of its original size in your page layout, consider scaling it down in Photoshop CC instead, because InDesign can't sharpen image content.

Scanning Artwork

If you are incorporating flat artwork such as pen-and-ink drawings or paintings in your design, you have several choices for digitizing the artwork. If you have a good flatbed scanner, you may be able to capture the artwork without any special handling. To provide some flexibility in later usages of the scanned image, consider performing two scans at 100 percent: one at 300 ppi, and one at 600 ppi if your scanner supports it. Then, you have two robust images that can be resized for a wider range of uses.

If your flatbed scanner isn't up to the task, ask if your print service provider performs scanning. Many printers have high-end scanners capable of capturing and enlarging artwork. If you have transparencies or negative film that must be scanned, the printer's professional scanners can capture detail and perform enlargements with higher-quality results than are possible with consumer-level scanners.

Some materials, such as textured paper, dimensional paint (such as heavy acrylic or oil paint), metal, or transparent substrates, don't scan well. The scanner's illumination bounces off metallic components and often appears black in the scanned image. Because of the even, frontal lighting of the scanner, texture is subdued or lost. And you can't very well pin a statue under the lid of your scanner. If you have to capture a challenging art piece, the best solution might be to hire a photographer who specializes in capturing fine art pieces and has experience lighting and photographing such projects.

Cropping and Transforming Images

It would be great if you could anticipate the exact size, crop, and angle at which you'll want to use an image in your page layout. But it may be difficult to see that far down the line at the moment you're pressing the button on your camera, or slipping a print under the lid of your flatbed scanner. Oh, and watch out for that little gust of wind that comes along just as you're putting the scanner lid down...

Cropping

Should you crop your images? Maybe. If you're certain about future image use, feel free to crop. Leave a reasonable rind around the image area you intend to use to provide some elbow room when you place the image in the final page, so you have room to reposition the image, or to provide bleed for the page. However, if you think there's even a remote chance that you'll want to use more of the image in the near future—maybe you're not sure if you might want to show a row of four buildings instead of just the one in the middle—then it's worth keeping the whole shebang. While you may be reluctant to store an entire image just to keep the part with the 2-inch golf ball that you're sure you will silhouette, give yourself a safety net and at least keep an uncropped backup copy of the image. Hard drive space is plentiful and you can always crop it later. It's hard to recover that extra person you lopped off last week who turns out to be the CEO of the company.

Rotating Images

Almost any transformation, whether resizing or rotating, causes interpolation of pixel information. The only safe rotations are 90-degree increments—anything else will result in softening of detail (see **Figure 4.4**). Think of those rows and columns of pixels, much like the grid of a needlepoint pattern. Imagine what a challenge it would be to redraw that pattern at a 42-degree angle. It should give you a little sympathy for the math Photoshop has to do.

Figure 4.4 *Repeated rotations of an image can result in cumulative erosion of detail (original image on the left, rotated image on the right). The exaggerated sharpening in the image on the right is a result of Photoshop's attempt to compensate for softening of detail.*

All these cautions about transformations such as scaling and rotating are not intended to strike terror in your heart. Don't be afraid to enlarge, reduce, or rotate if you need to. Just be prepared for the slight but unavoidable loss of detail and the degradation of the image's appearance. Try to resize in even increments, and beware of oddball rotations such as 1.25 degrees in the interest of maintaining as much information as possible.

Successive transformations—scaling and then rotating, for example—are particularly destructive. Let your conscience be your guide. How important is the detail in the image? If it's a key product shot, it's worth rescanning (if possible). If it's a less important image, such as a ghosted background or a decorative bit, you needn't feel quite so guilty about the transformation.

Where to Transform: Image Editor vs. Page-Layout Application

If you are going to transform images, does it matter where the transformation takes place? If you use Photoshop to scale an image, is the result superior to the outcome of scaling within your page-layout application?

The answer is an unqualified, "It depends."

If you perform your scaling and rotation in Photoshop or another image-editing application, and then place the resulting image in a page layout at 100 percent with no rotation, you do have a pretty good idea of how the image will look when it's printed.

If, however, you induce the scaling or rotation in a page layout, you've only *requested* those transformations—you haven't actually *performed* the transformations. They don't really take place until the job is processed by a RIP. This puts you at the mercy of that RIP's implementation of scaling and rotation algorithms. If you generate and submit PDFs, the rotations or distortions within that PDF are still pending, and they are implemented only when the PDF is processed by a RIP. In other words, the original image information is contained in the PDF, unchanged, but earmarked for its ultimate transformation in the RIP.

Be comforted by the fact that late-model RIPs can chew a lot more information in a shorter time than they used to. Rotating a few images here and there won't prevent the processing of your job. However, despite the improvements in RIP technology, it is still possible (although rare) to build a job that can't be processed by a RIP. (Please don't take that remark as a personal challenge.)

Keep in mind, too, that if you've rotated an image in Photoshop and then subsequently applied additional scaling or rotation in a page layout, you've transformed it twice. It's not the end of the world, but you may see some slight softening of detail in the finished piece.

Appropriate Image Formats for Print

How you should save your raster images is governed largely by how you intend to use them. Often, you will be placing images into InDesign or Illustrator, so you're limited to the formats supported by those applications. The application may be willing to let you place a wide variety of file formats, but that doesn't necessarily serve as an endorsement of file format wonderfulness. In the olden days, the most commonly used image formats were TIFF and EPS. However, native Photoshop files (PSD) and Photoshop PDF files are much more flexible, and both formats are supported by InDesign and Illustrator. So, there's not much reason to use other formats unless you're handing off your images to users of other applications, such as Microsoft PowerPoint or Word.

NOTE When you receive a JPEG image, it's a good idea to immediately resave it as a PSD or TIFF to avoid further erosion to image content. Repeatedly opening, modifying, and resaving a JPEG can result in compromised quality if aggressive compression is used.

TIFF

If you need to blindly send an image out into the world, TIFF (tagged image file format) is one of the most widely supported image file formats. It's happy being imported into Illustrator, InDesign, Microsoft Word, and even some text editors—almost any application that accepts images. The TIFF image format supports multiple layers as well as RGB and CMYK color spaces, and even allows an image to contain spot-color channels (although some applications, such as Word, do not support such nontraditional contents in a TIFF).

Photoshop EPS

Some equate the acronym EPS (Encapsulated PostScript) with vector artwork, but the *encapsulated* part of the format's name gives a hint about the flexibility of the format. It's a *container* for artwork, and it can transport vector art, raster images, or a combination of raster and vector content. EPS is, as the name implies, PostScript in a bag (see the sidebar, "EPS: Raster or Vector?"). The historic reasons for saving an image as a Photoshop EPS were to preserve the special function of a PostScript-based vector clipping path used to silhouette an image or to preserve an image set up to image as a duotone. If you're using InDesign and Illustrator, that's no longer necessary.

EPS: Raster or Vector?

It may be a bit confusing that there are raster-based EPSs (saved from an image-editing program such as Photoshop) and vector-based EPSs (saved from a vector drawing program such as Adobe Illustrator or Adobe [formerly Macromedia] FreeHand). The uninitiated sometimes think that saving an image as an EPS magically vectorizes it. Not so. Think of the EPS format as a type of container. The pixels within an EPS are no different from those in their TIFF brethren. They're just contained and presented in a different way.

As applications and RIPs have progressed, you're no longer required to save such images as Photoshop EPS. Pixel for pixel, a Photoshop native PSD is a smaller file than an equivalent EPS and offers support for clipping paths as well as duotone definitions.

This doesn't mean you need to hunt down your legacy Photoshop EPS files and resave them as PSD (unless you're terribly bored). Just know that unless you need to accommodate someone else's requirements, there's no advantage to saving as Photoshop EPS now.

Photoshop Native (PSD)

> **TRANSPARENCY TIP:** Although Illustrator and InDesign accept and correctly handle *opacity* settings in a placed native Photoshop file, they do not correctly handle *blending modes* in a Photoshop file. There are some workarounds for InDesign, detailed in Chapter 12, "InDesign Production Tips."

In ancient times, the native PSD (Photoshop document) format was used solely for working files in Photoshop. Copies of those working files were flattened and saved in TIFF or EPS formats for placement in a page-layout program. While PageMaker allowed placement of native Photoshop files (yes, really—although it did not honor transparency), QuarkXPress required TIFF or EPS instead. Old habits die hard, and TIFF and EPS have long been the standard of the industry. Not that there's anything truly wrong with that.

However, Illustrator and InDesign can take advantage of the layers and transparency in Photoshop native files, eliminating the need to go back through two generations of an image to make corrections to an original file. Today, there's no need to maintain two separate images: the working image and the finished file are now the same file.

Photoshop PDF

A Photoshop PDF (Portable Document Format) contains the same pixels as a garden-variety PSD, but those pixels are encased in a PDF wrapper—it's like the chocolate-covered cherry of file formats. A Photoshop PDF comes in handy on special occasions, because it can contain vector and type elements without rasterizing the vector content, and it allows nondestructive round-trip editing in Photoshop.

A Photoshop EPS can contain vectors and text, but the vector content will be converted to pixels if the file is reopened in Photoshop, losing the crisp vector edge—so you lose the ability to edit text or vector content. A native Photoshop PSD can contain vector components, but page-layout programs rasterize the content. However, Photoshop PDFs preserve vector content when placed in other applications (see **Table 4.1** for a feature comparison of common image formats).

Table 4.1 *Image format features*

Supported Feature	TIFF	EPS	PSD	JPEG	PDF
RGB color space	X	X	X	X	X
CMYK color space	X	X	X	X	X
Grayscale	X	X	X	X	X
ICC profiles	X	X	X	X	X
Clipping paths	X	X	X	X	X
Layers	X	—	X	—	X
Alpha channels	X	—	X	—	X
Spot color channels	X	1	X	—	X
Duotones	—	X	X	—	X
Bitmap (bi-level content)	X	X	X	—	X
Vector data	—	2	3	—	X
Transparency	X	—	X	—	X

[1] If saved as DCS 2.0 (a variant of the EPS format)
[2] EPSs cannot be reopened in Photoshop with vector content intact
[3] Page-layout applications rasterize vector content in PSDs

Moving to Native PSD and PDF

Is there any compelling reason to continue using old-fashioned TIFFs and EPSs? It may seem adventurous to use such new-fangled files, but workflow is changing. The demarcation between photo-compositing and page layout is blurring, and designers demand more power and flexibility from software. RIPs are more robust than ever, networks are faster, and hard drives are huge. It's still important to know the imaging challenges posed by using native files (such as transparency), and it's wise to communicate with your printer before you embark on the all-native path. You're still at the mercy of the equipment and processes used by the printer, and if they're lagging a bit behind the latest software and hardware developments, you may be limited by their capabilities.

Bitmap Images

Also called "line art images," bitmap images contain only black and white pixels, with no intermediate shades of gray. If you need to scan a signature to add to an editorial page or scan a pen and ink sketch, a bitmap scan can provide a sharp, clean image. Because of the compact nature of bitmap scans, they can be very high resolution (usually 600–1200 ppi) but still produce small file sizes (**Figure 4.5**).

Figure 4.5 *This 1200 ppi bitmap scan prints nearly as sharply as vector art. It weighs in at less than 1 MB; a grayscale image of this size and resolution would be nearly 10 MB. Magnified to 300 percent, it may look a bit rough, but at 100 percent it's crisp and clean.*

Special Case: Screen Captures

If you're creating software documentation for print, or you want to show an image of a Web page in your project, you may need to include screen captures of software interface components such as menus or panels in your page layouts. Screen captures are easy to make using a system utility or dedicated screen-capture software, but they require some special handling to print clearly. When they're part of software documentation or instructional materials, it's important that the details are as sharply rendered as possible.

You should understand this about screen captures: Whether you take them by using your system's built-in screen-capture functionality or a third-party screen-capture application, you are merely intercepting *information* that eventually becomes pixels on your monitor. Regardless of your current monitor resolution, there is a one-to-one relationship between the fixed number of pixels that an application (and your system) uses to render panels and menus and the number of pixels you see on your screen, even if you use a zoom utility. Of course, the size of the overall image you see is a function of your current monitor resolution, but the *pixel dimensions* of panels, menus, and tools will be identical, regardless of resolution. (**Figure 4.6**)

An application panel that measures 244 pixels by 117 pixels appears larger when your screen resolution is set to 800 by 600, and it's almost unreadably small when your monitor is set to 1920 by 1200. However, the panel is made of exactly the same number of pixels in both instances. So it doesn't matter what resolution your monitor is using, or how large the panels may appear onscreen, or whether you use a utility to zoom in. The captured image of a panel or menu will be the same in terms of pixel dimensions, regardless of the monitor resolution setting, and the resulting image will be 72 ppi.

TIP Do an experiment: In the software of your choice, open a panel and position it in the middle of the screen. Take screen shots at two different resolutions. Make a loose selection of the panel in one image, copy it, and place it into the other image. You'll see that they're identical in pixel count. The overall images will be different sizes because of the different monitor resolutions, but the number of pixels used by interface components such as panels, menus, and tools will be identical.

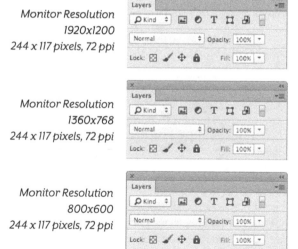

Monitor Resolution 1920x1200 244 x 117 pixels, 72 ppi

Monitor Resolution 1360x768 244 x 117 pixels, 72 ppi

Monitor Resolution 800x600 244 x 117 pixels, 72 ppi

Monitor Resolution 1920x1200, zoomed using OS X Accessibility Zoom feature 244 x 117 pixels, 72 ppi

Figure 4.6 *The resolution setting of your monitor has no effect on the number of pixels used by panels and menus. Although this panel was captured at three different monitor resolutions, the three captures are identical, each consisting of exactly the same number of pixels.*

Since it's been drilled into you that 300 ppi is the Holy Grail of image resolution, it's tempting to try to improve screen captures by increasing the resolution. Unfortunately, this usually makes them look worse by softening small details during interpolation.

If you plan to use a screen capture at 100 percent enlargement, just leave it at 72 ppi (go ahead and freak out). Yes, the print service provider's prepress department will raise a flag, but the examples below show why screen captures are not improved by increasing their resolution.

As you can see in **Figure 4.7**, the original 72 ppi screen capture seems a bit coarse, but it's readable. Increasing the resolution to 300 ppi in Photoshop may sound like a good idea, but the interpolation will soften detail in the image.

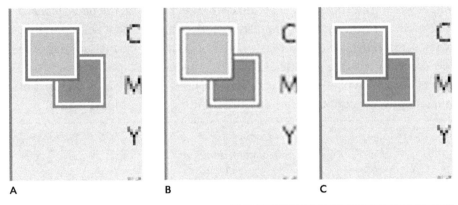

A   B   C

Figure 4.7 *Image A is the original 72 ppi screen shot. Image B is the result of increasing the resolution to 300 ppi, using the default Bicubic method: Note blurry text and softened edges. Image C is the result of increasing the resolution to 288 ppi, using Nearest Neighbor.*

If you do feel compelled to increase the resolution of a screen capture, choose *Image > Image Size* in Photoshop, and then set the resolution to an even multiple of the original resolution; for example, resample a 72 ppi screen shot to 288 ppi. In that same dialog box, set the Resample Image option to Nearest Neighbor. This avoids interpolation by simply repeating pixels rather than attempting to create pixels. It's not an appropriate approach when scaling images of a photographic nature, but it's a helpful solution for screen captures, because of their special nature.

Converting Screen Captures to CMYK

Because screen captures are generated as RGB images, they must usually be converted to CMYK for print. When performing that conversion, a special approach is recommended to maintain the best rendering of black type. The default conversion of RGB to CMYK in Photoshop will render black as a four-color mix (**Figure 4.8**), with the possibility that slight misregistration on press will turn tiny details to mush.

CYAN

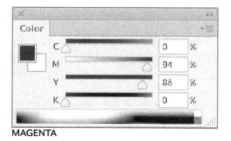

MAGENTA

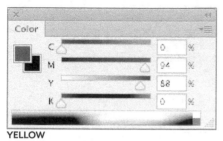

YELLOW

BLACK

Figure 4.8 *A conventional conversion from RGB to CMYK produces four-color equivalents of the gray and black parts of a screen capture. Press misregistration will turn text and other black or gray elements to an out-of-focus rainbow. Festive, but hard to read.*

To simplify printing of screen captures, use a color-separation recipe that ensures that all neutral black or gray areas of the image will print only in black ink during the RGB-to-CMYK conversion. Neutral areas in an RGB image are those areas in which the RGB values are equal; for example, R128–G128–B128 would constitute a midtone gray.

To create this custom screen-capture conversion recipe in Photoshop, choose *Edit > Color Settings* to access the color-separation controls. Under Working Spaces, choose *Custom* for the CMYK setting (**Figure 4.9**).

Figure 4.9 *In the Color Settings dialog box, select Custom CMYK from the CMYK menu.*

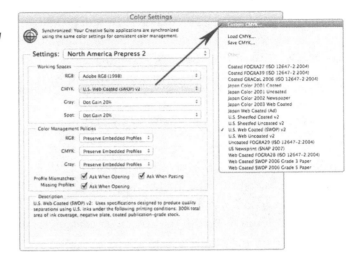

In the Custom CMYK dialog box, select *Maximum Black Generation* (**Figure 4.10**). The curve you see may seem odd, but it merely indicates that all equivalent RGB values are being replaced with black. The appearance of color elements won't be compromised.

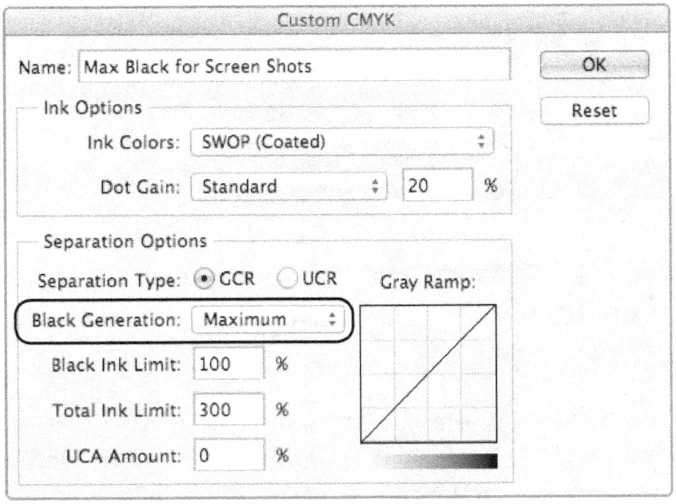

Figure 4.10 *In the Custom CMYK dialog box, select the Maximum Black Generation setting. This consolidates all gray-equivalent values to the black channel, minimizing issues with registration.*

Color elements will be composed of four colors in the final CMYK image. But black and gray elements will be rendered only in black (**Figure 4.11**). While this may look odd, it results in cleaner printing of the screen capture, because there aren't four colors piling up in most of the image.

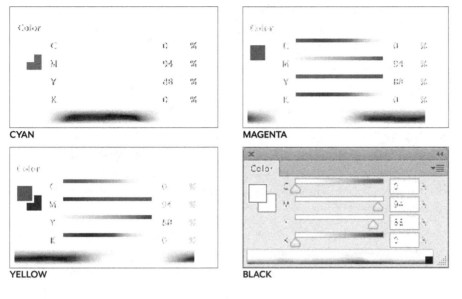

CYAN   **MAGENTA**

YELLOW   **BLACK**

Figure 4.11 *All the color components appear on the cyan, magenta, and yellow plates. Black and gray areas appear only on the black plate. This special treatment ensures that screen shots print cleanly.*

RGB vs. CMYK

Since the dawn of desktop publishing, it's been unquestioned that Thou Shalt Convert to CMYK. Those who submitted RGB files were considered uninformed, even uncivilized.

The rules are changing, though, because of the increased use of digital printing. Although these devices may use inks or toners named *cyan*, *magenta*, *yellow*, and *black*, those inks and toners have a different pigment makeup than the namesake inks used on offset presses, and they have a wider color gamut than offset inks. Inkjet devices such as large-format printers utilize additional inks such as light cyan, pink, light yellow, orange, and green, further extending the range of colors that they can print.

This seems like a good time to open a can of multicolored worms. After you've been told by printers for years that you should convert your images to CMYK before submitting, I'm now going to tell you that you might not have to do so. That's because many digital devices happily digest RGB and can provide more vibrant output by rendering RGB content.

When you convert to CMYK, ranges of colors outside the CMYK gamut are remapped to fall within the CMYK printable gamut, and some of your most vibrant colors are lost forever.

If you happen to have some very colorful RGB images (tropical birds would do the trick), try this little experiment:

1. Open the RGB image in Photoshop, and maybe make it even more vibrant by using Hue/Saturation or Vibrance. Get carried away; this is for science, after all, not for art.

2. Choose *Edit > Color Settings*. At the top of the dialog box, choose *North America Prepress 2* from the menu and click OK.

3. Choose *View > Proof Colors*. The difference in appearance may not be huge, but try toggling Proof Colors on and off quickly by using the keyboard shortcut (PC: Ctrl-Y; Mac: Cmd-Y) and watch for differences in bright blues and greens. Neon greens provide a particularly noticeable difference.

4. Choose *View > Gamut Warning*. The gray areas are areas whose current RGB color will be remapped (and probably become duller) when converted to CMYK, because of the smaller color gamut of CMYK.

This gives you an idea of the color range that you'll lose when you convert to CMYK—and much of that color range can be imaged on many digital devices. Of course, ask the print service provider before you submit your work to ensure that you're sending what they want. Just don't be surprised if they say "RGB is OK."

RGB as a Working Format

Because the RGB gamut is larger than that of CMYK, it's often preferable to perform color corrections and compositing with RGB files, converting to CMYK (if necessary) as late in the process as possible. If you are participating in a fully color-managed workflow, you will keep your images as RGB with ICC profiles. The International Color Consortium (ICC) was formed by a group of graphic arts industry vendors, with the goal of promoting the use and standardization of color management tools. ICC profiles are methods of describing the characteristics of devices such as scanners, presses, and printers for optimal results. Conversion will not take place until the job is imaged. Much of today's software offers sophisticated support of color management. For example, when exporting a PDF or printing, InDesign will perform the same conversion of RGB to CMYK that Photoshop would (assuming you've synchronized your color settings across all your Creative Cloud applications).

What if the Printer Demands CMYK Images?

Some print service providers and their customers have fully adopted color-managed workflows as part of their regular operation. But many print service providers (especially in North America) expect CMYK when you submit your job, believing that it's what Nature intended, especially when the job will be printed on an offset press (as opposed to a digital printer). Consult with your printer to see what they prefer. If you're using digital photography or scanning your own artwork, they should be able to provide you with their preferred settings, so you can make appropriate conversions to CMYK.

Inappropriate Image Formats for Print

Some image formats are intended primarily for onscreen and Web use. **Portable Network Graphics** (PNG) images can contain RGB and indexed color as well as transparency. While PNG can be high resolution, it has no support for the CMYK color space.

The Windows format **BMP** (an abbreviation for bitmap) supports color depths from one-bit (black and white, with no shades of gray) to 32-bit (millions of colors) but lacks support for CMYK. BMP is not appropriate in projects intended for print.

Graphics Interchange Format (GIF) is appropriate only for Web use because of its inherently low resolution and an indexed color palette limited to a maximum of 256 colors. Don't use GIF for print.

JPEG (Joint Photographic Experts Group), named after the committee that created it, has an unsavory reputation in graphic arts. Just whisper "jay-peg" and watch prepress operators cringe. It is a lossy compression scheme, meaning that it discards information to make a smaller digital file. But some of the fear of JPEGs is out of proportion to the amount of damage that takes place when a JPEG is created. Assuming an image has adequate resolution, a very slight amount of initial JPEG compression doesn't noticeably impair image quality, but aggressive compression introduces ugly rectangular artifacts, especially in detailed areas (**Figure 4.12**).

Figure 4.12 *There's good JPEG, and there's bad JPEG:*

A. Original PSD

B. JPEG saved with Maximum Quality setting

C. JPEG saved with lowest quality setting

Each time you open an image, make a change, then resave the image as a JPEG, you recompress it. Prepress paranoids will shriek that you're ruining your image, and there's a little bit of truth to that. While it's true that repeatedly resaving an image with low-quality compression settings would eventually visibly erode detail, the mere fact that an image has been saved as a JPEG does not render it unusable, especially if you use a minimal level of compression. Despite the reputation, JPEGs aren't inherently evil. They can be decent graphic citizens, even capable of containing high-resolution CMYK image data.

That said, when you acquire a JPEG image from your digital camera or a stock photo service, it's still advisable to immediately resave the image as a TIFF or PSD file to prevent further compression. However, JPEGs intended for Web use are low-resolution RGB files, inappropriate for print. If your client provides a low-resolution or aggressively compressed JPEG, there's not much you can do to improve it. Even with the refined Intelligent Upsampling in Photoshop CC, you can only go so far. They'll find that hard to believe, though, because they know there's a tool in Photoshop called the Magic Wand. Good luck explaining it to them.

Vector Graphics

5

While raster images are made up of pixels, vector graphics are refreshingly pixel free—they're made of math. As such, vector graphics are not subject to the scaling restrictions that plague raster images (**Figure 5.1**). The smooth shapes of a purely vector drawing have no inherent resolution, so vector art can be enlarged and reduced with no penalty.

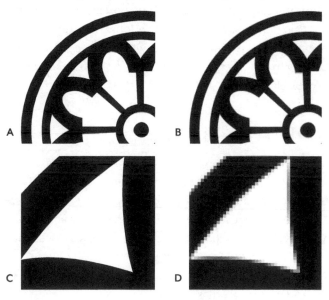

Figure 5.1 *Vector drawings (A) are mathematically generated smooth lines, whereas raster images (B) are composed of pixels.*

Vector art can be scaled up with no limit (C). Raster images, however, don't fare well at extreme enlargements (D).

While there are other vector drawing programs, such as CorelDRAW and FreeHand (still sold but no longer updated), the power and flexibility of Illustrator is unmatched, and its tight integration with other Adobe applications makes it indispensable.

Vector File Formats

TIP If you need to share Illustrator files with users of CAD programs or sign-creation software, you may need to save your file as an older version EPS so it can be correctly interpreted by other software. Illustrator allows you to save to files compatible with versions back to Illustrator 3 (hello, 1990!).

Because the *File > Save* and *File > Export* dialog boxes in Adobe Illustrator offer a dizzying list of prospective file types, it's important to know what's acceptable for print and what's not.

Native Illustrator (AI)

Welcome to the future: Unless you are submitting a vector file for use in a workflow that doesn't support native Adobe Illustrator files, there is rarely any reason to save an Illustrator file as EPS in the current environment, and a number of reasons in favor of using the native Illustrator (.AI) format.

If you're planning to place the artwork into InDesign, there is plenty of motivation to go native. InDesign honors transparency and blending modes in a native Illustrator file. This means that a placed Illustrator file can interact with other artwork in InDesign, allowing you to create some interesting opacity and blending effects that would not be possible with an EPS, whose internal contents are opaque to other applications. In addition, InDesign allows you to control the visibility of layers within a placed Illustrator native file without having to modify the file in Illustrator but doesn't provide that nifty flexibility for placed EPS files.

Encapsulated PostScript (EPS)

For years, the most common file format for containing vector artwork was EPS. In fact, the acronym EPS is so deeply associated with vector graphics that new entrants to the mysteries of graphic arts sometimes believe that merely saving a raster image in the EPS format magically converts it to vectors. They're subsequently disappointed when they discover that they must instead use the dreaded Pen tool to create vector art. (See Chapter 4, "Preparing Raster Images," for an explanation of the difference between raster EPS files and vector EPS files.)

Encapsulated PostScript is, as the name implies, a container for PostScript information that allows it to be understood by other applications. An EPS file may contain drawing information as well as font information and embedded raster images. A preview image is also usually included to provide an appearance for the file when it's placed into another application. Some programs can't correctly interpret the PostScript information, resulting in poor output. It isn't the fault of the EPS—it's the application's inability to utilize the PostScript contents.

EPS files can be placed in a wide range of applications, including InDesign, but those applications can't directly interact with the contents of an EPS, so any editing must be performed in the originating application.

Although the EPS spec is a public spec, not all applications create the same flavor of EPS. Consequently, there are cautions, even when opening EPS files generated by the most popular drawing programs. FreeHand can safely open EPS files created by FreeHand. Illustrator can successfully open its own Illustrator EPS files. This may not seem surprising, but it only works because each application adds extra information to create an editable EPS, allowing it to be reopened in the originating application.

If you attempt to use Illustrator to edit EPS files created by other applications (such as page-layout programs), the translations are not always successful. Text may become point text (little isolated clumps of editable text), and some special features such as shadows may not translate correctly. Some elements may completely disappear or become rasterized. It's best to keep such files in their own native habitat, if possible, to avoid problems.

Why is this? PostScript is a programming language that provides instructions for imaging. Thus, an EPS is more than a drawing in some sort of container. In essence, it's a tiny computer program. So, just as one programmer might not understand another's style of coding, one application may not correctly interpret an EPS produced by another program. Man was never meant to reopen EPS files, but you know what always happens in horror movies. They just *have* to pry open that EPS. They just *have* to go into that darkened room. With a flashlight. In a nightgown. Thus, some real-world advice: Make edits in the originating application.

Adobe PDF

If you are creating vector artwork for placement in another application such as a page-layout document, there's usually not much reason to save your file as a PDF. However, if the vector art is not destined for placement in a page layout, but will be submitted as finished art or sent to a client for approval, saving it as PDF allows you to discourage unwanted editing of your artwork.

NOTE Even if you save a PDF with security settings intended to prevent someone from altering it or trying to extract content, it isn't completely bulletproof—there are ways of bypassing the security protections. No, I'm not going to tell you.

And, unless you're using fonts that prevent embedding in a PDF (for shame!), saving as PDF eliminates the need to supply fonts separately with your job.

You may have heard that it's a bad idea to use PDFs as artwork; some of that caution is based on old wives' tales and mental scars from obsolete workflows. A badly made PDF created by an application that doesn't play by the official PDF-creation rules could be an issue, but PDFs generated by Illustrator or InDesign will be perfectly good graphic citizens. So don't be afraid to use them. In all cases, before you send your job as PDF, ask the print service provider to provide detailed specifications for PDF creation. Better yet, ask them to send the PDF preset so you can import it for use in InDesign and Illustrator.

Vector Formats Not Appropriate for Print

Not all vector formats are created equal. While page-layout programs may allow you to import them, some vector file formats are not the best choices for artwork you intend to print.

Microsoft Windows Metafile Format (WMF)

WMF is intended for placement in applications such as Microsoft Word and PowerPoint. While WMF can contain both vector and raster content, it offers no support for CMYK content. Curved shapes are rendered as choppy, chiseled sections (**Figure 5.2**). WMF is a very limited format and simply isn't appropriate for print.

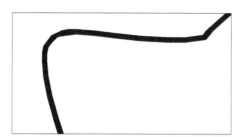

Figure 5.2 *WMF renders curved shapes as choppy approximations. While it may be acceptable in a Microsoft Word or PowerPoint file, WMF should not be used for print.*

Enhanced Metafile Format (EMF)

EMF, like WMF, is intended for use in applications such as Word and PowerPoint. While curves are smoother than those in a WMF, strokes become concentric shapes. EMF offers no support for CMYK, and some vector artwork may be rasterized. And, like WMF, EMF is not appropriate for print production.

Raster Formats

Illustrator offers options for exporting to raster formats such as TIFF, JPEG, PNG, and BMP. Of course, a vector format provides more flexibility and sharper output. But if you do need to rasterize the content of a vector artwork file (say, for Web use), choose *File > Export* and select the appropriate format and settings. The Illustrator file is unchanged; a new file is created during export.

TIP If you need to export Illustrator artwork for use in Microsoft Power-Point, use the Portable Network Graphics (PNG) format. It's a very flexible format; it supports high resolution, soft edges, and transparency.

Handling Text

When you include text in your vector artwork, you have to take steps to ensure that it will print as expected. Of course, you can use the same approach that's recommended for page-layout applications: Collect the fonts and linked artwork and include them when you submit your vector artwork to the print service provider. Illustrator CC provides the ability to package your work so you can provide the Illustrator document, fonts, and linked images to a print service provider. If you're using an older version of Illustrator, the Scoop plug-in (Mac only) from Worker 72a (www.worker72a. com) adds the package functionality for Illustrator CS3 through CS6.

Embedding Fonts

Provided that the font creator has not forbidden embedding, Illustrator embeds fonts in an EPS or AI file for placement in other programs. This means that font information is available for *display* and *printing*, but this does not make the font available for *editing* text in the EPS or AI. To edit text, you'll still need the appropriate fonts active on your system; embedding does not deliver the fonts to you. Not all applications can embed fonts in the EPSs they generate.

Some font vendors prevent embedding by placing a "don't embed" flag in their fonts. This won't prevent you from using these fonts to create artwork, nor will it prevent printing. But you will be unable to embed the font in any

AI, EPS, or PDF file that you create. This means you have to ensure that the print service provider also has the necessary fonts to print your job (more about this thorny issue in Chapter 6, "Fonts").

Even if you *can* embed fonts, there is no guarantee that the embedding will survive what the print service provider might do to your poor, innocent AI, PDF, or EPS file. If there is a problem that requires editing the file, they'll need to open the file. Opening the file without the necessary fonts loaded will result in the font embedding being destroyed. As long as the file is left unopened, it will print as expected when placed into a page-layout program such as InDesign.

Some workflows perform imposition by positioning EPS files in a page-layout application. Trapping, imposition, and RIP software all must correctly interpret font information. Each step has the potential to corrupt font information. Don't freak out; these are worst-case scenarios. But the prospects are worth considering.

Now that you fear for the safety of your fonts, what can you do to ensure successful imaging? Your best bet is to create a PDF. But some printers or publications may insist that you convert your text to outlines. Of course, save a second version of the file without outlined text to use as a working file in anticipation of possible corrections or the sobering discovery of a misspelled word. And run the spelling checker first.

Outlining Text

Fonts contain information, called *hinting*, which refines the display and printing of text. Consequently, some purists hold that those who outline text should be tarred and feathered. It's true that converting text to outlines eliminates hinting, so text may display onscreen as if slightly bloated, and it may print slightly heavier on desktop printers because of the lower resolution of those devices. However, the fattening is not usually apparent when outlined text is imaged on higher-resolution devices such as imagesetters and platesetters. If the device is capable of 600 dpi or higher, your text should look fine. It's worth mentioning that very small text or type with delicate serifs may lose definition when outlined, regardless of the output device or printing process.

Converting text to outlines eliminates the worry that font embedding might be undone by incautious editing or a process that fails to honor the embedded fonts. If you are submitting PDF files, it's unnecessary to outline fonts, because of the limited editability of PDF files.

Incorporating Images into Vector Files

It's possible to place images in vector drawings in much the same way they're placed in page layouts. It's accepted practice in page layout to *link* the images rather than *embed* them, and this same approach is an option when incorporating images in vector artwork. However, linking images rather than embedding them can cause some problems when the finished artwork is placed into another document, such as a page-layout file. If, in the heat of battle, you neglect to send the linked images along with the parent vector file, things will understandably fall apart.

One alternative is to embed the image in your vector drawing so that it can't fall by the wayside. Embedding, as you might expect, increases the size of the resulting file. It's pretty easy math. If you've embedded a 2 MB image, you'll be adding 2 MB to your final size. However, if that image subsequently requires retouching or color correction, how do you pull it back out of the Illustrator file?

Fortunately for us, we live in civilized times. Illustrator CC provides an option to unembed images and save them as independent files. They can then be edited, and linked or reimported into the Illustrator document.

A more flexible approach is to take advantage of the package function in Illustrator CC. When you're ready to send your project to a collaborator, client, or print service provider, just choose *File > Package*, and Illustrator gathers up the necessary fonts and linked images. There are licensing considerations when you package a file, though—the recipient is supposed to have purchased the same fonts so that they're legally entitled to use them. It's a bit of a quagmire, and we'll tackle that topic in Chapter 6, "Fonts."

> **NOTE** Please read the section on font licensing in Chapter Six, "Fonts." Not all font vendors allow you to outline text. This is probably a surprise to you, but it's an issue that you must consider.

> **NOTE** Subscribers to the Creative Cloud version of Illustrator CS6 also have the ability to package files and unembed images.

Avoiding Unnecessary Complexity

RIPs are more robust than ever, but there are still reasons to simplify vector artwork. Simpler drawings usually result in a smoother appearance, and they're easier to edit later. If you've used the drawing tools in Illustrator, you know that vector art is made of straight and curved lines called Bézier shapes. The anchor points and direction handles that allow you to modify such shapes are fairly confusing when you first use them. So, in our timid early experiments in drawing programs, we tend to tiptoe around shapes, using a bazillion clicks to create a drawing. Eventually, we become more comfortable with the tools and learn to do more with less.

Simplify Your Paths

Stop clicking. Really. Right now. More points do not equal a better drawing. In fact, fewer points—if they're the right points—result in a smoother drawing, as you can see in **Figure 5.3**. Of course, in the early stages of learning vector drawing tools, it's difficult to draw so elegantly. But even if your drawing is a bit lumpy, there are tools in Illustrator that smooth and simplify paths.

Figure 5.3 *Too many points (top row) result in a choppy drawing. Good Pen tool technique yields fewer points and a smoother finished drawing (bottom row).*

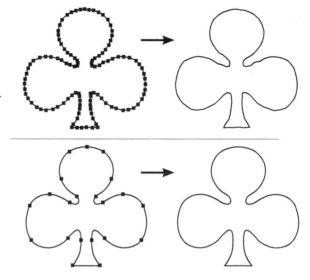

In the early days of desktop drawing, it was crucial to minimize the number of points in a drawing to ensure successful imaging. The overly busy shamrock on the top row of Figure 5.3 might have been called a RIP-buster in those ancient days, resulting in glacially slow print times and the possibility that it would produce the dreaded limitcheck error and fail to be processed by the RIP. Modern RIPs are much more robust and computers are exponentially faster, but smoothness is still a strong motivation to master the Zen of fewer clicks while drawing. And your mouse will last longer.

Recommended Approaches to Document Construction

The original purpose of vector drawing programs was to create logos and other geometric shapes. With each release, these programs add features that delight artists and frighten print service providers. Illustrator 9.0 went beyond basic vector capabilities by adding transparency, soft edges, shadows, and glows. As the distinctions between painting and drawing are blurred, you must decide which is the best tool to create your artwork. If you want to mimic the look of a watercolor painting, use Photoshop CC or a painting program such as Corel Painter. For multiple pages with lots of text and images, you might be saner if you use InDesign rather than Illustrator.

It's a Drawing Program

Well, *duh*, you're thinking. Of course it is! And that's the point; Illustrator is a drawing program, not a page-layout program.

If you are creating a single-page piece such as a magazine ad and you're more comfortable working in a drawing program, it's acceptable to use Illustrator, provided you correctly build in any necessary bleed.

But if you're contemplating creating something like an annual report, it's time to consider learning a dedicated page-layout application. As you will see in Chapter 11, "Illustrator Production Tips," it is possible to have multiple Artboards in Illustrator, so it may seem that the distinctions are becoming blurred between InDesign and Illustrator. However, Illustrator is still intended for illustration, and it lacks the dedicated page-layout features that InDesign boasts, such as master pages, automatic page numbering, hyperlinks, cross-references, and the ability to generate a table of contents or an index.

Understandably, if you're most comfortable in Illustrator, it's easy for it to become the graphic hammer with which you smack every design nail. But think of Illustrator, Photoshop, and InDesign as an ecosystem: Each application has its strengths, but together they make a powerful team. Make sure you're using each player for the job it does best.

Fonts

6

We have a love-hate relationship with fonts. We love their chiseled serifs, we swoon over their graceful swashes, we kern them to the verge of claustrophobia. We painstakingly track text to perfection and agonize over minuscule changes in leading values. Wait a minute. This is starting to sound like a romance novel. That would be the *love* part of the equation. Alas, this chapter is more about the *hate* part.

Font Flavors

Fonts come in several formats: OpenType, PostScript (often also referred to as Type 1), and TrueType. Within those major species, there are subspecies, but it's sufficient to know the major species. If you're a Mac user, you also have Apple's data-fork–based TrueType format fonts, called dfonts.

PostScript (Type 1) Fonts

PostScript fonts consist of two files: A bitmap "screen font" component for onscreen display and a printer component that contains PostScript instructions for actually printing the character. Since it's made of pixels, the bitmap component alone can't provide acceptable resolution for output, so if you misplace the printer font, you're out of luck. Don't discard the screen font either: It contains additional resources required by the system.

Whereas the screen font was once necessary for onscreen display of a Post-Script font, current Mac and Windows operating systems can rasterize a printer font for onscreen display once it's activated, without needing a companion screen font to do so. Font activation applications, such as Extensis™ Suitcase Fusion or FontAgent Pro from Insider Software won't activate a lone printer font without its companion screen font. Some applications, such as Adobe InDesign, will activate printer fonts placed in their own private fonts folders. Placing a PostScript printer font in InDesign's fonts folder makes it available to InDesign on both Windows and Mac. In either case, the operating system handles the onscreen display without having a screen font.

InDesign's dedicated fonts folder can be found here:

- Windows: Program Files\Adobe\Adobe InDesign CC\Fonts
- Mac: Applications/Adobe/Adobe InDesign CC/Fonts

If you have only the screen font suitcase, you're out of luck: neither the operating system, a font management program, or InDesign can use it to activate or use the font.

TrueType Fonts

We were all raised to believe that PostScript fonts were the Only Right Way and convinced that any other font format was evil. In the earlier days of desktop publishing, this was a well-founded belief because some RIPs couldn't handle TrueType. That was rectified long ago, but some users still believe the myth. Let it go.

The TrueType format was the result of a collaboration between Apple Computer and Microsoft and consists of a single file (that is, no separate screen and printer font components). Thus there is no need to keep track of two separate files to constitute a usable font. However, in more primitive times—say, 1993—just mentioning TrueType could strike terror in the heart of a prepress operator, because earlier PostScript RIPs could not interpret TrueType fonts.

Fast-forward to current times. It's no longer necessary to jump through these treacherous hoops. RIPs can now process TrueType just as easily as PostScript fonts. Really. There is no longer any need to sneer at TrueType fonts as being somehow inferior. Understandably, if you buy TrueType fonts in a $9.95 font collection called Larry's Boatload o'Fonts, there's a chance that they won't be well behaved. But that isn't because they're TrueType fonts. It's because Larry builds lousy fonts.

OpenType Fonts

OpenType fonts are single-file fonts and do not have separate screen and printer fonts to keep track of. But here's where the real font fun begins. OpenType fonts are cross-platform. This doesn't mean that Adobe Garamond Pro comes in a Mac version and an identical Windows version. Instead, the same font file can be used on a Mac or on a PC without any special handling.

But, as the late-night TV ads say: Wait, there's more. Whereas PostScript fonts are limited to a paltry 256 characters (isn't that enough?), OpenType fonts can contain more than 65,000 glyphs. A *glyph* is any distinct letterform, such as a number, a lowercase *p*, a dingbat, or an ampersand. This allows a font designer to include swashes, contextual ligatures, titling alternates, alternate versions of characters—even fractions—all in one font. The entire range of characters that previously required separate expert and titling sets can now be contained in one font. See **Figure 6.1** for a glimpse of just a few of OpenType's possibilities.

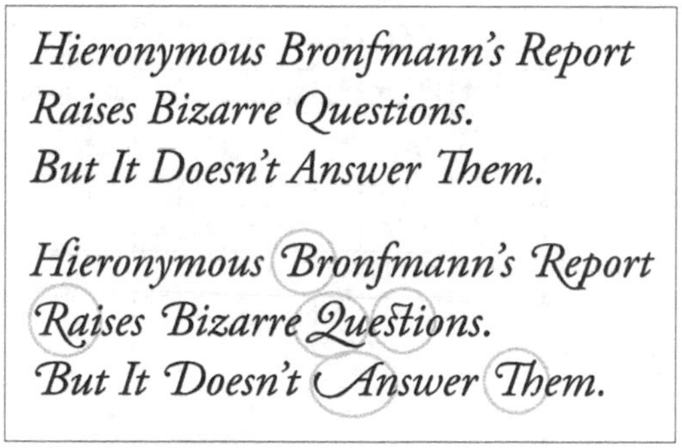

> **TIP** You may have heard the word *dingbat* used as a pejorative, but it's actually a perfectly lovely decorative typeface component. You're probably familiar with Zapf Dingbats, which is nothing but dingbats. Carta, Wingdings, Webdings, and Adobe Woodtype Ornaments are all dingbat fonts.
>
> Dingbat characters are also sprinkled throughout many OpenType fonts. Some of the hidden gems in Adobe Caslon Pro, for example are ✤, ✿, and ❦. To find them, just choose Ornaments from the Show menu in the Glyphs panel. It starts to become a typographic treasure hunt.

Hieronymous Bronfmann's Report Raises Bizarre Questions. But It Doesn't Answer Them.

Hieronymous Bronfmann's Report Raises Bizarre Questions. But It Doesn't Answer Them.

Figure 6.1 *Adobe Garamond Pro is a lovely font even without invoking its special OpenType features (top).*

But look what happens when Swashes and Discretionary Ligatures are turned on (bottom).

Not all OpenType fonts contain glyphs in every one of those 65,000 available character positions. For example, one font may have swashes but another may not. However, the adherence to Unicode mapping ensures that each character exists in the same position from font to font. Unicode is a standard that provides a unique universal identifier for every character, regardless of language, application, or platform. For more information, visit the Unicode Web site (www.unicode.org). If you set text using some of the special diacritical characters (special language characters, such as á, ä, and ç) in Caslon Pro, for example, and then change the font used to Myriad Pro, the diacritical marks are intact because they exist in both fonts. Not all OpenType fonts contain the same glyphs, but a glyph occupies the same position in all fonts in which it's contained.

Table 6.1 *Consistency of diacritical marks across OpenType fonts*

Adobe Caslon Pro	Myriad Pro	Adobe Garamond Pro	Bickham Script Pro
façade	façade	façade	*façade*
Rückumlaut	Rückumlaut	Rückumlaut	*Rückumlaut*
à la mode	à la mode	à la mode	*à la mode*

The benefits of OpenType extend far beyond typographic beauty. One of the motivations for the OpenType format was to provide multilingual support. In **Figure 6.2**, you can see the extensive character set in just one font, Myriad Pro from Adobe Systems.

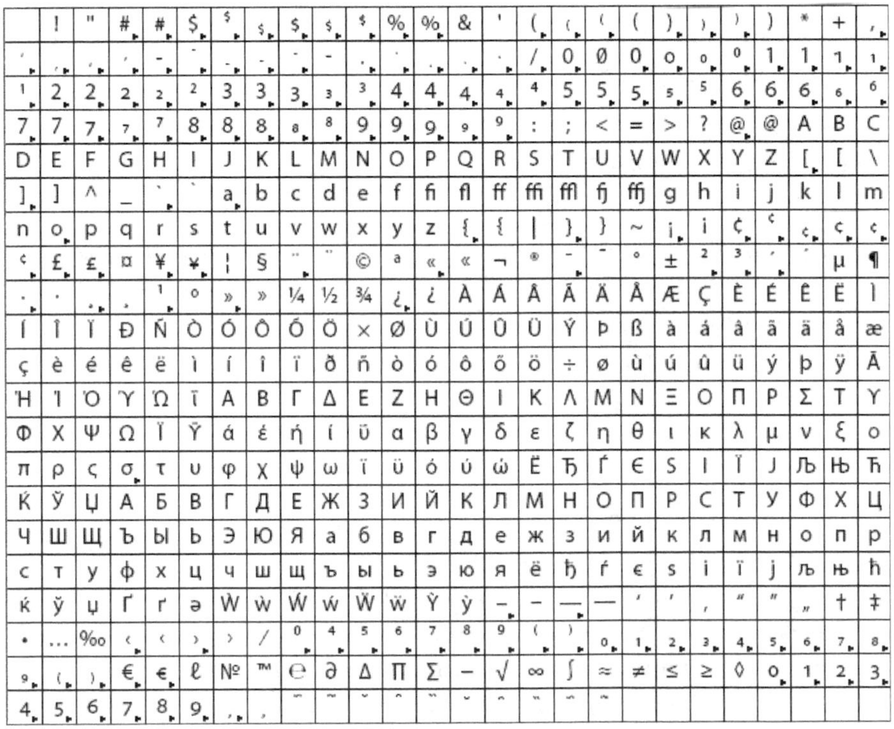

Figure 6.2 *OpenType support for up to 65,536 glyphs makes it possible for the font designer to include multiple language characters, diacriticals, and more. You say that doesn't look like 65,000 glyphs? The tiny triangles by some icons indicate alternate characters.*

You won't be able to use all 65,536 glyphs unless you're using software that recognizes the additional features. Adobe InDesign, Illustrator, and Photoshop can see and use the entire contents of an OpenType font, whereas QuarkXPress through version 6.5 has blinders on, and it can only utilize the same old 256 characters. QuarkXPress 7.0 introduced support for the complete range of OpenType features.

You can use OpenType fonts without fear of imaging problems. They are compatible with all recent RIPs, and all current font-management software supports OpenType. Not using font-management software? OpenType fonts can be activated by the built-in Font Book application on the Mac and by the Windows Fonts control panel. Or you can drop them in the Mac system fonts folders to make them available to all applications (although it's preferable to use font-management software). And having OpenType fonts doesn't mean you have to stop using the PostScript and TrueType fonts you might already have.

Adobe has converted its entire font library to OpenType and will no longer be offering PostScript Type 1 fonts. It's easy to spot OpenType fonts from Adobe: They have Std or Pro as part of their names. Adobe is not the only font vendor marketing OpenType fonts. Most major font vendors now offer OpenType. Given the linguistic support and the enhanced typographic features offered by OpenType fonts, it's easy to see that it's the font format of the future. And it's here today, unlike those flying automobiles we've all been waiting for.

NOTE In fonts from Adobe, the inclusion of Std in a font name indicates an Adobe OpenType version of a previously available PostScript Type 1 font.

Adobe OpenType fonts with the Pro indicator have more expanded glyph sets, including multilanguage characters, and are often the result of combining what once were expert font sets and their base companions. Other font foundries don't necessarily follow the same naming convention.

Glyphs and Characters

It's easy to confuse the terms character and glyph, but they describe different concepts. A character corresponds to a single position in the Unicode standard, which is a uniform, agreed-upon mapping system for the contents of a font. A glyph, however, is a distinct letterform. Multiple glyphs may exist for a single character position in an OpenType font, such as Q and 🌸 for the uppercase Q in Adobe Caslon Pro. Have some fun exploring the Glyphs panel in InDesign and Illustrator.

Mac OS X System Fonts

Mac system fonts such as Geneva, Monaco, Chicago, and Charcoal had traditionally been easy to spot because of their distinctive names. But with the introduction of OS X, Apple threw a monkey wrench into the font wars by including system fonts with names such as Helvetica, Helvetica Neue, and Times Roman, identical to the names of their PostScript cousins. Under the hood, these are TrueType fonts, but you'll see them described as dfonts, a moniker derived from the fact that the fonts are data-only and not a two-headed file consisting of a data fork and a resource fork. (If this doesn't mean much to you, don't worry.)

Mac dfonts aren't inherently evil, but they are problematic because their names are indistinguishable from their PostScript counterparts. If the job is created by multiple people who are using different versions of a font, this may result in font substitution and consequent text reflow. Since they're system fonts, they're active by default. To use the PostScript fonts of the same names, you have to sneak up on the dfonts to control their activation or deactivation by using options in font-management software such as Extensis Suitcase Fusion.

With the advent of OS X on the Mac, there were issues with the operating system's default fonts having the same name as popular PostScript fonts. When Leopard (10.5) was released, this became more of an issue: Leopard insists on having certain fonts available to it. Try to disable them, and, like zombies in bad B-movies, they keep coming back. If you're a fan of Helvetica or Helvetica Neue, your PostScript fonts will conflict with the insistent system fonts. Solution? Purchase the OpenType versions of those fonts, and ignore the aggressive versions forced on you by the operating system. Why not just use the dfonts? Because they can be problematic for some imaging devices, and their font metrics may differ from those of the PostScript versions. If you have created projects using the PostScript versions, then use the dfonts in substitution, you may have text reflow and altered line breaks.

OpenType fonts are innocent bystanders in this battle. Their unique names distinguish them from TrueType, PostScript, and dfont files. As you can see in **Figure 6.3**, the OpenType version of Times is named TimesLTStd, making it much easier to pick it out of the pack.

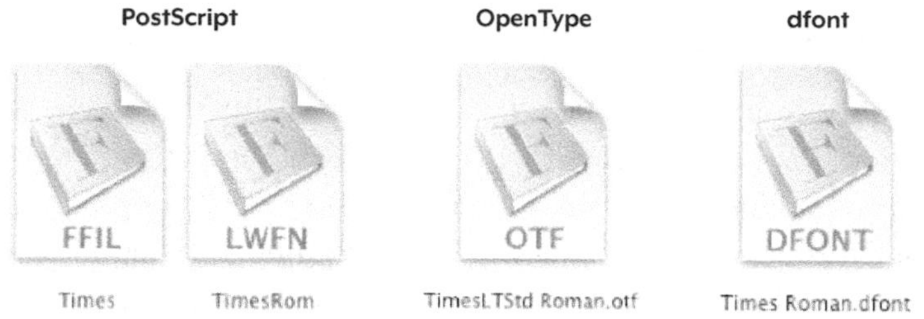

PostScript   OpenType   dfont

Times   TimesRom   TimesLTStd Roman.otf   Times Roman.dfont

Figure 6.3 *Distinguishing the font species. While they look the same at a casual glance, note the identifiers:*

FFIL: PostScript screen font

LWFN: PostScript printer font

OTF: OpenType font

DFONT: Mac OS system font

Windows System Fonts

PC users may now revel in the fact that, starting with Windows 2000, their system fonts are OpenType fonts. As a result, Windows users don't experience the naming conflict between system fonts and PostScript fonts. In fact, the birth of OpenType is the result of a collaboration between Adobe Systems and Microsoft. The Arial system font has the ability to display an extensive character set, including Greek, Hebrew, and Arabic characters.

Multiple Master Fonts

The term Multiple Master probably elicits as much fear in a prepress department as yelling "rush job!" Adobe's Multiple Master fonts were a great idea: Start with a PostScript font, and then give users the ability to create multiple weights, angles, and widths (such as condensed or extended) of a single font. It was an enlightened idea. The problems arose from a lack of education. It wasn't obvious how to make all the cool variants, how to collect the variants necessary for your job, or how to ensure that the print service provider knew how to use them. So the Multiple Master concept sort of died on the vine. Its creative promise was never fully realized, and it's been phased out as an available font product. However, Multiple Master technology is still used for display and printing when fonts are missing in a PDF and for displaying text when fonts are unavailable for an InDesign or Illustrator file.

Substituting One Font Species for Another

When you collaborate on designs, try to avoid substituting a TrueType version of a font for a PostScript version, or vice versa. Don't use an OpenType font instead of the file creator's original font choice, despite your conviction that it's somehow better. You may get lucky, but you're still risking type reflow, which can wreck your carefully crafted line breaks, munge your perfect table of contents, and just plain break your heart.

This is particularly treacherous if you move a job between platforms. A Windows font and its Mac namesake may both be PostScript, but that's still no guarantee that they were created by the same foundry with the same nuances. The solution to this dilemma, of course, is to use OpenType fonts because of their cross-platform usability. The Creative Cloud installs a generous helping of OpenType fonts to get you started.

The default system font directory for CC-installed fonts is:

- Mac: <System Disk>/Library/Fonts
- Windows: <System Disk>:\Windows\Fonts

Fonts Installed by Creative Cloud

CC Font Set 1:

AdobeArabic-Bold	KozGoPr6N-ExtraLight	MyriadPro-BoldCond
AdobeArabic-BoldItalic	KozGoPr6N-Heavy	MyriadPro-BoldCondIt
AdobeArabic-Italic	KozGoPr6N-Light	MyriadPro-BoldIt
AdobeArabic-Regular	KozGoPr6N-Medium	MyriadPro-Cond
AdobeDevanagari-Bold	KozMinPr6N-Regular	MyriadPro-CondIt
AdobeDevanagari-BoldItalic	KozMinPr6N-Bold	MyriadPro-It
AdobeDevanagari-Italic	KozMinPr6N-ExtraLight	MyriadPro-Semibold
AdobeDevanagari-Regular	KozMinPr6N-Heavy	MyriadPro-SemiboldIt
AdobeGurmukhi-Regular	KozMinPr6N-Light	MyriadHebrew-Bold
AdobeGurmukhi-Bold	KozMinPr6N-Medium	MyriadHebrew-BoldIt
AdobeHebrew-Bold	LetterGothicStd	MyriadHebrew-It
AdobeHebrew-BoldItalic	LetterGothicStd-Bold	MyriadHebrew-Regular
AdobeHebrew-Italic	LetterGothicStd-BoldSlanted	AdobeNaskh-Medium
AdobeHebrew-Regular	LetterGothicStd-Slanted	ACaslonPro-Bold
AdobeMingStd-Light	MinionPro-Regular	ACaslonPro-BoldItalic
AdobeMyungjoStd-Medium	MinionPro-It	ACaslonPro-Italic
AdobeSongStd-Light	MinionPro-Bold	ACaslonPro-Regular
KozGoPr6N-Regular	MinionPro-BoldIt	ACaslonPro-Semibold
KozGoPr6N-Bold	MyriadPro-Regular	ACaslonPro-SemiboldItalic
	MyriadPro-Bold	AdobeHeitiStd-Regular

AdobeFangsongStd-Regular	KozGoPro-Regular	OCRAStd
AdobeFanHeitiStd-Bold	KozMinPro-Bold	OratorStd
AdobeGothicStd-Bold	KozMinPro-ExtraLight	PoplarStd
AdobeKaitiStd-Regular	KozMinPro-Heavy	PrestigeEliteStd-Bd
AGaramondPro-Bold	KozMinPro-Light	SourceSansPro-ExtraLight
AGaramondPro-BoldItalic	KozMinPro-Medium	SourceSansPro-ExtraLight-
AGaramondPro-Italic	KozMinPro-Regular	Italic
AGaramondPro-Regular	LithosPro-Black	SourceSansPro-Light
BirchStd	LithosPro-Regular	SourceSansPro-LightItalic
BlackoakStd	MinionPro-BoldCn	SourceSansPro-Regular
BrushScriptStd	MinionPro-BoldCnIt	SourceSansPro-RegularItalic
ChaparralPro-Bold	MinionPro-Medium	SourceSansPro-Semibold
ChaparralPro-BoldIt	MinionPro-MediumIt	SourceSansPro-SemiboldItalic
ChaparralPro-LightItalic	MinionPro-Semibold	SourceSansPro-Bold
ChaparralPro-Italic	MinionPro-SemiboldIt	SourceSansPro-BoldItalic
ChaparralPro-Regular	MyriadArabic-Bold	SourceSansPro-Black
CharlemagneStd-Bold	MyriadArabic-BoldIt	SourceSansPro-BlackItalic
HoboStd	MyriadArabic-It	TektonPro-Bold
KozGoPro-Bold	MyriadArabic-Regular	TektonPro-BoldCond
KozGoPro-ExtraLight	NuevaStd-Bold	TektonPro-BoldExt
KozGoPro-Heavy	NuevaStd-BoldCond	TektonPro-BoldObl
KozGoPro-Light	NuevaStd-Italic	TrajanPro3-Bold
KozGoPro-Medium	NuevaStd-Cond	TrajanPro3-Regular

Activating Fonts in the Operating System

Just having a font somewhere on your hard drive isn't enough. You must activate it to make it available to all the applications on your computer. Both Windows and the Mac provide built-in font activation. If you tend to use the same fonts, and don't need to frequently add fonts, the built-in font activation schemes may be sufficient for your needs.

TIP Some applications must be restarted to recognize a font after it's activated. Adobe applications immediately recognize fonts, whether they're activated by the operating system or a font-management program.

Apple Font Book

Apple's free Font Book utility ships as part of OS X. If you're using a limited selection of fonts for the majority of your work and don't need the control afforded by creating font sets, Font Book is probably adequate. Font Book copies fonts into *Users/[username]/Library/Fonts* to activate them. It deactivates fonts when Font Book's collections are disabled and removes the font files from the Library/Fonts folder.

Windows Control Panel

Windows users can activate fonts by using the Fonts option in the Control panel. The Fonts option in the Control panel provides a common system location so that fonts are available to applications. Deleting a font from Windows' Fonts puts it in the Recycle Bin. There is no provision for creating sets of fonts. Activated fonts are stored together in a single folder, and they're all awake, all the time.

Font-Management Programs

It's important to note that the font activation methods provided by your operating system are just that—font *activation*, not font *management*. As an application launches, it takes note of all the activated fonts. If you have hundreds of fonts active, you're adding to system overhead and slowing down all your applications. If you're tired of taking ten minutes to get from A to H in your overly long font listings, it's a sign that it's time to adopt some sort of font management.

Font-management programs allow you to selectively activate and deactivate fonts as necessary to reduce system overhead. These programs also allow you to create custom sets of fonts, so you can easily activate all the fonts needed for a job or a particular customer with just one click.

Some of the commonly used font-management applications include Extensis Suitcase Fusion (Mac and Windows), FontAgent Pro from Insider Software (Mac and Windows), and Linotype Font Explorer X Pro (Mac and Windows). Which solution should you choose? There's no easy answer: It depends on your own tastes. All of these products provide approximately the same functionality, so your choice will likely depend on your fondness for a particular interface. Download a trial version of the software, give it a spin, and see if it fits with your workflow and requirements.

Automatic Font Activation

In addition to allowing you to create and activate font sets, some font-management solutions install plug-ins or extensions that provide the ability to automatically activate fonts as needed when document files are launched.

Occasionally, an auto-activation plug-in can conflict with other plug-ins in some applications. Symptoms may include minor effects such as display glitches or pauses while fonts are activated. Such glitches are rarely dangerous, but be prepared for them.

Font Conflicts

It is possible to have multiple font files with the same name: For example, over the years you may have bought a PostScript Type 1 version of Helvetica and a TrueType version, and then found that those legacy fonts now conflict with the Mac system font also named Helvetica (**Figure 6.4**). How do you know which font is the "right" font?

Figure 6.4 *Attempting to activate a PostScript version of Helvetica prompts an alert because the OS already has its own version of Helvetica.*

This can happen when the desired font has the same name as an operating system font; take advantage of your font-management application's ability to manage system fonts to resolve the conflict, if possible. It also pays to perform some font house-cleaning. Use a utility such as FontGear's FontDoctor™ (available for both Mac and Windows) to check for damaged and duplicate fonts. FontDoctor also organizes fonts into a sensible library to make your font life easier.

Once again, OpenType can come to the rescue. The unique names of OpenType fonts preclude such conflicts. The OpenType format is like a wonder drug—with no bad side effects.

Typekit Desktop Fonts

Creative Cloud has introduced an entirely new way to obtain and manage fonts—Typekit desktop fonts. There's no installer, and you don't need a font-management program to activate Typekit desktop fonts; the fonts automatically appear in the font menus of all your applications (even non-Adobe applications such as Microsoft Word).

To access Typekit desktop fonts on Windows, launch the Creative Cloud desktop app by clicking its icon on your desktop. On the Mac, click the small Cloud icon in your menu bar. Once the Creative Cloud desktop app is launched, select the Fonts option, and click Browse Fonts on Typekit. You can refine your search by parameters such as font classification, weight, and x-height, or search for a font by name.

This is all managed through the Creative Cloud desktop application, as long as your Creative Cloud membership is active.

Typekit desktop fonts are OpenType® fonts—they're no different from any other OpenType fonts you have purchased conventionally and can be used as you would use any active fonts on your system. They can be embedded in PDFs, EPUBs, SWF files, and DPS projects, and can be converted to outlines.

If you are collaborating with someone who is not a Creative Cloud member, they can either join Creative Cloud or subscribe to Typekit alone and have access to all the same fonts you are using in projects. They can also purchase the necessary fonts from the type foundry.

But you need to be aware of one very important difference with Typekit desktop fonts. Because of licensing restrictions, Typekit desktop fonts are *not* packaged by InDesign or Illustrator. Conventionally licensed fonts will still be included in InDesign or Illustrator packages. If you send packaged files to a printer who also subscribes to Creative Cloud, they already have access to the same fonts through Typekit, so this will not be an issue.

The font files themselves are invisible on your system, so forget about packaging them manually.

In a homogenous environment, where all users are subscribed to Creative Cloud, this will be seamless. However, if you are designing work for clients who are using pre-CC versions of the software (for example, building templates for a company to use), either avoid using Typekit desktop fonts or advise the client to subscribe to the Typekit service (www.typekit.com) separately, or to purchase the necessary fonts conventionally from the font foundry.

Font Licensing Issues

You probably don't think of fonts as software, but that's how fonts are distributed and licensed. They're not just little drawings of letters. Fonts also contain instructions for font appearance and imaging. Consider the prodigious amount of work that goes into creating a font, and perhaps you'll understand why you shouldn't just freely distribute fonts. Each character must be painstakingly drawn. The font designer must take into consideration how characters fit together, how they will look at various sizes, create hinting information, and much more. Professional font-creation software is expensive and complex because designing fonts is not a simple undertaking. Consider that a copy of the FontLab font-editing application costs $650—that should give you an idea of the nontrivial nature of font creation and font editing. And just imagine the work that goes into creating an elaborate OpenType font with contextual alternates, swashes, and arbitrary fractions.

End User License Agreements (EULAs)

I'm sure you read the EULAs that come with all the fonts that you purchase (you did purchase them, didn't you?). Most font foundries allow use of a purchased font on several workstations and one or two printing devices, so if you've bought a font for a three-person workgroup that shares one networked printer, you're probably abiding by the EULA (commonly pronounced *yoo-la*).

The licensing situation is more complex than you may have realized. When you send your job to a print service provider, you probably gather up all the necessary files, including fonts. Surprise—you're probably in violation of the EULA for doing so. Here's an excerpt from a major font foundry's EULA:

> You may send a copy of any font along with your documents to a commercial printer or other service bureau to enable the editing or printing of your document, *provided that such party has informed you that it owns a valid license to use that particular font software.* [Italics added]

In other words, to be in compliance with the EULA, both you and the print service provider must have purchased licenses for the font. You may have never read the fine print for fonts you're using, but some of your fonts may

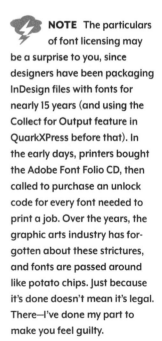

NOTE The particulars of font licensing may be a surprise to you, since designers have been packaging InDesign files with fonts for nearly 15 years (and using the Collect for Output feature in QuarkXPress before that). In the early days, printers bought the Adobe Font Folio CD, then called to purchase an unlock code for every font needed to print a job. Over the years, the graphic arts industry has forgotten about these strictures, and fonts are passed around like potato chips. Just because it's done doesn't mean it's legal. There—I've done my part to make you feel guilty.

specify this limitation. In other words, your inclusion of the font in a collection of job files submitted to the printer is not legal if the printer doesn't also own the font. What are the chances that your printer owns every font?

If you doubt that the printer owns the same exotic fonts you've used, you have two alternative solutions—send a PDF with embedded fonts, or convert the text to outlines.

Embedding Fonts in PDFs

You may think that no font vendor would object to an end user embedding a licensed font in a PDF. Well, some do. (The surprises just keep coming, don't they?) While we're not aware of any method for extracting a font from a PDF, apparently some font vendors fear that it is (or may become) possible. To forestall such thievery, some have included clauses in their EULAs that prescribe that fonts must be *subset*. Subsetting embeds only the characters needed to image the PDF file rather than the entire font (Illustrator and InDesign automatically subset any embedded fonts in exported PDFs). Some font foundries further stipulate that only one copy of the PDF must be supplied to the recipient. But beyond these two fairly harmless requirements, there's a rather sinister stipulation: Some foundries insist that the PDF must contain security settings to allow only viewing and printing.

PDFs with security settings may be rejected by many workflow segments, such as imposition. Of course, you can supply the secret unlock password with the PDF so the printer can disable the protection, but that defeats the purpose of locking it down in the first place (frustrated yet?). Note that some font vendors sell what is called a service bureau license at a reduced price; this is considered an extension of your license and may be exercised by the print service provider only for output of your jobs.

The sanest legal approach is to truly read the EULAs for fonts you own, and take the measures necessary to be in compliance with their stipulations, even if it means purchasing additional licenses for your print service provider. It's a small addition to job cost in the interest of legality.

Adobe does not place any restrictions on font embedding in PDFs, but you would be wise to pore over the EULA for any fonts you're thinking of buying from other vendors, keeping these issues in mind.

There are also some fonts that contain a "don't embed" flag that prevents these fonts from being embedded in a PDF. Such fonts are rare, and you will be warned that you have used an unembeddable font if you attempt to create a PDF in InDesign or Illustrator. You will have to substitute a font that does allow embedding, or convert the text to outlines (assuming the EULA for the font allows conversion to outlines).

Converting Text to Outlines

By now you're probably thinking, "Surely I can just convert my text to outlines and completely avoid the Font Police." Surprisingly (or perhaps not, at this point), converting text to outlines does not sidestep the provisions of the font vendor's EULA. In fact, while most font vendors' licensing allows conversion of text to outlines, some expressly forbid it.

Additionally, you must consider that, even if a font vendor's EULA permits outlining fonts, you may see some slight loss of quality when printing outlined text to low-resolution devices such as in-house printers, especially with small serif text.

What's a concerned citizen to do? First and foremost, read the license before you purchase fonts. If you're purchasing fonts online, the vendor should make the EULA available to you before you commit to purchasing a font. You'll find that some font foundries are less restrictive than others on issues such as font embedding and outlining. Either patronize those with less stringent EULAs, purchase fonts for your print service provider… or learn how to create your own fonts. That might give you some sympathy for what font designers do.

And please don't name your firstborn child Eula, or she won't be able to go anywhere or do anything.

Sending Fonts to the Print Service Provider

If you have studied the fine print in the licensing agreements for all the fonts you're using in a project, and you've determined that you and your print service provider are in full compliance with any applicable licenses, remember to gather up all the necessary fonts when you submit your files for printing. See Chapter 11, "Illustrator Production Tips," and Chapter 12,

"InDesign Production Tips," for specific information on preparing page-layout files (including fonts) for the print service provider.

If you submit PDF files, make sure you've correctly embedded the fonts. See Chapter 13, "Acrobat Production Tips," for general information about font handling in PDF files. For detailed information about creating PDF files from an individual application, see the appropriate chapter.

Cross-Platform Issues 7

Allegiance to an operating system can be a tribal issue, rivaling politics as a trigger for heated discussions, innuendo, condescension, and insults regarding parentage and one's fitness for procreation. It's an integral part of the fun of using computers.

In the early 1990s, this chapter would not have been necessary. In fact, it would have been fairly pointless (depending on your platform preference, you may feel that it's pointless now). In those days, if you were involved in graphic arts, you were using a Mac. Period. End of story. Windows users were treated like second-class citizens when they dared take their jobs to a print service provider. If you wanted to clear out a prepress department in 1992, all you had to do was yell "PC job!" It was much like yelling "Fire!" in a crowded theater.

Fast-forward to the present day: It's not a Mac-only world. The Creative Cloud applications such as InDesign, Illustrator, Photoshop, and Acrobat are almost indistinguishable across platforms. But while the applications themselves are generally compatible, operating system issues still must be addressed if we're all to get along peacefully. Now, please put down that wooden stake.

Crossing the Great Divide

Gone are the days when we needed special translation software to even read files from the Other Side. Whereas network connections once required arcane geek incantations and burnt offerings, mere mortals can now point, click, and magically access a networked PC from their Mac, and vice versa (assuming the IT department has set things up correctly). We live in wonderful times.

But that doesn't mean things are perfect or painless. Windows users have to accept that many Mac users don't consider file extensions important (even though the current Mac OS uses them). Mac users must learn to avoid florid naming conventions. And everybody still needs to gather up the fonts before they send a job out the door.

While setting up a network is outside the scope of this book, the assumption is that you've figured out some way to get your stuff to wherever it needs to be. We've come a long way from floppies (*Grandma, what are floppies?*) and SyQuest drives. It was very chic to have huge whopping 44 MB SyQuest cartridges ten years ago, and blank CDs cost nearly 20 dollars apiece. Now, we have large-capacity CDs, DVDs, USB memory sticks, and cloud storage—and none of the current methods is platform-specific. Pardon the flashback. The author suddenly feels very, ah, mature.

Naming Files

It's great to be creative while you're designing an annual report or sales brochure. But when it's time to name and save files, control your imagination. Both Windows and Mac computers, as well as popular server platforms, are more forgiving than in the days of the old eight-dot-three naming conventions (eight-character filename, followed by a three-letter file extension). In those days, a Mac user wanting to share with a PC user had to be fairly creative to come up with filenames such as *AnRepCov.eps*, *AnRepCv2.eps*, and so on. You get the idea.

Let's Have a Lot of Brevity

Fortunately, the ancient eight-dot-three limitation was lifted many years ago. With the expanded freedom in naming files, some of us get a little carried away. Here's a file from one of the author's clients, slightly altered to protect the innocent: *SSGC holiday wreath photos and logos -- Publisher (10-19-05).pub*. Because spaces, periods, and parentheses all count, that's a 64-character filename. Windows and Mac platforms currently allow a total of 255 characters, which is perhaps overly generous—that's an entire paragraph.

While Windows allows filenames of 255 characters, it limits a *total path designation* to 260 characters. Path designation is the literal pathway to the file's location. For example, a file named *Test.doc* stored at the root level of a PC's C drive would have a path designation of *C:\Test.doc*, a total of 11 characters. File extensions such as *.doc* or *.pdf* are included in the total character count for a filename. Think of file naming as a game: What's the shortest name you can think of but still find useful?

Filenames Don't Need Punctuation. Period.

Length is not the only issue affecting proper naming of files. There are certain characters—even certain names—that should be avoided. A good rule of thumb is this: Don't include any characters traditionally used in comic strips to indicate profanity, such as !@#$*% (pardon my language). Stick to alphanumeric contents—uppercase and lowercase letters, coupled with numerals, spaces, underscores, and hyphens. There's an urban myth that spaces are forbidden in filenames, but this doesn't usually matter in a graphic arts environment. In Web work, however, it's best to omit spaces from filenames because some server platforms don't correctly handle spaces: A space will be replaced with the characters "%20."

Avoid colons and slashes because those characters are reserved to mark directory breaks. Although the Mac OS won't prevent you from naming a file with forward or backward slashes, slashes will be replaced with bullets when you copy it to a Windows drive. PCs prevent the problem by stopping you in your tracks when you press either a forward or backward slash key, displaying an alert listing forbidden characters. And Mac CD-burning applications will convert slashes to underscores during the creation of a data CD.

If you're creating your job on the Mac and sending it to a print service provider who will be handling it on a Mac, why should you care about slashes? Because they'll probably copy your job to a server for storage. If it's a Windows server, they'll have to rename your files to even allow copying, which will then munge all your image links, forcing them to update your images. Ouch. Since you have no control over where your files may land, forestall such problems by getting in the habit of using safe filenames.

Both Windows and Mac OS X prevent you from typing colons in filenames, and neither operating system allows you to begin a file or folder name with a period. An initial period renders a file invisible under Unix, which includes Mac OS X.

Although current operating systems prevent much of this filenaming misbehavior, beware of legacy files created before the Mac adopted Unix under the hood. Files whose names begin with a period were not problematic under Mac OS 9, but they'll cause problems when you attempt to use them under Mac OS X—they'll disappear.

While some filenaming purists object to using multiple periods as visual separators in filenames, such as *Smith.Brochure.new.pdf*, newer Windows and Mac systems don't care, although this practice may cause problems with some persnickety applications. Some older server processes may modify the name by substituting underscores for extra periods, or by truncating the filename. Rather than risk this reaction, consider using underscores (*Smith_Brochure_new.pdf*) or capitalization (*SmithBrochureNew.pdf*) as a way to add visual separators.

Watch Your Language

Although the Mac OS has no objection to using any combination of letters and numbers in filenames, some combinations are reserved by Windows. Names such as *com1*, *com2*, all the way through *com9* are reserved for communication ports on the PC. If you create a Word file named *com1.doc* on the Mac, you might successfully copy it to a Windows drive, but you'll be unable to open it under Windows. Other forbidden names include *lpt1* through *lpt9* (reserved for printer ports), as well as *prn*, *con*, and *nul*.

Add File Extensions

Like two-button mice, file extensions, such as *.txt* and *.doc*, have long been considered by some Mac users as signs of consorting with the Dark Side. On early Mac operating systems, file extensions were not required. In those days, files consisted of two forks—a data fork and a resource fork. The data fork held the true guts of the file, while the resource fork told the system which icon to use and how to open the file.

Under Unix-based OS X, there's no more fork in the road, and file extensions now identify the species of a file. In truth, the header information in a file usually makes it possible for the file to be recognized by the proper application, even without a file extension.

File extensions are also helpful for human identification of files, and they're crucial for cross-platform compatibility. On both Macs and PCs, you can choose to hide those extensions, but they are there nonetheless.

Most file extensions consist of three letters, but some applications create files with longer extensions, such as *.html* (Web page), *.indd* (InDesign), and what is possibly the world's longest file extension, *.joboptions* (Acrobat). A period always separates the filename from its extension, as in *Image.tif* or *Brochure.indd*.

Failure to append the correct file extension on the Mac can prevent a Windows user from being able to open the file. In addition, lack of a file extension may prevent accessing such a file in other ways, such as attempting to import or place the file in another document. Of course, it's easy to add the extension if you encounter this problem, but it's better to just develop the habit of making sure the extension is added when you save the file. All Windows applications and most Mac OS X applications are smart enough to do this for you.

Whereas even the most ancient Windows file will be sporting a file extension, Mac files saved under pre-OS X may be extension-free. So as you dig up old files for new jobs you're creating on Mac OS X, either manually add the appropriate extension or open the file in the appropriate application by choosing *File > Open* from within the program. Then resave the file with a shiny new extension.

Fonts

The best way to ensure that there will be no font-related issues with a job you submit for print is to create a print-ready PDF with all the fonts embedded. But if you are asked to package your print job and include the required fonts, there are some issues with fonts when you jump platforms. A few things you might want to know:

- OpenType fonts can be used on both Macs and PCs.

- Windows TrueType fonts can be used on Macs and PCs.

- Mac TrueType fonts work on Macs, but not on PCs (you'll need a Windows-specific TrueType version of the fonts).

- Mac system fonts (dfonts) do not work on PCs.

- Mac PostScript (aka Type 1) fonts don't work on PCs, and Windows PostScript fonts don't automatically work on a Mac. However, Windows PostScript fonts can be tricked into working for Adobe applications on a Mac by placing them in [user]/Library/Application Support/Adobe/Fonts.

A number of utilities are available to convert PC fonts to Mac fonts, and vice versa. Keep in mind that the end-user license agreement for a font (EULA) may forbid such trickery. Even if the EULA permits the conversion, there may be unwanted alterations to the font metrics, so text may not be identical between platforms—so this is not an ideal solution.

The most common motivation for such gyrations is to submit a Windows-based job to a Mac-based print service provider. There is only one correct way for the print service provider to treat the job, but unfortunately it's not what usually happens. The common solutions range from bad to acceptable.

- **Bad idea:** Copy the job to a Mac and use the closest available fonts. "Gee...Helvetica is pretty much the same as Arial, isn't it?" No. No, it absolutely is not.

- **Painful compromise:** If the font vendor's licensing agreement allows it, convert the PC fonts to Mac versions with a high-end font-editing program such as FontLab or Fontographer (both now owned by FontLab). Check the converted file carefully against the hard copy; or, better yet, a PDF supplied by the creator of the file.

- **Better approach:** The printer should keep the files in their native habitat. It's not that hard to just bite the bullet and learn the basics of Windows, and avoid any conversion. PCs are really not as scary or neurotic as they used to be. If you're designing on Windows computers, have a heart-to-heart conversation with the print service provider before submitting your job. Elicit some assurance that they will not use either of the first two approaches above. If that assurance is not forthcoming, submit print-ready PDFs to avoid font issues.

- **Best approach:** Switch to OpenType fonts. They're completely cross-platform and full of tempting typographical features. If you use OpenType fonts exclusively, you don't have to worry about the platform fate of your document. If the printer goes against the grain and opens your Windows file on a Mac, nothing will reflow, nothing will fall off. Life is good. Well, at least your fonts are.

- **Smart Approach:** Send PDFs. Fonts are embedded, regardless of the originating platform. See "Embedding Fonts in PDFs" in Chapter 6 for more information.

Sending Files from Mac to Windows

If you're a Mac user who shares files with Windows users, you should be aware that there are little invisible files in Mac directories that become visible on a Windows computer.

In **Figure 7.1**, the genuine document files are at the bottom. The files with names such as ._Fish.ai are not document files. Having the dot at the beginning of the name drives these files to the top of a directory list, and, because they're the first files seen as a user opens a directory, it's naturally tempting to double-click on them.

Name	Date modified	Type	Size
.DS_Store	1/13/2010 2:07 PM	DS_STORE File	7 KB
._Collateral.ai	11/20/2011 8:07 AM	Adobe Illustrator ...	5 KB
._Fish.ai	11/20/2011 8:07 AM	Adobe Illustrator ...	5 KB
Collateral.ai	2/17/2009 10:38 PM	Adobe Illustrator ...	998 KB
Fish.ai	8/16/2009 8:43 PM	Adobe Illustrator ...	3,800 KB

Figure 7.1 *The contents of a Mac directory copied to a Windows computer displays files that are invisible when the same directory is viewed on a Mac.*

What are the mystery files? The .DS_Store file stores folder viewer preferences or any custom attributes of a folder, including the position of the folder window, and which view mode—icon, list, column, or Cover Flow—is selected. If you're curious, "DS" stands for *Desktop Services*.

When Mac files are copied to a PC drive, their data forks are represented by the file's "real" name, and additional Mac HFS (Hierarchical File System) information, such as the resource fork and creator codes, is stored in a second file whose name starts with "._".

What happens when such a directory is opened on a Windows computer? While the formerly invisible files are not problematic, they can be confusing when they're mistaken for document files. When a Windows user double-clicks on one of the mystery files, an error message is displayed (**Figure 7.2**). Shortly thereafter, you'll receive a phone call or email asking why you sent the wrong files.

Figure 7.2 *Because the Windows operating system doesn't know what to do with the hidden directory files, attempting to open them yields an error message.*

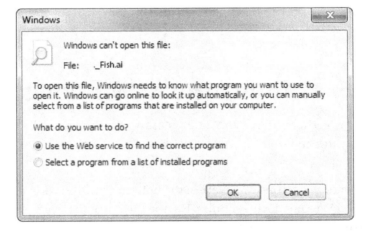

Because the extra files serve no purpose on Windows, they can safely be deleted. If the Windows user sends the same back to a Mac, shorn of the mystery files, it doesn't matter; the Mac will re-create them as necessary.

Sending Files from Windows to Mac

I'll make this short and sweet: It's no big deal. Because the Mac recognizes file extensions, you should have no difficulty opening Windows files on the Mac unless the Mac user doesn't have the proper application to open the file.

Graphics Formats

All current graphics and document formats—including TIFF, PSD, EPS, AI, JPEG, PDF, and more—are perfectly happy jumping platforms. Just don't forget the file extensions. That was easy, wasn't it?

Compressing Files

The most common file compression format on both Mac and Windows platforms is the ZIP format. A number of applications can create and open ZIP archives, including StuffIt on both Mac and Windows, and WinZip for Windows. The ability to ZIP files and folders is built into Mac OS X; just select a file or folder and choose *File > Compress [filename]*. On the Mac, just double-click a ZIP archive to decompress it and unleash the files.

NOTE Why is it called *ZIP* compression? Because of the association of the word "zip" with the notion of moving at high speed. Understandably, compressed files transfer more quickly than the original fluffy files.

Job Submission 8

You need to start planning how your job will be printed long before you send your files to the print service provider. As you've seen in the preceding chapters, it's wise to anticipate the challenges presented by the physical processes of printing. It's less traumatic to prevent problems early in the game than to frantically fix something as the deadline looms. And it's not just the big stuff that bites you. It's no fun to be leaning blearily over a printed sheet on a 3 a.m. press check and have a pressman remark, "Hey, didja notice that this guy's name is spelled three different ways in this brochure?"

In the heat of battle, it's easy to overlook the basics while you're focused on the tricky parts of the job. Tunnel vision (and lack of sleep) can cause you to lose sight of the big picture. But if you break the process into smaller chunks, it's easier to catch problems at each stage.

This chapter is intended to serve as a reminder of some of the issues covered in earlier chapters, and it provides a number of checklists to use while you're preparing to send your job to the printer. You'll find expanded information on many of these topics in the application-specific chapters, but this chapter is meant to call your attention to key issues.

Preparations During the Design Process

It's exciting to get started on a new project, and there's no such thing as too much time to do a job. However, before you wade right into the project, take a breath. In fact, take two.

Lean back and consider the end product. Try to isolate the most challenging aspects of manufacturing the printed piece.

- Does it involve spot colors or varnishes?

- Do you plan to use exotic stock?

- Does it require special finishing treatments such as die cutting, embossing, or foil stamping?

- Is it an odd size?

- Does it involve multiple collateral pieces that need to fit together, such as a pocket folder with inserted literature and a business reply card?

As you sketch out the job in your mind, start having conversations with the printer. In the very earliest stage of the job, you may not always have the luxury of knowing who the print service provider will be. But as soon as you do, start paving the way for a successful print project by opening the lines of communication. Their staff can help you build your project successfully, and you will have prepared them for the incoming job. In printing, as in any kind of manufacturing, *surprise* is rarely a good word.

Talking with the Printer

Your first contact at the printing company will probably be with a salesperson. The ideal salesperson asks questions about your expectations for the job, advises you of any potential problems if your job contains some challenging aspects such as special stock or fancy finishing requirements, and gives you a realistic idea of the outcome. The salesperson will gather your initial information, and give you an estimate of job costs and a timeline for the steps along the way. The timeline will include such events as when your files must be submitted, when you can expect the first proofs, when the press run will take place, and when the final job will be delivered. Finally, the salesperson will hand you and your job off to a customer service representative (CSR).

If you're fortunate, your CSR will be an experienced print professional who can give you some insight into your job's special needs. If you find yourself dealing with someone who seems to know less about the print process than you do, you might try to expand your list of contacts at the printing company. A few print service providers frown on allowing customers to talk to production personnel, but it really does make life easier for everyone if you can deal with knowledgeable operators. Your salesman may be able to smooth the way if necessary. But speaking as a production person, I'll volunteer that most production personnel welcome a customer who's interested in providing a job that's not a nightmare. There's a fine line between being a conscientious client and being a pest, but you, of course, would never cross that line. You shouldn't call the prepress department unnecessarily (they'll start hiding from you), and it's important that you keep the CSR in the loop if you are allowed to contact production staff directly. The CSR is the common contact point for jobs and is expected to know everything about a job. So, don't forget to inform the CSR immediately if anything about the job needs to be changed.

In your initial conversations with the salesman and the CSR, make sure they're aware of any special issues with your job. Here are a few topics you may need to discuss:

- **Unusual stock.** Substrates such as metallic stock or paper with pronounced texture or of unusually thick (or thin) weight may require additional time to order, and may also dictate which press will be used for the job.

- **Special mixed inks.** If you need something beyond what's available in the PANTONE, Toyo, or other swatch libraries, you can request a special, custom-mixed ink. Since this ink is not picked from an existing swatch book, you will need to see ink draw-down samples on the final stock before the job is printed. A draw-down sample is created by spreading a thin coating of the desired ink on the intended stock to present a realistic preview of how the ink will look on press.

- **Varnishes or other coatings.** Special add-ons such as spot varnishes, aqueous coatings, or scratch-off spots require planning because their use may dictate which press will be used to print the job.

HERE'S the best story I've heard about custom-mix spot colors. A fast-food chain wanted a poster to show the color of correctly fried chicken, so the printer needed to create a custom ink. The ink technician, using a plate of fried chicken pieces as a guide, mixed a special ink to be used on press. The proof for color check when the job was running on press? A large tray of fried chicken. It's probably the first time in history that the pressmen ate the proofs.

- **Custom finishing.** Operations such as perforation, die cutting, embossing, foil stamping, or unusual folds require advance planning and equipment setup. Because custom finishing can take extra time, adequate time must be included in the schedule for the job. Complicated folding may also require modifications to the standard configurations of the folding equipment to ensure that the folds occur in the proper manner. See Chapter 3, "Binding and Finishing," for more information on issues with finishing processes.

- **Unusual content.** If you require special print add-ons such as customized content for variable data printing (VDP) or custom addressing, it may be necessary to add time for programming and acquisition of data such as mailing list files.

For your sanity—and the printer's—make sure you obtain the following crucial information from the printer:

- A detailed schedule that includes dates for intermediate events such as random proofs, page proofs, bluelines, and any press checks. Of course, the final delivery date is important, but unless you're aware of all the intermediate dates, you'll jeopardize the final goal.

- Contact information for all the people who are (or should be) familiar with your job, including the salesman, the CSR, and any prepress staff you've been told you can call with questions. Make sure they know how to contact you if questions arise. And keep in mind that printing plants often operate 24 hours a day. You may not be accustomed to phone calls after midnight, but if your job is on a tight schedule and there's a problem during night shift, your phone may ring. This prospect alone may be a strong incentive to check your job thoroughly before you submit it.

Planning for Print

As your files take shape, it's important to build from the ground up. It's not much fun to deconstruct a complex file and then reassemble it because it was built one-half inch too big, or to modify artwork because the file uses the wrong six spot colors. Before you choose *File > New*, make sure you've established the following important specifications:

- **External document size.** If you're printing letterheads, that's easy. But if you're creating a piece that folds, such as a trifold brochure or a pocket folder, whip out the ruler and make sure you know the correct external dimensions before you go too far.

- **Adequate bleed.** While the standard bleed is one-eighth of an inch, some print service providers may request a larger value, especially on packaging or large-format output.

- **Internal panel sizes.** In folding pieces such as trifold brochures, remember that you have to allow for shorter panels that fold in (see Chapter 3, "Binding and Finishing"). In your page-layout program, set up guidelines to help you position content. In fact, your print service provider may be able to provide a template to use if you're building to a common size.

- **Artwork interactions with folds, perforations, or die-cut trims.** If artwork stops at a fold, special handling may be required to ensure that it doesn't dribble over onto the next panel, especially on packaging. Your printer can provide some guidance for preparing artwork, especially if you're printing on heavy stock whose thickness has a bearing on how thick the folded edge will be.

- **Correct number of pages.** In a common-format, multipage document (facing pages), the number of pages should be divisible by four. If you were inspired to pull the staples out of a magazine while you were reading Chapter 3, look at the loose pages and note that each loose sheet consists of four pages—two front, two back. In a longer document, such as a textbook, you (or the printer) can take up the slack by providing blank pages for notes.

- **Correct inks.** If it's not a 27-color job, there shouldn't be 27 spot colors in your application's swatches panel. Delete unnecessary colors, or convert them to CMYK if they're not intended to print as spot colors.

Checking Raster Images

As you've seen in Chapter 4, "Preparing Raster Images," it's important that your images are of sufficient resolution at final size. In addition, be sure you've saved the images in an appropriate file format and in the correct color space.

TIP There are exceptions to the 300 ppi rule—for example, large-format output such as posters, store signage, and billboards. Because readers will probably be at least several feet away from the finished poster or large sign, the net effect is the same as viewing a smaller image at a shorter distance. In other words, a 150 ppi image viewed from a distance of several feet is the equivalent of a smaller 300 ppi image viewed up close.

Check images in Photoshop or the application in which you created them. Consult your print service provider to make sure you know their requirements, but here are some general guidelines:

☐ **Resolution.** Raster images should usually be at least 300 ppi (pixels per inch) at their final imaging size for offset printing.

☐ **It may be necessary to create images of higher resolution for high line-screen work (200 lpi or higher).** If you are creating images for special printed pieces such as art prints or art books, you may be asked to supply images at higher than 300 ppi. Keep in mind that it's best if the original scan or digital photograph is of adequate size and resolution. Scaling up or increasing resolution through interpolation never produces results equivalent to healthy original images.

☐ **Color space.** Images usually come in one of five major flavors for printing purposes: CMYK, RGB, grayscale, monochrome (bitmap black and white, with no shades of gray), and duotone. Unless you're working in a color-managed environment, you'll be asked to provide CMYK images for color images. If your print service provider utilizes color management, ensure that you've tagged your RGB images with the appropriate color profile. Make sure that grayscale images are truly black-only files, not gray-appearing RGB or CMYK images.

☐ **Retouching.** If you're not comfortable performing retouching work beyond simple blemish removal, let the print service provider know that you'd like their staff to perform the work instead. It's helpful if you print the images in question and then mark up the problems you'd like them to fix. It's likely that you'll incur additional job charges for this service.

☐ **Rotations and scaling.** You'll achieve the best results if your scans or digital photographs are created at the proper size and rotation for final use. But let's be realistic. You can't always anticipate how you'll use an image. If you've simply flipped an image horizontally or vertically in a page layout, don't worry about it. If you've rotated an image by increments of 90 degrees, don't worry about that. But, if you rotate an image in a page layout by anything other than 90-degree increments, or if you scale—or if you do both—you'll see some slight softening of detail in the final output. For more information on performing transformations on images, see Chapter 4, "Preparing Raster Images."

☐ **Filenames.** Avoid using periods, asterisks, and other characters to drive files to the top of a directory, and be mindful of characters that cause problems when going cross-platform (see Chapter 7, "Cross-Platform Issues"). Even if you and your print service provider are both using Macs, remember that your files may be copied to a server based on Unix or Windows.

Checking Vector Artwork

Because Illustrator allows you to place raster images as content, you have to consider some of the same issues that you encounter in page-layout applications. Don't forget to check the following:

☐ **Correct colors.** If you'll be placing vector art into a page-layout program, try to avoid multiple instances of what should be a single spot color. If the job uses PANTONE 384, for example, make sure that the color isn't called *PANTONE 384C* in your illustration program and *PMS 384CVC* in the final page-layout document. Ensure that color naming is consistent across all constituent files.

NOTE The naming of PANTONE colors across the Adobe products is consistent, so you're likely to encounter the C/CV/CVC nonsense only with ancient files created in other applications.

☐ **Images.** Illustrator offers the choice of embedding or linking placed images. Embedding increases the file size and ensures that all the pieces are in place. However, it may limit editing if the print service provider needs to modify the image. If you anticipate the need to color correct or retouch images placed in Illustrator, send the image files along just to be safe. As long as the printer is using the Creative Cloud version of Illustrator, the image can be unembedded easily for editing.

☐ **Fonts.** Embed fonts or outline text (the font EULA permitting). Note that while Illustrator enables the embedding of fonts with proper permissions, this only facilitates correct imaging. The fonts are not available for text editing unless the user (in this case, the printer) also has the fonts active on their system. If you're tempted to convert text to outlines, be advised that some text effects such as underlining or strikethrough may be lost when you outline the text. Another consequence of outlining text to consider: Fonts contain special information called hinting, which is lost when text is converted to outlines. As a result, outlined text will not be as crisp as the original text when printed on a desktop printer. However, on a high-resolution output device such as an imagesetter or platesetter, outlined text should be satisfactory.

☐ **Text.** Proofread and run spell-check on the content, and check for pesky little empty remnants of text where you may have unintentionally clicked with the Type tool in Illustrator (it happens to all of us sooner or later). Those clicks create empty point text entries that may result in preflight reports of a font being needed. This can result in time wasted troubleshooting something that isn't truly a problem if the font isn't used anywhere else.

☐ **Bleed.** Ensure that you've included adequate bleed if any artwork goes to the edge of the artboard.

Checking Page Layout Files

At each step of the process, through your design stages and the successive proofing stages at the printer, there are multiple opportunities for things to go awry. While you're focused on kerning an important headline on the cover, it's easy to overlook a typographical error on the last page of the publication. After all, we all get tired.

Tiny errors can lead to expensive problems. Tunnel vision is unavoidable, especially in complex projects. That's why proofing is so important. It's also helpful to solicit input from someone who hasn't been staring at the job as long as you have. An innocent bystander can often spot errors you've missed: "Hey, this looks great, but shouldn't there be a picture in this big empty white box?"

Once you've determined that your raster images and vector artwork pieces are healthy, you still need to examine any page-layout file that combines that content to make sure that additional errors are not introduced. Don't forget to do the following:

☐ **Proofread.** It's important to weed out typing errors, but be particularly careful with product names and proper names. You also need to check for mistakes that spell-checkers don't catch, such as grammatical errors and words that are spelled correctly but aren't what you intend. You don't want to go to press with a headline that reads "The Clam Before the Storm."

☐ **Delete extra junk.** Clean off the pasteboard, and eliminate any empty elements.

☐ **Delete double spaces.** If you were still setting type with a typewriter, double spaces would be fine. But you're not. Double spaces in computer typesetting are large, airy gaps. Perform a find-and-replace to replace double spaces with single spaces. And quit hitting that spacebar. If you've used double spaces in folios to separate page numbers from footer text, replace them with em spaces. Do all of this before you generate a table of contents, so text reflow does not render an existing TOC invalid.

☐ **Check for scaling and rotation.** While a few rotations here and there aren't a problem, and it's permissible to scale within a reasonable range (70–125 percent), an image-heavy document with lots of such transformations can be slow to RIP. Especially if you are greatly reducing many large images, consider doing those transformations in Photoshop and then updating the images in the page layout so they can be handled without rotation.

☐ **Provide printouts of your job.** They're really helpful to CSRs, planners, estimators, and prepress operators at the printer for quick visual aids. It's best if printouts are actual size, but if the piece is too large to print at final size (or you don't feel like tiling output and taping pieces of paper together), mark the printout prominently with the scale factor. This is especially important if the print service provider will be scanning transparencies or other artwork for you. The scanner operator will need to measure your transparencies, measure your printouts, and then determine the proper scale factor for each image. If you indicate the scale factor used in your printout, you reduce the chance for error by alerting the scanner operator and by providing an important factor in the scaling equation.

☐ **Preflight your job.** The term preflight comes from the aviation industry. If you are about to become airborne in a 150,000-pound metal tube, you check all the operating systems before you pull back on the stick. If you want to minimize problems in a print job, you check all the contents. The preflight profiles in Adobe InDesign can be customized to perform very granular examinations of a file, checking issues from spelling to bleed and live area violations. You might also consider using dedicated preflight software to do the job for you. FlightCheck from Markzware (www.markzware.com) can automate preflighting of multiple InDesign, Illustrator, Photoshop, Acrobat, and many other document types.

NOTE Ask the printer to provide a custom InDesign preflight profile to ensure your files are set up correctly for printing conditions.

☐ **Have realistic expectations.** Your monitor and your desktop printer's approximation of the final printed piece may be fairly good if you calibrate your monitor and you're using a high-end printer along with careful color management. Otherwise, you have to wait for contract proofs from the print service provider to have a good idea of the appearance of the final output.

Sending Job Files

The print service provider should give you some guidelines for submitting job files. Some prefer PDF files, while some would rather have application files such as InDesign or Illustrator documents. Usually, you'll be asked to provide multipage documents in *reader's spreads*, which is how you normally build such documents, with page 2 facing page 3, and so on. If you're asked to provide *printer's spreads*—imposed for plating—you should be suspicious that the printer doesn't have dedicated software to perform imposition. This may be a sign that the printer lacks other important capabilities.

Submitting PDF Files

If the printer requests that you submit PDF files, they should give you specifications for creating PDF files, or recommend using a standard such as PDF/X-4. While PDF creation is discussed in other chapters, be sure to address these crucial issues:

☐ **Preflight PDFs before submitting.** Even if you have performed a preflight on the application files that generated the PDF files, it's a good idea to preflight the PDF files themselves. Markzware's FlightCheck Designer and FlightCheck Professional products can preflight PDF files. The print production tools in Acrobat Professional offer extensive preflighting features as well.

☐ **Follow print service provider specifications.** Faithfully follow the specifications that are provided for creating PDF files. Restrict your PDF to the version your printer requests. That is, don't send them an Acrobat 9.0 file if they've asked for an Acrobat 4.0 file. Ask the print service provider to send you PDF job options files (.joboptions) so you can easily create the correct type of PDF for their workflow. Creative Cloud applications share a common repository of PDF-creation settings, and importing the options into any one of the applications makes those settings available to other Creative Cloud applications.

☐ **Embed fonts.** By default, Illustrator and InDesign correctly embed fonts in generated PDFs. Although it's uncommon, if you've used fonts whose vendor forbids embedding or forbids supplying the fonts separately, you must either request that the print service provider purchase the same fonts, or you'll have to substitute fonts that can be embedded. Consult the end user licensing agreement (EULA) for your fonts to be sure that you're in compliance.

☐ **Ensure safe transit.** Even though it's easy to think of PDF files as being hermetically sealed, they can sometimes be corrupted when sent as email attachments unless they're first compressed with a utility such as StuffIt on the Mac or WinZip on Windows. Encasing the PDF files in a compressed archive protects them in transit. If you are submitting the job on digital media, this isn't an issue, and you don't need to compress the PDF files.

Packaging Application Files

It isn't sufficient to send only your finished page-layout file to the print service provider. The page-layout file is like a recipe for the printed piece. And a recipe is not much good without all the necessary ingredients. The fonts and images used in your page layout are the ingredients, and you must supply all those constituent parts for the print service provider to complete your job. While you're working on your project, you may be using images and vector art stored in multiple locations on your hard drive or on a server. Graphics files are simply linked to your page-layout file and referenced by the page-layout file, as are the fonts you've used. By default, images and vector art components are not embedded in the page-layout file, so the graphics and fonts must be gathered up to constitute a complete kit for your project. (While it's possible to embed images and vector art, doing so adds to the file size of a page-layout file.) Fortunately, InDesign provides methods for gathering up all the necessary images and vector files, as well as fonts.

When you're sure all your work is in good shape, the Package function in both InDesign and Illustrator makes it easy to gather up all the pieces necessary for printing a file, including linked graphics and necessary fonts.

In InDesign and Illustrator, choose *File > Package*. (For more about packaging see Chapter 11, "Illustrator Production Tips," and Chapter 12, "InDesign Production Tips.")

NOTE If you place a linked image in an Illustrator document, then place the Illustrator file into an InDesign layout, the linked image required by the Illustrator file is not packaged by InDesign. Either include the image manually, embed it in the Illustrator file, or use Markzware's FlightCheck to package the job—it will gather up everything.

Before you exercise the Package feature in InDesign or Illustrator, make sure that all necessary fonts are active (use *Type > Find Font*), and that all graphic links are current (*Window > Links*). Make sure that no graphics are missing or in need of updating. Carefully examine the packaged job folder. The final package for an InDesign or Illustrator file should contain the following components:

- The InDesign or Illustrator file.

- Files for all graphics, including all raster images and all vector artwork. Also include any raster images that have been placed in vector drawings from Illustrator (unless you embedded the images in Illustrator).

- All necessary fonts, including those needed by support art such as Illustrator or Photoshop files. Be mindful of the EULAs for the fonts you've used—some forbid supplying fonts to print service providers (see Chapter 6, "Fonts").

Handling Layered Image Files

If you have created any elaborate compositions with multilayered Photoshop files, and you choose to use a flattened, simplified version of the image in your page-layout file, include the layered working file with the job. The flattened image may be your final file, but if the printer needs to make any corrections to the image, it is easier to modify your working, layered Photoshop file than to work with the flattened image. Keep in mind that unless the Photoshop file is enormous or you want to thwart easy editing, there's no need to flatten it before placing it into InDesign or Illustrator. And there's no need to squash Illustrator files into a single layer.

Version Issues

Because software is constantly being updated, make sure the printer knows which version of the page-layout application you are using. If you like to upgrade the minute new software is released, don't assume that your printer is quite so avid. You might think that printers would be the first to update their software, but they're just like many users—they don't update software until they have to do so.

This leads to another important thought. If you are using an earlier version of software than the printer, this may present problems if the printer needs to perform any corrections to your files and then return them to you for future use. Most printers maintain earlier versions of software so they can keep client files in their original version. But not all printers are so conscientious, so it's worthwhile to mention that you're using an earlier version than the current release in the marketplace. If you're one version behind them in InDesign or Illustrator, they can save your files to your earlier version. Don't forget that while it's possible to save an InDesign CC file to InDesign CS4, there's no provision for saving back from InDesign CS4 to InDesign CS2. That highway doesn't exist. If you have no intentions of upgrading, this may become an issue for you. Discuss this with your printer. You may have to perform any corrections on your files using your own, earlier version of the software and then submit new, corrected files.

Platform Issues

Generally speaking, it's preferable to keep a job on one platform throughout its lifespan. While sending files across platforms is not the major undertaking it once was, fonts remain an issue. If you're using all OpenType fonts, there's no need to worry. But if you are using PostScript or TrueType fonts on Windows, and your print service provider is Mac-only, you should insist on submitting your job in PDF format. While there may be Mac fonts with the same names as your Windows fonts, they aren't necessarily identical in terms of font metrics, and there may be text reflow as a result of opening the job on a Mac (see Chapter 7, "Cross-Platform Issues"). Most printers sensibly keep Windows files in their native habitat for this reason. If you're using Windows, it's worth mentioning this concern early in your discussions with the CSR.

Sending Files

Ask the print service provider about their preferred method of file submission. If they provide a way of submitting files online via FTP (File Transfer Protocol), they'll give you directions for accessing the correct target directory. Use a file-compression program such as StuffIt (Mac and Windows) or

WinZip (Windows) to consolidate the job into a single archive and to reduce the amount of data you're uploading. Additionally, both Max OS X and Windows have built-in file compression utilities. On the Mac, select a file or folder and right-click (or Control-click) to select *Compress* from the context menu that appears. In Windows, select a folder, right-click, and select *Send To > Compressed (zipped) Folder*. The utility will then create a compressed archive of the folder and its contents.

While CDs and DVDs are probably the most commonly used physical methods of transporting files, the printer will usually have an FTP portal for direct file submission.

In addition to the files themselves, it's helpful if you provide these collateral materials to the print service provider:

- Your contact information, along with any alternate contacts such as other members of your design team, or appropriate client contacts if you're acting as an intermediary.

- Comprehensive mockups of the job if there's anything tricky about the final piece, such as inserts or foldout panels.

Preparing for Proofing Cycles

Depending on the workflow of your print service provider and the nature of the job you are submitting, you may be asked to check proofs at several points during the life of the job. You've probably been looking at the same content for so long that it all starts to look alike, and it's easy to develop blind spots when you're in a hurry to approve a proof. Here are some checklists to help you remember key issues at each stage.

Checking Image Proofs

Image proofs are sometimes referred to as *random proofs* or *scatter proofs* because they are proofs of just the images without any page-layout context. If you're unsure of how your own scans or digital photos will reproduce, or if the printer has performed scans of supplied artwork or transparencies, you may want to proof images before going ahead with the remaining print production steps. Check these issues:

☐ **Size.** Are images the correct size? If some images are used multiple times at different sizes within the project, are there separate images for wide variations in scale factor?

☐ **Crop.** Is there sufficient image to fill the intended area when you place it in the page layout? Make sure nothing important has been cropped out. Also, if you need only a small portion of a large image, it's OK to crop out unused image area in Photoshop to save storage space and processing time.

☐ **Orientation.** Does the image need to be flipped vertically or horizontally for use in the final layout?

☐ **Angle.** Is the image at the correct angle for the final piece?

☐ **Matching the original artwork.** Is the proof a fair rendering of the transparency, reflective art, or digital photo? Matching the art is sometimes a subjective evaluation but, given the limitations of CMYK pigments, is it a reasonable match to the original?

☐ **Color.** Is it too dark? Too light? Does it lack contrast? Are neutral areas such as whites, grays, and blacks free of any tinge of unwanted color? For example, check gray areas such as concrete or paved road and make sure there's no reddish, bluish, or greenish tinge (called a color cast).

☐ **Detail.** Is there discernible detail in the highlight and shadow areas? If the original image or original artwork lacks detail, it can't be manu-factured, but any existing detail should be maintained.

☐ **Moiré.** Especially when photographing or scanning patterned originals such as woven fabric or geometric patterns, it may be necessary to give special treatment to all or part of an image. Sometimes slight blurring may be used in Photoshop to subdue the moiré. You may have to decide which is more objectionable—the unwanted pattern or the loss of detail due to blurring.

☐ **Silhouettes.** This is a good opportunity to check the edges of any silhouettes, whether you've created them or asked the print service provider to create them. An edge that looks acceptable onscreen may need some cleanup once you see a proof of the image.

☐ **Retouching.** If you've requested retouching, does the proof show that it's been done? Does it need additional work to accomplish what you intended? Are there problems that weren't apparent before, that now should be retouched?

Checking Page Proofs

Not every printer creates proofs of individual pages. Some may show you imposed proofs, which serve a dual purpose: You can check page content and color as well as correct pagination (page position as a result of imposition). When viewing page proofs, you should check for the following:

☐ **Correct size.** Make sure the page dimensions are correct.

☐ **Bleed.** Make sure there is adequate bleed. If images must bleed, make sure they don't fall short.

☐ **Live area.** Make sure no artwork or text falls too close to the trim edge or interior spine. Such artwork will be at risk of trimming out or disappearing into a fold.

☐ **Overset text.** Check the end of text flows to make sure the last line is intact. It's helpful if you put your own printout over the proof and hold it up to a light source to check for disparities between your prints and the printer's proof.

☐ **Text reflow.** Compare your printout to the printer's proof, checking for changes in line breaks.

☐ **Correct images.** Make sure correct images are used, especially if intermediate retouching or color corrections have been performed.

☐ **Crop.** Make sure images are cropped as you intended.

☐ **Special effects.** If you are using drop shadows or transparency effects created in Photoshop, InDesign, or Illustrator, make sure the effects are correctly rendered, especially where they interact with spot-color content. Look for missing shadows, portions of objects printing as white shapes, or discoloration around transparent elements.

☐ **Rules and other strokes.** Make sure rules are unbroken and uniform in weight.

☐ **Trapping.** While there should be no misregistration on proofs, look for any unattractive dark lines where trapping has been performed. Some darkening may be unavoidable, but it's possible to mitigate the effect by changing trap settings, especially where light colors interact.

☐ **Overprint.** Make sure black text and art don't knock out of underlying areas if they're not intended to do so.

☐ **Rich blacks.** Check that rich blacks have been created for large black coverage areas, or ask the printer to assure you that such areas will not be anemic or mottled when printed. The same cautions apply to large single-color areas other than black, such as spot-color areas. If the job will be printed on a toner-based digital press such as the Xerox iGen, rich blacks are unnecessary; the black toner is sufficiently dense.

☐ **Moiré in screen tints or images.** While patterns and woven pieces are prone to moiré, the effect can also occur in some combinations of flat-color screen tints, such as combinations of yellow and black. Moiré in an image can occur when a patterned original, such as fabric, is scanned, but it may not be apparent when you view the scanned image on your monitor. When such an image is rendered as a halftone, the combination of fabric pattern and the halftone pattern can produce an unattractive moiré. If you notice the effect at the proofing stage, don't ignore it. Consult with the printer to determine if additional work such as rescanning, softening the pattern, or perhaps even changing the screen angles might improve the outcome.

☐ **Crossover art.** Check the alignment and color match for artwork that crosses from one page to another. Make sure that crossover text isn't awkwardly divided and that any art that should stop at the spine does stop at the spine without falling over onto the facing page.

☐ **Spot colors.** Check any color bars to make sure there are no unnecessary spot colors.

TIP For some jobs, the printer may not supply "hard" proofs (i.e., physical paper proofs), opting instead to send PDFs. It's not easy comparing two PDFs onscreen to find the differences. Acrobat Pro includes a method for comparing two PDFs (*View > Compare Documents*), but because your own PDF and the printer's proof PDF may be generated by different processes, the Compare function might yield ambiguous results. You can always print the proof PDF and sandwich it with your own print, hold it up to a light, and try to spot the differences.

Checking Corrections

By now, you're probably tired of looking at this job. It's particularly hard to focus on corrections because they tend to consist of small details such as typographical errors. It's helpful to place a marked-up intermediate proof on top of a later proof, and then hold the "sandwich" up to a light source to look for the corrected areas.

Checking Imposed Bluelines

Before a multipage job goes to press, the printer will usually create a dummy booklet of the job, commonly called a *blueline*. The name dates back to older methods of creating the dummies from imposed film. The term is still used, even though such proofs are now usually created on large-format color inkjet printers and are no longer just blue. Because bluelines are created in the final stages of the job, just before press, scrutinize them carefully for problems. Check:

- [ ] **Crossover art.** Make sure that no text or artwork is incorrectly cropped at the spine where pages meet. Make sure that nothing falls short of the spine if it's intended to go all the way to the center of the spread.

- [ ] **Correct pagination.** Refer to the folding dummy created by the print service provider's planner or imposition department, and check the imposed blueline against the pagination in the original folding dummy.

- [ ] **Changes from page proof stage.** Make sure nothing has moved or disappeared, especially if corrections have been made since an earlier stage of the job.

Signing Off on Proofs

When you sign off on a proof, you're indicating that you are satisfied with the work. This places responsibility on both you and the printer. If the printer fails to match the signed proof in subsequent steps, those mistakes should be fixed at no cost to you. However, if you fail to notice problems before you sign off on the proof, you will incur costs (and possible schedule upheavals) when you ask the printer to make changes.

Attending a Press Check

The printer may invite you to be present for the running of your job; this is called a *press check*. Not all jobs warrant a press check. If all the intermediate proofs have been satisfactory, and the job doesn't involve exotic stock or ink effects, there may be no need for the printer to invite a customer to sign off on a live press run. However, there are numerous reasons for holding a press check: There may be concerns about printing on challenging stock, or there may be the need to ensure the successful outcome of a high-profile job such as an annual report. Don't be intimidated by the atmosphere of a press check. The roar and bustle of a pressroom can be overwhelming, but just take a deep breath—a good whiff of all those solvents may actually have a calming effect.

Because printing plants often run around the clock, a press check may be held at any hour of the day or night. The printer will attempt to give you an idea of the time, but problems with other jobs may change the schedule for your own job. You may find yourself camping out at the printer or waiting to be called.

During a press check, watch for the following:

- ☐ **Accuracy.** Make sure the press sheet matches the approved intermediate proofs (page proofs and bluelines). Check images, text, content, and overall color.

- ☐ **Ink on paper.** Watch for flaws in registration, color, and ink coverage. Look for smearing, and check small details for distortion. Small text (especially white text reversed out of multiple colors) may close up. Check color consistency in elements that repeat on separate pages. Check that crossover art matches from page to page—you may need to fold up printed sheets to lay the pages side by side to check the match.

- ☐ **Alterations.** Minor color adjustments can be made on press, but major problems on an offset job—such as the need for a second hit of a solid color or the creation of a rich black—will require pulling the job off press, reworking the job, replating, and going through makeready all over again.

- ☐ **Stock behavior.** Watch for flaking or picking (small fibers of paper breaking off after printing, leaving unprinted areas), especially with heavily textured stock. Watch for wrinkling in thin stock. Check for showthrough from the other side of the sheet. To some extent, the pressman can compensate for stock behavior, but if the stock proves unwieldy, you may have to reconsider your choice of paper. Such a drastic change will result in the job being pulled off press. New stock will have to be located (or ordered), and your job will have to be rescheduled. An ink draw-down sample might have established that the inks would look satisfactory when applied to the stock manually, but the combined effects of multiple ink impressions over large areas of the paper and the mechanical actions of paper being pulled through the press may produce unexpected results when the job is actually printed.

- ☐ **Debris and scratches.** Keep an eye out for hickeys—small white halos in solid color areas that are caused by foreign particles stuck to the plate or press blanket. Hickeys are fairly easily fixed by wiping the particle away. Watch for scratches in text or large areas of color coverage.

It is largely the job of the press crew (especially the lead pressman) to catch such problems during the makeready stage before the true press run begins, but your presence at the press check gives you an opportunity to serve as another set of eyes. Understandably, you're focused on the aspects of the job that are most important to you, such as product color and the overall look of the job.

While the prospect of stopping a press and juggling the complexities of corrections and rescheduling may seem distasteful, the costs incurred at this stage may still pale in comparison to the expense of completely reprinting a job if the printed outcome is not satisfactory to your own client.

This is no time to make trivial changes: Stopping a job because you want to move a photo a fraction of an inch will incur thousands of dollars in press time and alteration charges, and will drive the pressman crazy. Your job deadline may suffer a considerable impact, so it's wise to consider the huge ramifications before suggesting any changes so late in the game.

Creative Cloud

With the decision to make future versions of its creative software available only by subscription, Adobe has drawn some virtual lines in the digital sand. Some users have been reluctant to jump to the Creative Cloud, because of newness of the Cloud concept, the prospect of a continuing expense, or because they had not traditionally upgraded to each new release and want to stick with the version they already know.

What does this mean to you? You may be asked to collaborate with users of older versions of Adobe Illustrator or InDesign, or to create content for clients or publications that are still using older versions. Although most printers stay current on software, you might occasionally have to work with small printers that are not up to date.

Although it's best to keep documents in their native habitat, the Creative Cloud applications do provide methods for backsaving for users of older versions. And PDFs are a reliable format for submitting work to printers and publications. So don't panic.

Understanding Creative Cloud

Because the subscription model is new for Adobe software, some users are still confused (or misinformed) about how to obtain and install software. It might be helpful to have clarification in regard to some of the persistent myths about the Cloud.

Debunking Persistent Myths

TIP For detailed information about compatibility and system requirements for Creative Cloud, visit www.adobe.com.

Twenty minutes spent on the Adobe Web site would clear up these misconceptions, but secondhand Tweets and ambiguous blog posts seem to take on a life of their own, until eventually they're taken as fact. Let's clear the air.

- **You have to be online to use Creative Cloud software:** No, you don't. You go online to select the applications you want, install the software on your computer, and then you can pull out the Ethernet cable. Just be online about once every 30 days so the software can verify that your subscription is paid up (as if you could stand to be offline that long).

- **Creative Cloud subscriptions cost more:** For users who traditionally upgraded each time a new version of Creative Suite was released, Creative Cloud is actually less expensive. But if you always skipped versions, yes, the yearly fee is a bit higher than the total you would have paid for upgrades. To be fair, this rewards loyal Adobe users.

- **I have two computers; I shouldn't have to buy two memberships:** You don't. Licensing for the Creative Cloud is the same as for perpetually licensed Adobe software—you are allowed to install the software on two of *your* computers (not yours and your brother-in-law's). Because you're downloading software rather than purchasing disks, here's a bonus—one computer could be a Mac and the other could be Windows. In the days of perpetual licensing, you would have had to purchase the second platform version with a crossgrade fee.

- **I don't want to store my files in the Cloud:** Then don't. The online storage offered with Creative Cloud is much like Dropbox; files are stored on your local hard drive and synced to their Cloud versions. You can access the Cloud stored files from anywhere using a web browser. But you are not required to use Cloud storage; it's there if you want it.

- **I'll be forced to upgrade my software every time a new version appears in the Cloud:** When new features become available (or new versions), you're notified but not forced to install the updated software.

- **I won't be able to use my older perpetually licensed programs:** Yes, you will. The Creative Cloud versions of Adobe programs coexist quite nicely with their ancestors; there's no requirement (or reason) to uninstall the older applications, unless you need the disk space.

- **I won't be able to collaborate with people who aren't using Creative Cloud:** While users of older versions can't directly open CC documents, you can backsave from Creative Cloud applications:

    Photoshop files saved with the default *Maximize PSD and PSB File Compatibility* option can be opened in older versions of Photoshop.

    Illustrator allows backsaving all the way to Illustrator 3 (that's 14 versions back, if you're counting).

    InDesign exports to the InDesign Markup Language (IDML) format, which can be opened by InDesign CS4 or newer.

- **I'll lose my files if I cancel my membership:** Any files you have created and stored *locally* aren't going to disappear. You'll be downgraded to a free account, which includes 2GB of Cloud storage. If you have more than 2GB stored through Creative Cloud, you have 90 days to drain the online repository down to the allowed 2GB. If you anticipate canceling your Creative Cloud membership, take the time to open files and resave them as older versions (see above). Keep in mind that some aspects of your files may not be retained through backsaves, depending on how far back in time you're going.

- **I don't want to lease my software:** If leasing a car were like the Creative Cloud membership, you'd go out to the garage one morning and discover that you now have heated seats. A month later, the car would suddenly have a sunroof. You aren't leasing unchanging software; constant improvements are the most appealing aspect of Creative Cloud.

- **I don't want to have to pay every month:** Resellers such as Amazon offer prepaid one-year memberships to Creative Cloud.

TIP Perhaps it's splitting hairs to mention that when you buy software, what you're really purchasing is a *license to use* the software. In the strictest sense, true ownership of the software code belongs to the creator of the code (or the company that markets the software). The same is true of fonts, because although you may not think of them this way, fonts are software, too. You own a *license* to use fonts and software.

Where Is the Cloud?

I had suspected that Adobe purchased the planet Mars and covered it with server farms, but actually Creative Cloud is hosted on Amazon Web Services (AWS), including Amazon Elastic Compute Cloud (Amazon EC2) and Amazon Simple Storage Service (Amazon S3), in the United States, European Union, and Asia Pacific. Customer data is stored in Amazon S3, and Adobe determines the physical region where customers' data and servers are located. The hosting for Creative Cloud is designed so that downtime is virtually eliminated.

Version Determination

The first release of Creative Suite was just referred to as *CS*, but subsequent releases were numbered—*CS2*, *CS3*, and so on. Creative Cloud is relatively new as of this writing, and the only identifier is the patch number seen in the About screen. For example, Photoshop at the moment is 14.1.2 x 64, InDesign is 9.1, and Illustrator is 17.0; of course, that may change by tomorrow morning (and almost certainly by the time you read this).

Will there be yearly designations for different releases—CC2014, CC2015, and so on? Will there be a CC2 and CC3? Will there be animal names—Barracuda, Dolphin, Moose? There's no way of knowing whether there will be clear demarcations of versions within CC, or whether it will be more of a continuum, with frequent introduction of new features. Whatever the labels might be, compatibility shouldn't be a problem. Let's say you decide to maintain your Creative Cloud membership but choose to decline patches and improvements for several years. You would still have access to the necessary version of an application if you needed to open a document sent by a user who had stayed current all along.

Creating Work for Users of Older Versions

I frequently build templates for clients in the architecture, real estate, and construction industries, and historically they don't update when a new version is released; most are using CS5.5 or CS6. Fortunately, distributed over several old laptops, I have at least 10 years' worth of old software for both Mac and Windows (I'm sentimental). When I'm building a template, I use the same version that the client uses. If they're using common OpenType fonts, I can safely build the templates on either Mac or Windows. Unless the client has a stand-alone subscription to a Portfolio, Performance, or Business plan from Typekit (www.typekit.com), I avoid using Typekit desktop fonts.

Why don't I just use InDesign CC and export IDML for the client? I suppose you could attribute it to paranoia. On a past project, I had built files in CS4 and performed time travel to send InDesign Interchange (.inx) files to a client using InDesign CS3, but I experienced the heartbreak of text reflow as a result. The issue stemmed from paragraph styles based on other styles; the changes in the "child" style were lost in translation during the export to the Interchange format. Understandably, I'm now more cautious than ever about jumping versions. You should be, too.

Backsaving: Illustrator

Although Adobe Illustrator gives you options for saving back to versions as old as Illustrator 3, elements created by newer features may be modified or lost during the trip back through time. Illustrator tries to maintain the appearance of such content, often at the expense of editability. Type is often converted to outlines and, depending on how far back you go, drop shadows become embedded images, and individual artboards may be lost. See **Table 9.1** for a list of major changes to consider.

Table 9.1 *Changes when backsaving from Illustrator CC*

If you save back to this version...	...these features may be expanded or lost
CS6	· Images in brushes · Auto-generated corners in Pattern brushes (the pattern is expanded)
CS5	· Gradients on strokes
CS4	· Variable-width strokes · Bristle brush strokes
CS3	· Multiple artboards · Transparency in gradients · Objects adhered to Perspective Grid
CS2	· Crop area
CS	· Live Paint areas · Live Trace objects
10	· Live 3D effects · Paragraph and character styles · Type on a path · Scribble effect
9	· Symbols · Warping · Envelope distortion
8	· Drop shadows and glows · Transparency
3 or Japanese Illustrator 3	· Gradients · Gradient mesh · Graphs

Backsaving: InDesign

TIP Before exporting a file to IDML from InDesign CC, it's a good idea to also export a PDF. Open the IDML file in the intended older version of InDesign and place the PDF in a separate layer. Toggle the visibility of the PDF layer off and on to check for text reflow and other unwanted changes. Be sure to send the PDF to your client or collaborator with the IDML file and links.

InDesign CC exports IDML files that can be opened by users of CS4 and newer. If you own versions older than CS4, you could continue the process even farther back, resulting in even more types of content being modified or lost. **Table 9.2** concentrates on the results of a direct export to IDML from InDesign CC, which can be opened by CS4 and later.

Table 9.2 *Changes when backsaving from InDesign CC*

If you save back to this version...	...these features may be modified or lost
CS6	• Editable QR codes
CS5/5.5	• Alternate layouts • Liquid layout rules • Linked stories • Auto-size text frames • PDF form fields (except buttons)
CS4	• Multiple page sizes • Span columns • Split columns • Balanced columns • Vertical text justification in nonrectangular frames • Live corner effects • Live captions • Animation • Multi-state objects • Color labels for page thumbnails • Support for Digital Publishing Suite

Backsaving: Photoshop

This is an easy one: Save with the *Maximize PSD and PSB File Compatibility* option turned on (it's on by default), and even users of ancient versions of Photoshop can open the file.

Photoshop Production Tips

10

Countless books and Web sites are devoted to using Adobe Photoshop for the entire spectrum of skill levels, from beginner to Master of the Pixel-Based Universe. We're assuming you understand the basics of Photoshop, so you won't find any basic how-to instructions here. Nor is this a Hot Tips & Tricks compendium. What you *will* find are tips to help you create print-ready files and some heads-up warnings regarding tricks that the software can play on you. Because Photoshop is used for a wide variety of purposes, from Web to print and video, it provides multiple methods for accomplishing what you want to do to an image. The method that might be ideal for Web is not necessarily appropriate to use on an image intended for print.

Off to a Good Start

Before you start slinging pixels around, do a bit of planning. You may just be stuck with a low-quality supplied image, with no control over how it began life. In that case, you may have to make some compromises for print. But if you have some control over the birth of an image, you can prepare for a better outcome. You might glance at Chapter 4, "Preparing Raster Images," for some general image guidelines.

Know the Fate of the Image

Before you photograph a subject with a digital camera, or scan a piece of art-work, it's helpful to know how the image will ultimately be used. Consider some important issues:

- **At what scale factor will the image be used?** If possible, shoot or scan the image to the final size rather than scaling the image in Photoshop or a page-layout application.

- **Will the image be used at multiple sizes?** If the scale factors are fairly close (for example, the image is being used at 8-by-10 inches and at 6.5-by-8 inches), shoot for the larger size and just use scaling tools in the page-layout application for the smaller size. But if there is a substantial difference in scale factors—an image used at 8-by-10 inches and at 2.5-by-3 inches, for example—it's worth making a separate image for each use. Create the image for the larger scale factor, and then scale it down in Photoshop *(Image > Image Size)* using the Automatic resampling option (**Figure 10.1**). By performing the scaling in Photoshop, you have more control over the resampling and scaling quality. This also reduces the burden on the raster image processor (RIP) that ultimately handles your job because it doesn't have to process unnecessary pixels.

Figure 10.1 *Select the Automatic option to allow Photoshop to choose the right method for scaling.*

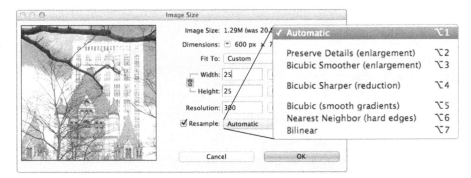

- **Will the image be rotated in its final use?** Shoot or scan the image at the correct angle. Photography may be more challenging ("Can you stand on your head just a little bit longer?"). As with scaling, you'll achieve better results by performing the rotation in Photoshop rather than in a page-layout program. Because multiple rotations may slightly erode image detail, it's best if you determine the correct final angle and perform a single rotation. If you anticipate doing a lot of experimentation with the angle of the image, consider using Smart Objects to minimize any data loss (see the section on Smart Objects later in this chapter).

- **What are the important elements in the image?** If the image is a product shot, concentrate your efforts on maintaining the best detail and most faithful color rendition in the product, even if that means slightly hurting the incidental contents of the image. For example, worry about the red in the product package rather than agonizing over the color of the two partial tulips accenting the upper-right corner of the shot.

- **Will the image be used on the Web as well as for print?** Consider keeping the image in RGB as you perform color corrections and retouching work. Then save an RGB version of the image to be used as the source file for Web work. Save another copy of the image as CMYK for print. You should also keep your RGB working file in case you need to do additional work; this lets you regenerate the Web and print images from a new parent image if necessary.

- **Will the image be printed on a digital press?** Ask the printer if you need to convert to CMYK; it may be acceptable (or even preferable) to leave the image as RGB.

Image Resolution

The rules for image resolution are the same as for image size because the concepts are intertwined. Start with as much image information as you can. You can always discard information, but you can't convincingly create it out of nothing.

What's the appropriate resolution? Generally speaking, 300 ppi at final size is sufficient for printing at 133–150 line screen (see Chapter 4, "Preparing Raster Images," for a discussion of resolution, and Chapter 2, "Ink on Paper," for information about line screen). If your project will be printed at a very high line screen (175 lpi or above), and it is important to maintain a high level of detail in the content—images of jewelry, fine art, or antiques, for example—it may be beneficial to maintain a resolution greater than 300 ppi. Consult with the print service provider to determine the proper resolution for the job.

Photoshop CC Resampling Options

Resampling is the process of changing the amount of data in an image when the dimensions or resolution of an image are altered. When you scale down an image, pixels are discarded during the resampling process. When you scale up an image, new pixels are created to fill in the space between the original pixels. Choosing a resampling method allows you to determine how the process is performed. Photoshop offers seven options for the resampling method. Here's how each method works.

- **Preserve Details (enlargement):** Uses Intelligent Upsampling and provides a Reduce Noise slider to prevent increased graininess in small detailed areas.

- **Automatic:** Photoshop examines the document and chooses an approach based on whether the image is being scaled up or down. Enlargements automatically use the Preserve Details option, but you're not presented with the Reduce Noise slider.

- **Bicubic Smoother (enlargement):** Attempts to smooth out pixelation artifacts from enlargement.

- **Bicubic Sharper (reduction):** Interpolates color from surrounding pixels, then adds some unsharp masking to compensate for detail loss.

- **Bicubic (smooth gradients):** Produces smoother tonal gradations in smooth areas and gradients than Bilinear.

- **Nearest Neighbor (hard edges):** Appropriate for screen captures.

- **Bilinear:** Averages the color values of surrounding pixels.

TIP Lab color uses a three-dimensional coordinate system, in which the *L* axis represents lightness, the *a* axis represents a linear path between red and green, and the *b* axis is a linear path between blue and yellow. Photoshop uses coordinates in Lab color space as reference points when converting images between RGB and CMYK.

Color Space

Our eyes see a gamut of colors approximated by the coordinates in Lab color, we view work on our color monitors in RGB, and we print (usually) with CMYK. As mentioned in Chapter 4, "Preparing Raster Images," RGB is the native tongue for digital cameras and scanners. Even though an image may be fated to printing in CMYK, there are advantages to keeping the image in RGB as you perform color correction, retouching, and compositing. The wider color gamut of RGB is beneficial when you make color corrections, and many useful Photoshop tools, such as Vanishing Point, are not available for CMYK images.

Once you convert an image to CMYK for a given printing condition, you lose some flexibility. Keeping the image in RGB allows you to defer the conversion until later in the workflow rather than locking you in to a particular print condition early in the life of the job.

The color landscape is changing. Because of the increasing use of digital presses and large-format inkjet devices, RGB is no longer a forbidden color mode. In fact, it offers substantial benefits for digital output: The file size of a three-channel RGB image is only 75% of the size of the CMYK version of the image, and the larger color gamut of digital devices makes it possible to render more vibrant colors that would be lost in the conversion to CMYK.

Converting RGB to CMYK

If your printer instructs you to submit CMYK images, ask if they can provide conversion settings customized for their presses as well as instructions on applying those settings. Lacking that, you may find that Photoshop's built-in conversion settings are serviceable. Choose *Edit > Color Settings,* and then select *North America Prepress 2*, or use the custom settings provided by your print service provider.

If you'd like to use an even better color setup, download and install the GRACoL (*General Requirements for Applications in Commercial Offset Lithography*) color settings files from the IDEAlliance Committee. The GRACoL committee produces guidelines and recommendations that are used as references throughout the printing industry.

A ZIP archive of the GRACoL color settings files can be downloaded from here: http://bit.ly/19ORztg.

Once you extract the files, install them according to your platform:

TIP The acronym GRACoL is pronounced "grackle"—like the bird.

- **Windows:** Documents and Settings\[Username]\Application Data\ Adobe\Color\Settings

- **Mac OS:** Users/[Username]/Library/Application Support/Adobe/ Color/Settings

To synchronize the color settings in all of the Creative Cloud applications simultaneously, launch Adobe Bridge and choose *Edit > Color Settings*. There are three color settings files within the download; choose the GRACoL setting that is appropriate for the kind of print work you are doing:

- **GRACoL_Coated1_AdobeRGB:** Commercial printing on high-quality Grade 1 or Grade 2 paper

- **SWOP_Coated3_AdobeRGB:** Publication printing on good-quality (Grade 3) paper

- **SWOP_Coated5_AdobeRGB:** Publication printing on lower-quality (Grade 5) paper

Photoshop applies these settings when you select *Image > Mode > CMYK Color* or *Image > Mode > Grayscale*, and also when you choose *Edit > Convert to Profile*. If you convert CMYK images to RGB to perform a color correction, or apply a filter that's only available in RGB mode, your conversion back to CMYK will result in color values that differ from the original image supplied to you, although the change may not be apparent on your monitor. As long as your color settings are not extreme, this will probably not result in a drastic alteration of the printed piece, but it's something you should consider before you begin repeatedly jumping between color spaces as you work on an image.

Working in Layers

While the intricacies of creating and editing Photoshop layers are beyond the scope of this chapter, it's worth mentioning some of the benefits of working with layered files. Layers can keep the individual components of a complicated composition from being glued together prematurely, giving you a safety net in case you change your mind. Being able to use Photoshop's History panel to backtrack is great during a working session, but it doesn't help if you've saved a file and realize—days later—that you've inadvertently cropped out something crucial, or performed a color correction that doesn't look so great.

Layers offer the advantage of using nondestructive methods for combining images, creating silhouette and soft-edged effects, and doing color corrections without permanently altering pixels.

Don't Erase That Pixel!

If you need to eliminate part of an image, it's tempting to just choose the Eraser tool from the Tools panel in Photoshop and get rid of it. When you permanently delete pixels, they're gone forever. If you accidentally erased the CEO's left ear in his portrait for the prestigious annual report, I hope you remember where you backed up the original image (**Figure 10.2**). I'll wait while you frantically search through that pile of CDs.

Figure 10.2 *Nice seashore! Well, it was. Too bad you accidentally erased the ocean and some of the scenic rocks (right). But you still have the original image somewhere. Don't you?*

There's a safer and more flexible way to eliminate pixels. Use the Layer Mask feature in Photoshop to selectively hide pixels without destroying them. If you can create a silhouette, you can create a layer mask.

1. Create a selection by using your favorite method, and make sure it's still an active selection. An active selection appears as a black-and-white dashed shape, often referred to as a selection marquee. Most users use the more colorful term "marching ants."

2. The layer must be a floating layer to use a layer mask. If the layer is named Background (and its name is italicized), it needs to first be converted to a floating layer. To do this, double-click the layer name. In the dialog box that is displayed, you can enter a new name for the layer or accept Photoshop's default name for the newly floating layer.

3. Make sure your ants are still marching, and then select *Layer > Layer Mask > Reveal Selection*, or just click the Add Layer Mask button on the bottom edge of the Layers panel. You should see the selected part of the image floating on a transparent background, and a mask icon will be added to the layer in the Layers panel (**Figure 10.3**).

Figure 10.3 *A layer mask hides and reveals content rather than erasing pixels. You can always modify the layer mask, to reveal or hide image contents in a non-destructive manner.*

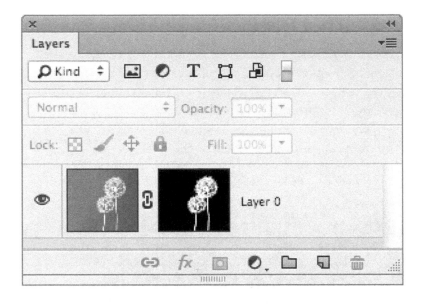

Color Corrections with a Safety Net

TIP Some of the color-correction options in Photoshop, including Shadow/Highlight, Match Color, and Replace Color, can only be applied directly to pixels in the image, which alters them permanently. If you're paranoid, duplicate the layer and apply the color correction to the duplicate layer.

Some of the most commonly used color corrections can be stored in adjustment layers, which are nondestructive. No pixels are harmed in this type of color correction, and you can always change your mind later. The Adjustments panel in Photoshop CC provides quick access to the 15 adjustments that can be performed nondestructively.

You can choose from a wide assortment of color-correction options, including Curves, Levels, Color Balance, Brightness/Contrast, and more. When you select an adjustment, the Adjustments panel changes to display the options for that adjustment (**Figure 10.4**). Controls on the bottom of the panel allow you to preview, reset, or cancel the adjustment.

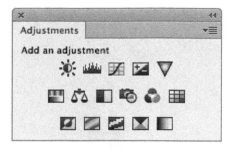

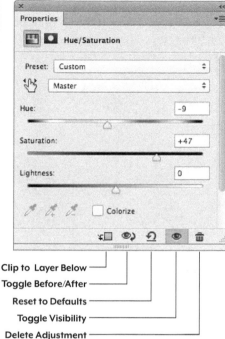

Clip to Layer Below ⎯⎯⎯⎯⎯⎯
Toggle Before/After ⎯⎯⎯⎯⎯⎯
Reset to Defaults ⎯⎯⎯⎯⎯⎯⎯
Toggle Visibility ⎯⎯⎯⎯⎯⎯⎯
Delete Adjustment ⎯⎯⎯⎯⎯⎯

Figure 10.4 *In the Adjustments panel, select an adjustment to perform or select one of the adjustment presets from the list (left). The Properties panel opens to show you the options for the adjustment (right).*

After performing an adjustment, you'll see a new entry in the Layers panel. You can control the visibility and opacity of an adjustment layer as you would any layer.

An adjustment layer consists of two components—the adjustment and a mask. Initially, the mask is empty (that is, it isn't hiding anything). But if you'd like to prevent the color correction from affecting some areas of the underlying image, use the Paintbrush tool to paint those areas of the mask with black. If you want to rework the color correction, double-click the icon in the adjustment layer to display the Properties panel, and change the options for the correction.

To disable the correction, click the eye icon to turn off the visibility of the adjustment layer. To permanently delete the adjustment layer, select the layer in the Layers panel, and then choose *Delete Layer* from the Layers panel menu, or drag the layer to the trash can at the bottom of the Layers panel (**Figure 10.5**).

Figure 10.5 *An adjustment layer performs a color correction without actually altering pixels. Don't like it? Delete it or click the eye icon next to the layer to hide the correction.*

Smart Objects

If you scale an image, then rotate it, then scale it again, Photoshop performs three separate sets of interpolation. As a result, you lose a bit of data (and, therefore, detail) in each transformation. To minimize the data loss that results from transformations such as scaling or rotation, use *Smart Objects* when possible.

When you create a Smart Object, you're embedding the original data of a raster or vector component in a Photoshop file. When you scale, distort, or rotate a Smart Object, Photoshop starts afresh with the stored data. This allows you to perform multiple transformations without multiple interpolations of data.

To embed a copy of a Photoshop, Illustrator, or PDF file, choose *File > Place* and select the file. Position and scale the artwork as necessary, and then press the Return or Enter key to finish the operation. A Smart Object is automatically created (**Figure 10.6**). To convert an existing raster layer to a Smart Object, choose *Convert to Smart Object* from the Layers panel menu. If you copy and paste from an open Illustrator file, you have an option to paste as a Smart Object.

There are important differences between a vector Smart Object and a pixel-based Smart Object. As you might expect, a vector Smart Object can be scaled up endlessly, whereas a pixel-based Smart Object can be scaled down without penalty, (but should not be scaled up much beyond its original size).

Figure 10.6 *A special icon identifies a layer designated as a Smart Object.*

To edit a Smart Object, double-click it in the Layers panel. You can also select a Smart Object and choose *Edit Contents* from the Layers panel menu. Raster image content will be opened in Photoshop, and PDF or vector content will be opened in Illustrator. Perform any edits, and then save the edited file. The edited information is sent back to Photoshop, and the parent Photoshop file is automatically updated. Remember that an embedded Smart Object has no link to the original raster or vector art; what you're editing is data that is embedded.

Sometimes Smart Objects Aren't So Smart

Vector Smart Objects do have one limitation: While other vector content—such as shape layers, vector masks, or vector text—can be rendered as true vector art if the file is saved as a Photoshop PDF, Smart Objects will always render at the resolution of the containing image. If this presents a problem, consider performing a bit of surgery on the Photoshop file to separate the vector and raster components. Double-click vector content to open it in Illustrator, and then choose Save As to create a stand-alone Illustrator file. Delete

TIP Adobe software provides multiple methods of accessing most commands, including menu choices, dialog boxes, panel menus, contextual menus, and keyboard shortcuts. Listing all of the options for every activity would double the size of this book. Although that would certainly result in a more impressive page count, it's overkill. I encourage you to explore the options and find out which approach suits your style.

or hide the vector Smart Object in the Photoshop image, and recombine the vector and raster components in Illustrator or InDesign.

Clipping Masks

A layer mask controls the visibility of the contents of a single layer, but a clipping mask controls the visibility of the contents of multiple layers. If you need to establish a common edge for multiple layers, this is a clever and flexible way to do so (**Figure 10.7**).

Figure 10.7 *The Clipping Mask feature allows a layer to serve as a mask for layers above it, providing a common edge for all the layers.*

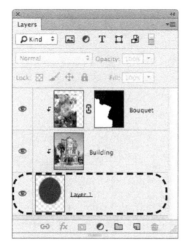

Using a clipping mask requires a bit of upside-down thinking, though. We're accustomed to a mask controlling what's underneath it, based on real-world examples such as the mat around a framed watercolor. But a clipping mask falls *below* the content it masks. The color of the painted area of the mask layer isn't important; it's the transparency or opacity of each pixel in the mask layer that governs the transparency and opacity of the layers above it in the group.

NOTE Clipping masks can be used to mask multiple individual layers, but cannot be applied to layer groups.

To create a clipping mask group, make sure the bottom (mask) layer is a floating layer (i.e., not a glued-down Background layer). Select the layers immediately above the mask layer that you want to mask (but *don't* select the mask layer), and choose *Create Clipping Mask* from the Layers panel menu. The indented appearance of upper layers and the downward-pointing arrows next to the layer icons indicate that the layers are being affected by the mask. To prevent one of the masked layers from being affected by the mask, select the affected layer (*not* the mask layer) and choose *Release from Clipping Mask* from the Layers panel menu.

Should You Flatten a Layered File?

Native Photoshop files offer the benefits of layers and transparency—what's not to love? Because Illustrator and InDesign support unflattened native Photoshop files, there's no need to flatten for compatibility if you're using the image in those applications.

Admittedly, if a Photoshop file has grown to hundreds of megabytes, it might be more efficient to use a flattened file for placement into a page layout. In addition, you may have to flatten a file for a client who is using an application that only supports flattened formats, such as JPEG. But you'd be wise to keep a copy of the original layered Photoshop file in case you need to do additional edits. To flatten a layered file, choose *Flatten Image* from the Layers panel menu. You can also merge several layers; select the layers and choose *Merge Layers* from the Layers panel menu.

Transparency

Adding effects such as ghosted areas or drop shadows is an easy way to add visual interest to images. Because you can incorporate Photoshop files into Illustrator drawings and Adobe InDesign pages, it's important to real-ize that you're governed by the limitations of those programs. Just because Photoshop can handle an effect doesn't mean that other programs can interpret that content correctly.

For example, Illustrator and InDesign both honor *opacity* in placed Photoshop files, but neither program correctly handles Photoshop *blending modes*. Opacity settings and blending modes both fall under the heading of transparency, but they're very different in how they're rendered.

Opacity is expressed in terms of percentage. For example, a white square with 20% opacity allows what's underneath to show through at 80% strength. Opacity settings in a Photoshop file are honored by InDesign and Illustrator, which enables you to create organic soft-edged mask effects and composite images together in InDesign or Illustrator files without having to combine the content in Photoshop.

However, blending modes involve much more complicated math. For example, drop shadows created in Photoshop by selecting *Layer > Layer Style > Drop Shadow* are set to use the Multiply blend mode with anything they encounter in Photoshop. This results in a realistic darkening of underlying image areas—but only within Photoshop.

Unfortunately, neither Illustrator or InDesign can understand blending modes within a Photoshop file. Consequently, drop shadows created in Photoshop do not interact correctly with underlying content when the native files are placed in Illustrator or InDesign (**Figure 10.8**). Instead of darkening underlying elements, Photoshop shadows knock out the shadow area, eliminating content beneath.

Figure 10.8 *When a Photoshop image containing a drop shadow is placed in another application, its shadow knocks out underlying color rather than darkening it (shown without the black plate).*

What can you do to fix this? If an element requires a simple, soft-edged drop shadow like the effect shown in Figure 10.8, the solution is simple: Don't create the shadow in Photoshop. Instead, wait until the image is placed in Illustrator or InDesign and create the shadow there, as both applications handle their own shadows correctly.

However, if you want a cast shadow, such as that cast by a vase on a tabletop, you'll have to perform a little trickery. See Chapter 12, "InDesign Production Tips," for instructions on the workaround.

Silhouettes and Masking

Frequently, you will need to separate a subject from its background in order to composite the subject into another image or so the image can overlap other content in a layout. The proper choice of masking method depends on the subject and its intended use.

Creating a Path: Right and Wrong

If you need to isolate a subject with well-defined edges, such as a book or ball, the Pen tool in Photoshop provides precision and smoothness. Some people aren't fond of the Pen tool, so they have instead become adept at avoiding the issue in several ways:

- Deciding that a square-cut image is much more tasteful

- Bribing someone else to draw the path

- Making a selection with the Magic Wand or Quick Selection tool and then converting the selection to a path

The first two options are acceptable, but using the Magic Wand or Quick Selection tool will result in a lousy path. The Magic Wand is not truly magic (sorry). It's acceptable for creating a selection to be used as a starting point for a mask, but it's not the way to make a suitable path.

Photoshop attempts to convert an active selection ("marching ants") to a clipping path, but the results are less than stellar. Because a selection follows the rectangular edges of pixels, it's not a very good basis for a smooth clipping path; the sawtoothed edge of the selection will be faithfully rendered in the resulting path.

In some instances, noodling with the Make Work Path tolerance setting on the Paths panel (*Window > Paths*) can soften the granularity of the generated path, but you'll have to keep reloading the selection and experimenting with the tolerance settings, because this function doesn't offer any preview of the quality of the outcome.

NOTE You will hear multiple terms in the printing industry for eliminating the background of a subject, including:

- Silhouette
- Silo
- Knockout
- KO
- Blockout
- Dropout
- Cutout

The black line in **Figure 10.9** shows the unsavory result of taking the easy way out by converting a selection to a path, using the tightest tolerance setting, 0.5 pixels. Not only does the path created from a selection have a whopping 1,916 points, it's unattractively irregular. The smooth gray line in the illustration was created, as you might suspect, with the Pen tool.

Figure 10.9 *Comparing a Pen tool path (gray line) with a path created from a Magic Wand selection (black line).*

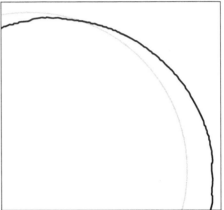

Using a 10-pixel tolerance setting smooths out the path but results in a path that doesn't fit the edge of the coin; it eliminates parts of the coin and includes slivers of the background. Face it: It's far better to bite the bullet and draw the path with the Pen tool. There's no need to obsessively follow every little imperfection. Because your goal is a reasonably faithful but smooth rendition of the object's edge, it's perfectly legal to take a bit of artistic license to improve the edge of the silhouetted image. For example, if you are creating a path to silhouette a gold ring that's being held in place by a bit of wax, you draw along the smooth rim of the ring—you don't include the lump of wax propping up the ring.

To use a path to knock out a subject when it's placed in Illustrator or InDesign, select the path in the Paths panel, choose *Save Path* from the Paths panel menu, and give the path a name.

If you're placing the image in Illustrator, you need to take one additional step: Return to the Paths panel menu and select *Clipping Path*. Choose your named path from the menu, and leave the Flatness field blank.

If you're using the image in InDesign, there's no need to designate the path as an official clipping path; just name and save the path. InDesign gives you the option to invoke the path for clipping if you want, or to ignore the path and display the unclipped image.

Path Flatness Settings

In the olden days of anemic RIPs, users were encouraged to set a high flatness value for paths to ease the burden on the RIP. Think of the RIP as constructing curved lines as a series of tiny straight segments. The fewer of those segments the RIP had to chisel— the flatter it could render curves—the faster the job would process. **Figure 10.10** shows a circle imaged with a high flatness setting. It might be easy on the RIP, but it's not easy on the eye.

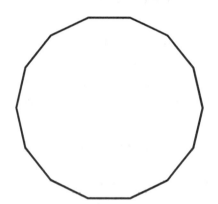

Figure 10.10 *A high flatness setting makes things easier for the RIP, but it results in a harsh, chiseled appearance for what should be curved lines.*

In reaction to seeing such clunky output, some people adopted the unfortunate habit of specifying very low flatness values in the Clipping Path dialog box, such as 0.2 device pixels, in the hopes that this would encourage the RIP to carve more petite segments. Forcing the RIP to chew this finely had the unpleasant side effect of slowing job processing and, in some cases, completely preventing the job from being processed by a RIP.

RIPs are more robust now, but the old habit of setting absurdly fine flatness settings persists. The truth is that it's actually best to leave the Flatness field blank (**Figure 10.11**), which allows the RIP to use an optimal flatness setting without additional calculations. So stop agonizing over what to put in the Flatness field. Just leave it empty, and the RIP will do what it knows is best.

Figure 10.11 *When specifying a clipping path, resist the urge to put a microscopic value in the Flatness field. Leaving it blank allows the imaging device to handle curves with an optimal setting.*

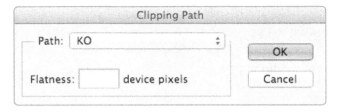

A dedicated tutorial on using the Pen tool is outside the scope of this book, but check the Appendix for some excellent references and tutorial resources.

Paths That Aren't Clipping Paths

When placed in a page-layout application, an image with an official clipping path can only display what's within the area of the clipping path—that's the whole point of a clipping path.

Consider an image that contains several elements that you'd like to use selectively in a page layout. If you're planning to use the clipping path approach to silhouetting those elements, you need to save multiple versions of the image, resulting in a separate image for each element you plan to use.

InDesign recognizes all paths in placed images, providing the option of choosing which path you'd like to use to silhouette the image (**Figure 10.12**). The paths just have to be named paths (an unsaved path, called *a work path*, will not be recognized). In InDesign, select the image, choose *Object > Clipping Path > Options*, and choose the name of the path to be used to silhouette the image.

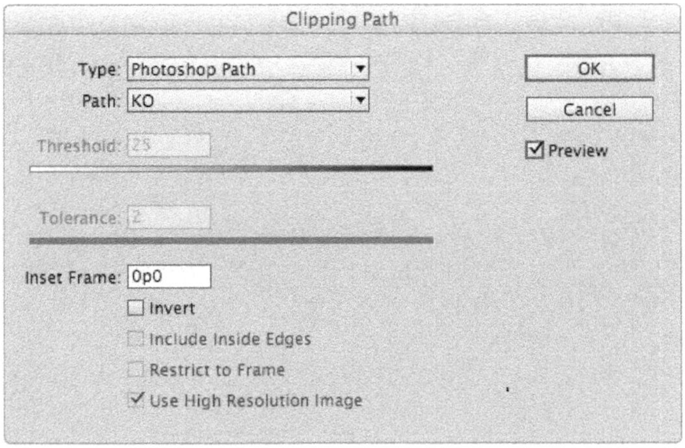

Figure 10.12 *InDesign allows you to specify which path to use for clipping. You can also ignore paths and just use the unclipped image.*

Taking this approach allows you to use the same image in multiple ways without saving multiple versions. In **Figure 10.13**, the same image provides seven uses—a square-cut version and the six individual silhouetted pens. There is no limit to the number of named paths you can have in an image.

Figure 10.13 *One image, multiple uses, thanks to optional paths in InDesign.*

Silhouetting Soft-Edged Subjects

Here's some good news for those who loathe the Pen tool—InDesign honors opacity in Photoshop images. In addition to providing liberation from the dreaded Pen tool, this also means that you can use layer masks to silhouette subjects with irregular, organic edges. Think of a mask as being much like a cardboard stencil. In a simple black-and-white mask, the black area is the equivalent of the cardboard; the white is equivalent to the hole cut out of the cardboard. But masks aren't limited to just black and white: Gray areas in a mask result in translucency (i.e., areas that are not fully opaque)—perfect for subjects such as ice cubes or glass, which are not truly opaque.

Intelligent Edge Detection

Soft-edged components, such as fur or flyaway hair, simply aren't candidates for the Pen tool (unless you're a masochist with too much time on your hands). The Magic Wand and Quick Selection tool aren't quite the answer, either; their selections can have harsh edges when they reach the end of a color area. But the *Refine Edge* feature can make all the difference.

Start with a Quick Selection or Magic Wand selection, then glance up in the Control panel: The Refine Edge option is available whenever you are using a selection tool and have an active selection. The Refine Edge functions let you preview and modify a potential mask, with sophisticated finessing features that really shine when you're trying to capture organic edges. Using the Smart Radius option in the Refine Edge dialog box, you can capture delicate details that would be impossible with the Magic Wand or Quick Selection tools—and certainly not with the Pen tool (**Figure 10.14**).

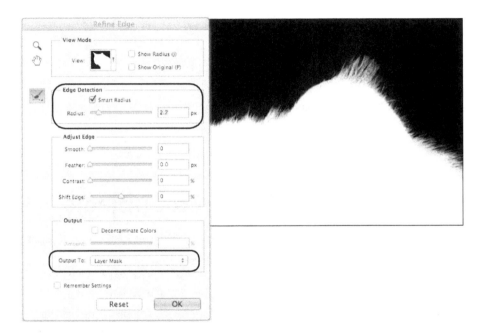

Figure 10.14 *The Edge Detection options in the Refine Edge dialog box make it possible to capture subtle organic edges.*

Using the resulting selection as a layer mask is nondestructive—no innocent pixels are destroyed. The masked image can be placed in Illustrator and InDesign documents, maintaining the soft edges beautifully (**Figure 10.15**).

Figure 10.15 *InDesign and Illustrator support soft-edged layer masks.*

Domestic Short-Hair Cats

A domestic short-haired cat doesn't belong to any particular recognized cat breed. In English, they are sometimes called as *moggies*. While domestic shorthairs are not a dedicated breed, they are the most popular cat in the United States. They're sometimes just referred to as "plain old house cats," but their varied personalities tend to make them popular and beloved companion

Creating Channel Masks

If a subject is photographed on a fairly consistent background (by which we don't mean plaid), you can create a density-based mask similar to that of the dandelion shown here by starting with one of the channels of the image. Open the Channels panel in Photoshop (*Window > Channels*) to inspect the channels. Click the name of each channel, one by one, until you find the channel with the most contrast between the subject and the background. It doesn't have to be perfect; you're just looking for the best starting point for a mask. In the case of the dandelion, the cyan channel is the most promising. The black channel is a close second choice, but the cyan has finer detail, so it's the winner (**Figure 10.16**).

TIP The Channel Mask technique isn't limited to CMYK images; it works equally well with RGB and grayscale images.

Figure 10.16 *Comparing channels to establish a good starting point for a mask. Either the cyan or black channel might work, but the cyan has more detail.*

Once you've decided on the channel that provides the best start for a mask, select it and choose *Duplicate Channel* from the Channels panel menu. You can name it something memorable in the dialog box that follows, or just accept the default name—in this case, *Cyan copy*.

The next step is to manipulate the contrast in the Cyan copy channel so that it becomes solid black and white. Note that because you want to affect only the mask channel, rather than performing a color correction on the color image, you can't use the Adjustments panel; adjustment layers can be applied to layers but not directly applied to channels.

Choose Levels (*Image > Adjustments > Levels*) or Curves (*Image > Adjustments > Curves*) to exaggerate the contrast in the mask channel (**Figure 10.17**). The goal with the dandelion image is to create a white dandelion-shaped hole in a black background. Because each image is different, you'll have to experiment with the values in your images.

Figure 10.17 *Using Levels to increase the contrast of the mask channel. There are no "best numbers" — correct values will vary for any given image.*

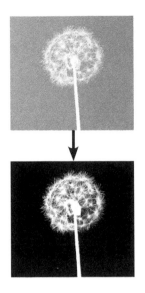

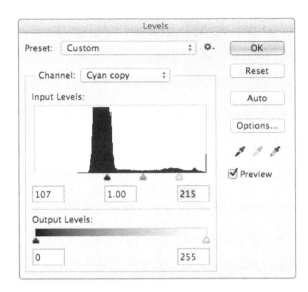

You'll almost always need to refine a mask with some manual touches. Paint with white to open up areas of the mask to reveal parts of the image. Paint with black to fill in the mask where you want to hide areas of the image. The mask is stored in an alpha channel (**Figure 10.18**). The alpha channel doesn't act as a mask until you load it as an active selection. Since the mask is derived from image contents, it creates a much more natural silhouette without the hard-edged cutout appearance that results from using a clipping path.

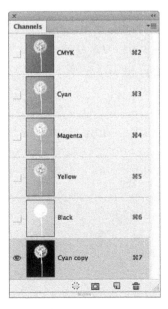

Figure 10.18 *When you create and save a mask, it's stored in an alpha channel. But it's just waiting there; it doesn't serve as a mask until you load it as an active selection.*

Beyond CMYK

You're not limited to just cyan, magenta, yellow, and black inks when you print a color image. You can create images that consist of combinations of CMYK and spot color, or even images that print only in spot colors.

Creating Duotones

A *duotone* image is composed of two colors, usually black and a spot color. Such images are a great way to add visual interest to a job with a limited color palette. There are variations on this theme, such as *tritones* (three colors), *quadtones* (four colors), and so on. Since these images contain spot-color components, it's important to create them correctly to ensure that they print as intended. Multitone images may be composed of all spot colors or a combination of spot colors and process colors. To create duotones and their kin, start with a grayscale image, and then choose *Image > Mode > Duotone*. Initially, the Duotone Options dialog is set to Type: Monotone; just select *Duotone* from the pulldown menu (**Figure 10.19**).

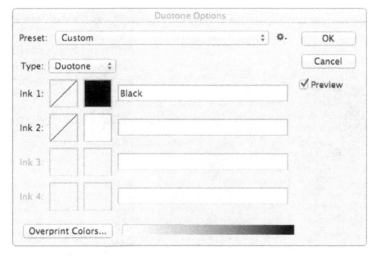

Figure 10.19 *When you choose the Duotone option, the Ink 1 position is populated by default with process black. Ink 2 is initially blank, unless you have previously created a duotone.*

The Black ink listed for Ink 1 in the Duotone Options dialog box is not a spot color. It's just the plain, old-fashioned process black of CMYK fame, and, unless the black component of the multitone image is intended to be a spot black, there's no need to change it. Unless you've created a duotone previously, Ink 2 is unspecified.

To choose the second ink, click the white square next to Ink 2. In the Color Picker, click the Color Libraries button, and then choose the appropriate color book, such as PANTONE+ Solid Coated (**Figure 10.20**).

Figure 10.20 *To assign a spot color to an ink, click Color Libraries and choose the color book in the Color Libraries dialog box.*

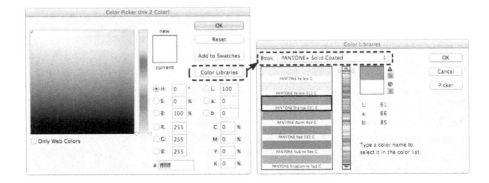

Under the hood, a duotone (or any multitone image) is actually still the original grayscale image, with an embedded recipe governing the generation of the specified spot colors (**Figure 10.21**). You'll notice that changing a grayscale to a duotone does not substantially increase the file size—that's why.

Figure 10.21 *Curves embedded in the duotone dictate the output on each plate.*

Black plate

Original grayscale image

Orange 021 plate

Adding Spot Color to a CMYK Image

Special handling may be needed to accentuate portions of an image or to ensure faithful rendering of a color that falls outside the CMYK gamut. In this approach—variously called *bump plate*, *touch plate*, or *kiss plate*—spot colors are added to the image. Bump plates are often used in high-end projects, such as fine art reproductions or crucial product shots, to ensure a closer rendition of the original artwork.

To add a spot color to a CMYK image, choose *New Spot Channel* from the Channels panel menu. Click on the Color block to select an ink color, and then click on the Color Libraries button to access the standard color books. Choose the correct ink from the color list, and then click OK. In the New Spot Channel dialog box, don't modify the name. The Solidity option controls visual opacity of the spot ink plate as it is displayed in Photoshop; it has nothing to do with how the plate will print. Varying the Solidity setting may make it easier for you to work on the spot channel, but the actual contents of the channel will not be affected by the Solidity setting (**Figure 10.22**).

NOTE In the past, it was necessary to save these images as DCS 2.0 files (Desktop Color Separations: a special flavor of EPS). Under the hood, these special images consist of all the individual color plates plus a low-resolution representation image for display. But DCS files present challenges when placed into some other applications, or into some older workflows. They're obsolete, and unnecessary in InDesign and Illustrator.

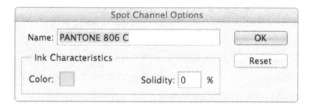

Figure 10.22 *Click the Color block to pick a color. The Solidity block controls the onscreen appearance, not how the ink prints.*

There's a bit of finesse involved in creating a bump plate, since it's usually intended to supplement or replace parts of the process components. The preview on your color monitor may suggest the results, but you'll need to see color proofs from the printer to truly judge the outcome.

In the rose image (**Figure 10.23**), the PANTONE+ 805 fluorescent pink plate was derived from the magenta plate; the magenta plate was lightened somewhat to "leave room" for the fluorescent spot color plate.

Figure 10.23 *The PANTONE 805 bump plate intensifies the pink color of the rose beyond what's possible with just the CMYK process inks.*

CYAN   MAGENTA   YELLOW   BLACK   PANTONE 805

Save the image as Photoshop PSD; it will print correctly when placed in InDesign or Illustrator. You may have to turn on Overprint Preview in those applications to make the bump plate visible, but you can easily check by choosing *Window > Separations Preview* in Illustrator or *Window > Output > Separations Preview* in InDesign. If the file contains vector content such as type or shape layers that should image as vector, you should save the file as a Photoshop PDF.

Creating a Spot Varnish Plate

TIP The color you assign to a varnish plate just serves to identify it when you view the file in Photoshop or place it into another application. The color does not affect the color appearance of the image when the file is output. The varnish plate that is generated during output will be used to print the spot varnish on press.

Even though it isn't usually colored, a *spot varnish* plate is handled just like a spot color ink. A spot varnish is a shaped application of varnish, commonly used to highlight an object, as opposed to an all-over flood varnish (for more information see "Coatings and Varnishes" in Chapter 2, "Ink on Paper").

To create a spot varnish plate, start as you would when creating a spot color: Choose *New Spot Channel* from the Channels panel menu. Name the varnish plate to be consistent with any existing art files (or ink already created in Illustrator or InDesign). Click the Color block in the Spot Channel dialog box and create a color mix in keeping with existing files. If you're starting fresh, consider naming the channel Spot Varnish and coloring it something obvious, such as an obnoxious bright green, so it will be easy to identify when placed into other applications.

Create the varnish area in the spot channel by painting or pasting content: Solid areas in the varnish channel represent the areas where the solid varnish will be printed (**Figure 10.24**).

Figure 10.24 *The spot varnish plate (right) will result in a gloss varnish printed to highlight parts of the antique motorcycle.*

When you place an image with a spot color or spot varnish plate into an Illustrator or InDesign document, the spot color is automatically added to the Swatches list.

Vector Content

Pixels and vectors can live together in graphic harmony, enabling you to combine smooth, sharp text with images for interesting results.

While Photoshop is primarily devoted to pixels, it is possible to add text and other vector elements to a Photoshop image. It's not appropriate to create body text in Photoshop, and most text should be typeset in an illustration or page-layout application. But if you want to bevel and emboss text (**Figure 10.25**), or give a special treatment to a vector logo, you may be compelled to handle it in Photoshop.

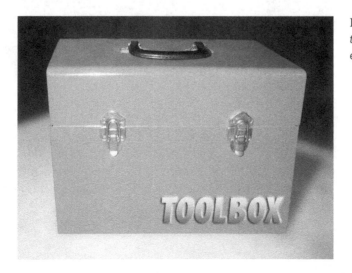

Figure 10.25 *Vector and text elements can be an interesting addition to an image.*

Vector elements in Photoshop do not have any inherent resolution, although any shading applied through effects such as embossing must be accomplished with pixels. Those pixels are just part of the effect, and they don't become literal pixels until the file is printed. Consequently, you can scale vector elements within the Photoshop image and the effects will be recalculated, growing new pixels of the appropriate resolution. Because the vector elements are truly vector, not pixels, they remain editable.

Unfortunately, when PSD files containing text or vector content are placed in an illustration or page-layout file, the vector edges are rendered as pixels during output, taking on the resolution of the underlying image.

The solution to this dilemma is to save the image as a Photoshop PDF. A Photoshop PDF can be reopened by Photoshop without rasterizing, and the vector content is imaged as vector when the file is placed into Illustrator and InDesign. Think of it as two files in one: Photoshop sees the original PSD, with its editable text and vector content, and other applications see the public face of the PDF file, with its nice, crisp edges. Fonts are embedded, so any text will print correctly (**Figure 10.26**).

Figure 10.26 *Text or vector components render as pixels in a PSD file (left) but correctly render as vector in a Photoshop PDF (right).*

Saving As a Photoshop PDF

To save a PDF that can be reopened by Photoshop, choose *File > Save As*, and then in the *Format* menu, select *Photoshop PDF*. When the Save Adobe PDF dialog is displayed, make sure the Preserve Photoshop Editing Capabilities box is checked.

To maintain transparency in the image when it is placed into Illustrator or InDesign, you must save with Acrobat 5.0 or above compatibility. If you open the file from within Photoshop, everything is still editable; layers and text are intact. If you double-click the file, it will launch Acrobat Pro or Adobe Reader, depending on your system's file associations. For more information on Acrobat and PDF files, see Chapter 13, "Acrobat Production Tips."

Saving for Other Applications

The old recommendations to save as TIFF or EPS were solid in their day, however, today native layered Photoshop files offer appealing features such as transparency, editable vector elements, and nondestructive color corrections. InDesign allows you to control the visibility of placed, layered, native Photoshop files (but not TIFFs). TIFF files can contain layers but offer no support for vector elements, so Photoshop PSDs and PDFs trump TIFF files for flexibility.

It's now acceptable to loosen up a bit. InDesign and Illustrator accept layered Photoshop files in all their glory, including transparency effects. There's no need to squeeze the fun out of your images before you place them into a page-layout document. But it's still worthwhile to do some housecleaning before you save and close your Photoshop file.

- Delete unused layers. Select an unwanted layer (or Shift-click to select multiple layers), and then choose *Delete Layer* from the Layers panel menu.

- Delete unused alpha channels. Select an unwanted channel (or Shift-click to select multiple channels), and then choose *Delete Channel* from the Channels panel menu.

- Delete unused paths. Select the unwanted path, and then choose *Delete Path* from the Paths panel menu. You'll have to delete paths one by one, as Shift-clicking doesn't allow you to select multiple paths in the panel.

- Make sure the image is in the correct color space for its final use.

- If you're certain about the final use of the image, crop out any unnecessary image content. But leave a rind of extra image around the outside, just in case you need a bit of elbow room when the image is placed in a page layout.

NOTE Shortly after viewing the 23rd proof of an image, your client may decide that *CoverPhoto_2.psd* was perfect. Clients are funny that way. That's why it's a good idea to keep all of the versions of a working image. Coffee helps, too.

- If you've created multiple, experimental files on your way to the final image, name the final image in a way that makes it clear It's The One, and put the older, obsolete files in a quarantine folder. Don't send a job to the print service provider with a folder full of images with names like *Final.psd, Final2.psd, NewFinal.psd, Newfinal2.psd, NewerFinal3.psd, NewestFinal.psd, OldFinalDon'tUse.psd,* and so on. If you're confused, think how they'll feel. Many graphic artists append an identifying suffix such as *r1* for Revision 1, or *v2* for Version 2. So the 23rd version of a cover image might be called *CoverPhoto_v23.psd*. Feel free to use a sensible naming convention that works for you.

11

Illustrator Production Tips

As Adobe Illustrator has evolved over the years, it has morphed from a relatively simple vector-drawing program into a full-featured graphic arts tool. The addition of live effects has blurred the line between drawing and painting, and the introduction of multiple artboards in Illustrator CS4 extended the concept of the drawing board beyond a single size of digital "paper."

Document Profile and Color Mode

As you begin a new Illustrator file, you're prompted to choose a New Document Profile as a starting point. You can choose from Print, Web, Mobile and Devices, Video and Film, Basic CMYK, and Basic RGB. Each profile has default settings for attributes such as dimensions, color mode, measurement units, and raster effects resolution. You can also base a new document on one of Illustrator's supplied templates, which contain more "furniture" (such as swatches, artboards, brushes, and artwork) than a simple document profile.

You can start with one of the canned settings, then modify its attributes by changing dimensions, color mode, bleed, or units of measurement (**Figure 11.1**). While these settings are in effect when the document is first created, all of the attributes can be changed over the life of the document.

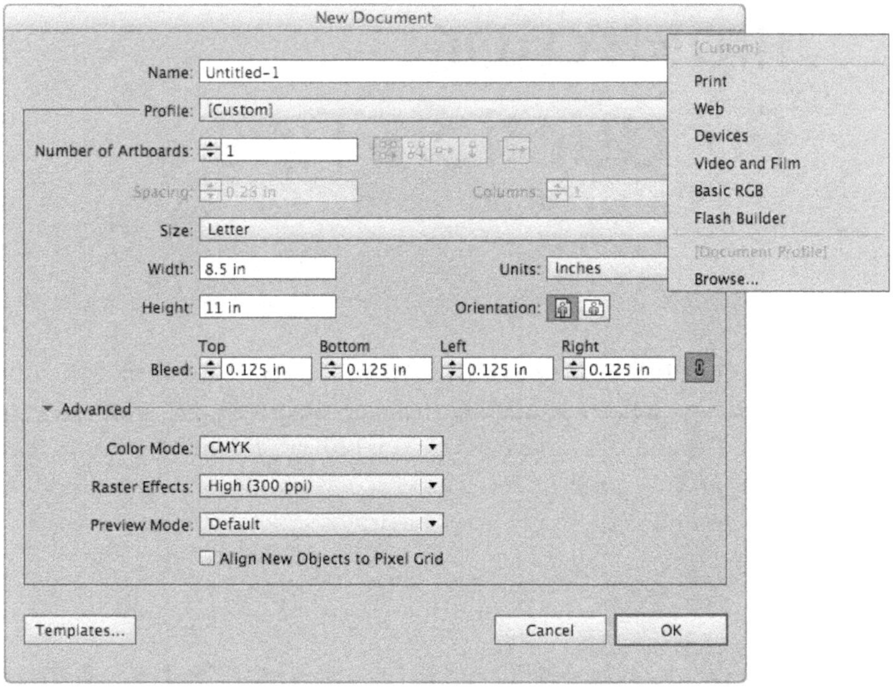

Figure 11.1 *Document profiles give you a head start on the settings for a new document. Click the triangle next to Advanced to reveal options for Color Mode, Raster Effects Resolution, and Preview Mode.*

All but two of the profiles are based on the RGB color mode. The Print document profile is set up as CMYK color, as is the generic CMYK profile. But what does this do to non-CMYK content?

Within a CMYK Illustrator file, you are allowed to specify colors as CMYK, RGB, or HSB (Hue-Saturation-Brightness). However, regardless of the color mode you might use to create a color, it takes on the color mode governing the document. For example, in a document with a CMYK color mode, an object set to an RGB value of R200-G40-B30 is converted to C2-M98-Y100-K0 if you save to PDF (provided your color-management options are set to North America Prepress 2). The CMYK value that's created depends on the current color-management settings, so your mileage (and CMYK values) may vary.

This keeps you out of trouble as you choose colors for objects, as long as you establish the correct color mode to begin with, and pay attention to the color space of linked images. If you didn't make the correct choice when you created the document, you can rectify that by choosing *File > Document Color Mode*. Objects created in Illustrator change to the new color mode. However, the color space of a placed image depends on whether an image is linked or embedded: An embedded image takes on the color space of the Illustrator file, but a linked image retains its original color space.

When you save an Illustrator file as a PDF, the color space of content in the PDF depends on the PDF settings used. For example, an Illustrator file set up in the RGB document color mode containing all RGB linked images will yield a CMYK PDF when the PDF/X-1a PDF creation setting is used. Spot color components remain spot color. For more information on the PDF/X-1a standard, see Chapter 13, "Acrobat Production Tips."

Artboards

Think of artboards as pieces of imaginary digital paper; you can create up to 100 artboards within the 227.54-square-inch area of an Illustrator file (**Figure 11.2**). The artboards can be repositioned and resized, unlike real paper.

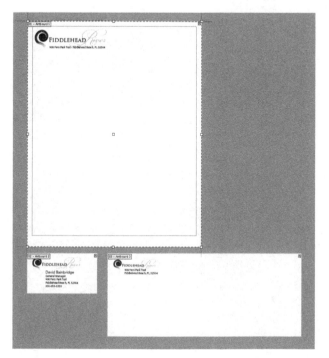

Figure 11.2 *Artboards make it convenient to create multiple job components within one document.*

Creating Artboards

As you begin a new document, you have the option to change both the dimensions and number of artboards in the New Document dialog.

To add an artboard to an existing document, click and drag with the Artboard tool (▢). The width and height of the new artboard is displayed next to the pointer as you drag, but it's challenging to create an exact size this way. Don't fret; to specify the dimensions of the artboard exactly, create the artboard at any size, and then press the Return or Enter key on the keyboard or click the Artboard Options icon (▤) in the Control panel to display the Artboard Options dialog box (**Figure 11.3**). You can also use the dimension fields in the Control panel to view and modify the dimensions of the selected artboard.

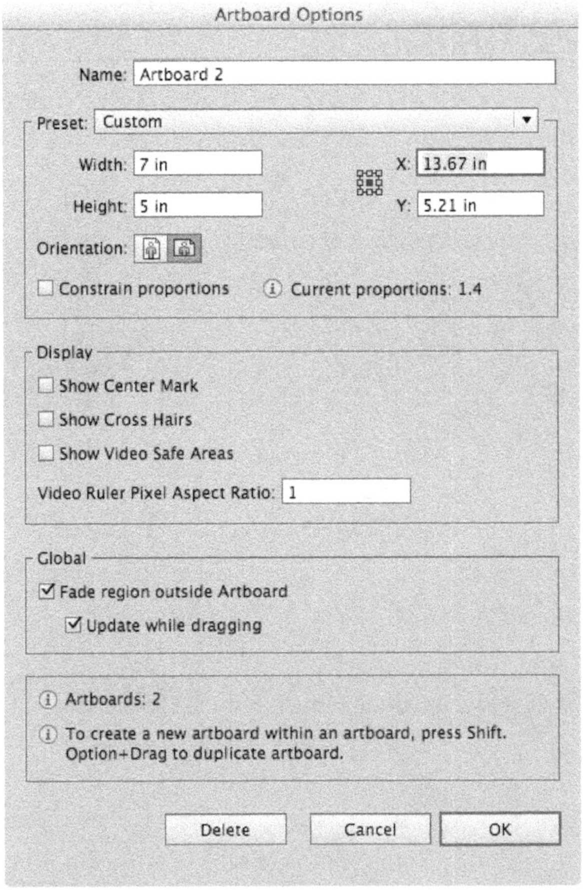

Figure 11.3 *Artboard options include dimensions, position, and orientation. The default global option to fade the region outside artboards makes it easier to identify artboard areas.*

Artboard Options

Name: Artboard 2

Preset: Custom ▼

Width: 7 in   X: 13.67 in
Height: 5 in   Y: 5.21 in
Orientation:
☐ Constrain proportions   ⓘ Current proportions: 1.4

Display
☐ Show Center Mark
☐ Show Cross Hairs
☐ Show Video Safe Areas
Video Ruler Pixel Aspect Ratio: 1

Global
☑ Fade region outside Artboard
    ☑ Update while dragging

ⓘ Artboards: 2
ⓘ To create a new artboard within an artboard, press Shift. Option+Drag to duplicate artboard.

Delete   Cancel   OK

You can create a custom size up to the maximum of 227.54 inches square (the dimensions of the Illustrator canvas environment). Artboards can be in any position within the overall canvas and can also overlap. Artboards are numbered according to the order in which they are created, but you can drag the artboard names in the Artboards panel to change their numbering. You can rename artboards in either the Artboards panel or the Control panel. Delete an artboard by clicking the "X" in its upper-right corner, or by clicking the trash can icon in the Artboards panel. All artboards share the same color space.

You can also create an artboard by clicking an existing object with the Artboard tool. If the object is rectangular, an artboard is created according to the dimensions of the rectangle. If the object is not a rectangle, the artboard corresponds to the object's bounding box (**Figure 11.4**).

Figure 11.4 *When you click an irregular object with the Artboard tool (left), a new artboard is created that corresponds to the bounding box of the object (right).*

To create an artboard on top of another artboard, hold down the Shift key as you click and begin dragging the new artboard. Release the Shift key before you release the mouse button if you don't want the artboard to be square—the Shift key is also a constrainer.

To hide artboards, choose *View > Hide Artboards*. If that option isn't available, it's because you have an Artboard selected.

To focus on a single artboard, select it with the Artboard tool and choose *View > Fit Artboard in Window*, select its name in the Artboards panel, or choose the artboard number from the status area at the lower-left corner of the application window.

Modifying Artboards

Unlike actual pieces of paper, artboards can be resized, repositioned relative to artwork, and deleted while leaving artwork intact.

Changing Dimensions

To change the dimensions of an artboard, select it with the Artboard tool, then enter new values in the dimension fields in the Control panel, drag the handles of the artboard, or press the Return or Enter key to open the Artboard Options dialog box and specify the new dimensions.

Repositioning Artboards

To reposition an artboard, select it with the Artboard tool and then drag to a new position. But what happens to artwork within the artboard area? It depends on the status of an easily overlooked option in the Control panel—the Move/Copy Artwork with Artboard tool (⬕). If this option is active (the default), any artwork that falls partially or completely within the area of an artboard will move with the artboard. If the Move/Copy option is deselected, a selected artboard moves independently of the artwork in it.

Because artboards can overlap, and larger artwork might fall across several artboards, be mindful of the Move/Copy setting before you move an artboard. If you want to duplicate an artboard and its artwork, choose the Artboard tool, and then hold down Option (Mac) or Alt (Windows) as you drag the artboard.

Deleting Artboards

You can delete all but one artboard in a document. As you delete artboards, the artboard identification numbers reset themselves. Artwork that falls within the deleted artboard area is not deleted (it remains in place on the canvas). Artwork outside artboards will be printed or exported only if *Ignore Artboards* is checked in the dialog box for export or print. If *Ignore Artboards* is checked, all content is regarded as one large illustration.

Bleed Settings

When you create a new Illustrator document, you have the option to specify a bleed value. You can also specify bleed in an existing document by choosing *File > Document Setup*. Bleeds can be asymmetrical and can be up to 1 inch in depth. The specified bleed value is applied to all artboards within an Illustrator file; there is no option to create a unique bleed setting for an individual artboard.

Please Don't Call Artboards "Pages"

The artboard concept is best suited for projects such as collateral pieces that share swatches and common bits of artwork, or projects with multiple versions. While it's tempting (and easy) to *refer* to artboards as pages, please don't *think* of them as pages: Think of them as sheets of drawing paper (well, actually, more like sheets of clear plastic). Perhaps that will help you resist being lured into building a 16-page brochure as an Illustrator file with 16 artboards; this will cause the prepress guys to refer to you in unflattering terms once you are out of earshot. Artboards don't provide basic page-layout features such as master pages, margin guides, and automatic page numbers. Consider those omissions to be nature's way of saying "Use InDesign."

Using Symbols

What if you need to create a school of 100 fish in Illustrator? You could draw 100 individual fish, which would be exhausting (but great for billing). Or you could draw one fish, and then copy and paste 99 duplicates; that's much faster but still tedious. And what do you do when your customer says the fish should be sharks rather than the 100 flounders you've just finished creating? You scream a lot, and then you start over—unless you were clever enough to use Illustrator's Symbol tools.

A symbol is a special kind of artwork that solves the need-a-lot-of-fish-in-a-hurry problem and makes it painless to change all those fish simultaneously. In addition to being powerful and flexible, the Symbol tools are amusingly named (**Figure 11.5**).

Figure 11.5 *The Symbol tools. From left to right: the Sprayer, Shifter, Scruncher, Sizer, Spinner, Stainer, Screener, and Styler.*

Artwork saved as a symbol can be reused multiple times in a document, and all the instances of the symbol retain a relationship to the original parent symbol. This offers several advantages:

- **Efficiency:** It's easy to populate the document with lots of instances of a symbol (think: school of fish, gaggle of geese, flock of sheep, etc.).

- **Quick corrections:** You can edit the original artwork in the ancestral symbol and all instances are automatically updated.

- **Smaller file size:** Using symbols can greatly reduce file size if you save in the native Illustrator AI format because you're just hauling around one copy of the artwork, rather than 100 copies.

To create a symbol, draw an object (or multiple objects), and then drag the selected artwork to the Symbols panel (*Window > Symbols*). You can also select an object and then choose New Symbol from the Symbols panel menu. Name the symbol and click OK; a thumbnail of the new symbol is added to the Symbols panel. Don't worry about the choice of Movie Clip or Graphic; either will work just fine if the file is to be used for print (**Figure 11.6**). The Registration reference point will be used if you scale or rotate an instance of the symbol; it overrides the current setting of the Transform proxy indicator (▦).

Figure 11.6 *Save as a Movie Clip if you are planning to export the Illustrator document to Flash. If the file will be used for print, it doesn't matter which option you choose.*

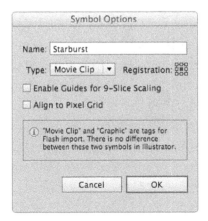

The symbol is stored in the current Illustrator file, not as a universally available symbol. However, you can import symbols from another file by choosing *Open Symbol Library > Other Library* from the Symbols panel menu. Navigate to the donor Illustrator file and click Open. Click the symbols you want to add to the internal Symbol library in the active document. You can also save symbols in a freestanding Symbol library by choosing *Save Symbol Library* from the Symbols panel menu (a Symbol library is actually just an Illustrator AI file containing the symbols).

To add a symbol to a drawing, either drag it from the Symbols panel onto the Illustrator document to create a single instance of the symbol, or (and this is much more fun) use the Symbol Sprayer to quickly populate the drawing with multiple instances. Tweak the distribution, size, and color of the symbols with the Symbol tools.

Once you've sprayed a bunch of symbols onto your Illustrator drawing, switch to Outline view (*View > Outline*). Notice that the symbol instances have no individual outlines; that's because symbols are live effects. Live effects can be continually added, removed, edited, and changed because they are not yet literal vector artwork. The underlying object is not altered by live effects. If you want to edit individual points on the artwork, expand the symbols to editable objects. Click the area occupied by the symbols, and then choose *Object > Expand*. If the original symbol used any effects, you may have to expand again or choose *Object > Expand Appearance* to fully release all objects for editing. You may also have to perform several rounds of ungrouping (*Object > Ungroup*) to completely dismantle aggregations of objects, depending on the internal complexity of the artwork. Some content, such as shadows and glows, will be converted to embedded image content.

Once you've expanded symbol instances, there's no link between the original symbol and the expanded artwork based on it. If you edit the parent symbol, changes will not be reflected in the expanded objects—as a result, you lose one of the big advantages of symbols. File size can increase as well, sometimes enormously, because of the complexity of the expanded artwork. Unless you need to edit individual pieces of symbol instances, there's no reason to expand symbols; expanding does not make such content print more predictably.

NOTE If you use a CMYK symbol in an Illustrator file whose document color mode is RGB, the symbol artwork, like placed images and other artwork, will also take on the RGB color space.

Simplifying Complex Artwork

Even though today's computers and current RIPs are significantly faster than their ancestors, there are still some benefits to eliminating complexity where possible. Pen paths with too many points can be lumpy and rough. And extraneous, empty points can result in incorrect boundaries for artwork, because the bounding box of an Illustrator file can be determined by the outermost points in the artwork (depending on how the file is saved as well as how it's imported into another application).

Fortunately, Illustrator offers some tools for polishing your drawing. Choose *Object > Path > Clean Up* to delete those little stray points that you might create with inadvertent pen clicks, objects with no fill and stroke, and those pesky empty text paths that spring up when you swear you didn't really click anywhere with the Type tool (**Figure 11.7**). Clean Up makes intelligent decisions: Although masks don't have a fill and stroke, the Clean Up function is clever enough to recognize and preserve them.

Figure 11.7 *Illustrator's Clean Up dialog box provides controls for eliminating extraneous paths and points, to create a much cleaner drawing.*

Given their names, it's easy to confuse Clean Up with another function, Simplify. Clean Up deletes unnecessary objects in the drawing, and it performs that task on a global basis—there's no need to select anything. By contrast, Simplify (*Object > Path > Simplify*) modifies *selected* objects by reducing the number of points in those objects (**Figure 11.8**). You can control the fidelity to the initial path with the Curve Precision slider: The higher the precision, the more points are retained.

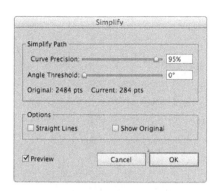

Figure 11.8 *Simplify, indeed. Note the striking reduction in number of points from 2484 to 284!*

When using Simplify, check Preview so you can immediately see the effect of your settings before you commit to the change. In general, keeping the Curve Precision value around 90–95% will achieve a satisfactory smoothing and a beneficial reduction in the number of points without significantly degrading detail (**Figure 11.9**).

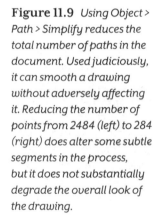

Figure 11.9 *Using Object > Path > Simplify reduces the total number of paths in the document. Used judiciously, it can smooth a drawing without adversely affecting it. Reducing the number of points from 2484 (left) to 284 (right) does alter some subtle segments in the process, but it does not substantially degrade the overall look of the drawing.*

However, it's possible to overdo things with the Simplify function. Dipping much below 90% for the Curve Precision value will quickly erode detail in the drawing by deleting too many points (**Figure 11.10**).

Figure 11.10 *Oversimplifying a path: The result of using a Curve Precision value of 50%.*

Live Effects

Illustrator offers a number of imaginative live effects that allow you to transform a simple object into something much more interesting with just a few clicks. Effects are "live," which means that you can modify how an object looks by editing effects in the Appearance panel without permanently altering the object itself. You can also hide or remove an effect to return an object to its original appearance.

Using Effects

The Effect menu is divided into two sections—*Illustrator Effects* and *Photoshop Effects*. The Illustrator Effects are applied to the interiors and the edges of vector objects, including objects being used as clipping masks for placed images. Photoshop Effects are applied only to the interior of vector objects, including those used as clipping masks (**Figure 11.11**).

Figure 11.11 *With the exception of the SVG filters, effects listed in the Illustrator Effects section of the Effect menu affect the interior and the edge of the object (top). The Photoshop Effects are applied only to the interior of the object (bottom). This example uses a placed image in a clipping mask. The SVG filters generate raster content for the interior of an object without modifying the edge of the object.*

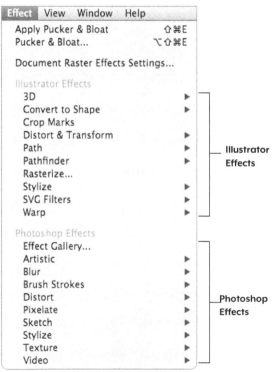

Some effects, such as glows or shadows, can only be accomplished with pixels. Such effects are potential pixels, not literal pixels; these effects don't become literal pixels until the file is exported or imaged.

Document Raster Effects Settings

To control the resolution for pixels generated by effects such as shadows or glows, choose *Effect > Document Raster Effects Settings* (**Figure 11.12**).

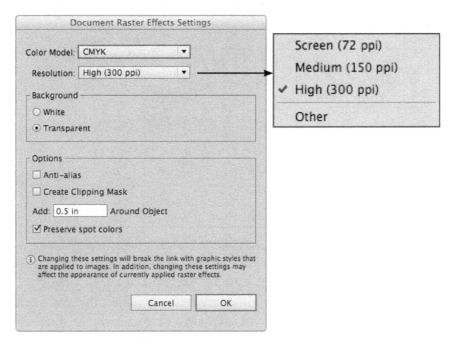

Figure 11.12 *The default resolution setting in the Document Raster Effects dialog box is 300 ppi, which is appropriate for artwork created to print at 100 percent size. If the artwork will be greatly scaled up (for example, if you are working at half size), you may want to increase the ppi accordingly. The default behavior is to preserve spot colors.*

The raster effects resolution setting governs all pixel-based effects, including drop shadows, feathering, the shading on 3D extrusions, and some graphic styles confections.

In a very complex document, rendering such effects at full resolution can cause your computer to slow to a crawl. Want to speed things up? You can work on your drawing with the raster effects resolution set to 72 ppi (or lower, if you like) and achieve pretty zippy performance. Then, when you're ready to finalize the drawing, change the setting to your final intended resolution. Because effects such as shadows aren't literal, changing the document's raster effects resolution causes these effects to regenerate at the new resolution value.

If the document uses lots of effects, be prepared for a slow redraw as the screen refreshes at the new resolution. Look on the bright side—you might use this as an opportunity to convince your boss that you really do need that newer, faster computer: "See how long this takes? You can't expect me to meet deadlines with this old, slow computer…"

There is no penalty (other than the time required for redraw) for repeatedly altering the raster effects resolution; any effects will redraw at the new resolution immediately (**Figure 11.13**). Because the pixels are generated on the fly, there is no resampling.

Figure 11.13 *Using a raster effects resolution of 72 ppi for effects (left) can speed up performance. Change the value to 300 ppi, and the shadow resolution changes immediately (right).*

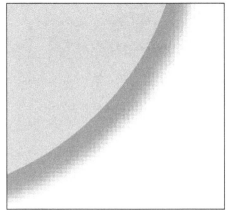

If you place a native Illustrator file into InDesign, the resolution of raster effects is not influenced by any settings in InDesign (such as the Transparency Flattener Preset). If you open the Illustrator file in Photoshop, the image will take on the resolution you assign in the Open dialog box. For example, if an Illustrator file with a raster effects resolution of 72 ppi is opened in Photoshop at 300 ppi, the image will be 300 ppi, but the raster effects will retain their coarse, pixelated appearance, as if they had been scaled to 300 ppi using the Nearest Neighbor setting.

When you create a new Illustrator document, the document profile or template you choose as a starting point dictates the raster effects resolution for the document. However, you can click the Advanced arrow to show more options, and choose from 72 ppi, 150 ppi, or 300 ppi instead of the default value of the profile or template. Once you have begun working in the document, you can change the raster effects resolution to any value you want.

TIP If you're using an older version of Illustrator, the directory path to document profiles may be different from the path shown in "Getting a Head Start." One easy way to find the document profiles directory is to do a search for a file-name corresponding to one of the existing profiles, such as "Video and Film." Find that and you've found all the document profiles.

Getting a Head Start

Illustrator provides templates and document profiles to get you started on new documents. But what if you want to make your own?

A custom document template or profile can be populated with custom swatches, symbols, graphic styles, and default stroke widths. You can even set the rulers to display automatically (a common request).

Templates: To create a template, create a new document, make the desired modifications, and then choose Illustrator Template (.ait) as the format in the Save dialog box. Illustrator takes you to the default template folder, but you can save it anywhere. To use the template, click the Templates button in the New Document dialog box and navigate to the template file. Illustrator opens a copy of the file as a new document.

New Document Profiles: Create and modify a new document and then save the file in the New Document Profiles folder (if you are using a non-English version of Illustrator, the "en_US" folder will be named differently):

- **Windows 7/8 64-bit:** C:\Users\[you]\AppData\Roaming\Adobe\Adobe Illustrator 17 Settings\en_US\x64\New Document Profiles
- **Mac:** [username]/Library/Application Support/Adobe/Adobe Illustrator 17/en_US/New Document Profiles

To reveal the user Library in the Finder on the Mac, hold the Option key and choose *Go > Library*.

Choose your custom document profile from the New Document Profile menu as you create a new document. Both custom document profiles and templates are available even if you reset Illustrator preferences.

Using the Appearance Panel

If you attempt to modify an effect by choosing its name from the Effect menu, an alert warns that if you continue, you'll apply another instance of the effect.

To edit an effect, select the object, and then open the Appearance panel (*Window > Appearance*). Click the name of the effect to open the options dialog box for that effect and modify the settings (**Figure 11.14**).

Figure 11.14 *To edit an effect, don't return to the Effect menu. Instead, click the name of the effect in the Appearance panel.*

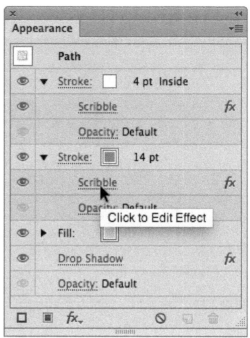

The Appearance panel is one of the handiest panels in Illustrator: It's actually one-stop shopping for choosing fill and stroke colors, stroke widths, opacity settings, blending modes, and effects options. You can add new effects by clicking the *fx* icon at the bottom of the panel and control the visibility of fills, strokes, and effects by clicking the eye icons next to those attributes. You can even add multiple strokes and fills to a single object by choosing *Add New Stroke*, *Add New Fill*, or *Duplicate Item* from the Appearance panel menu.

To modify a stroke, click its entry in the Appearance panel list. You don't have to visit the Swatches panel to change the stroke color: Click the color block in the stroke's row and it becomes a menu that expands to display a remote version of the Swatches panel (**Figure 11.15**). Press the Return or Enter key (or the Escape key) to dismiss the Swatches display.

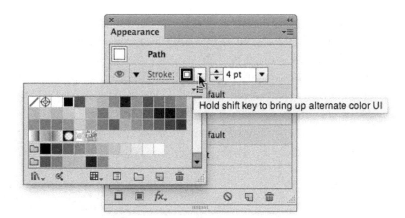

Figure 11.15 *There's no need to travel to the Swatches panel to change a stroke color; just click the Stroke color block in the Appearance panel to view swatches and pick a color.*

On the Appearance panel, click Stroke to display the Stroke panel (**Figure 11.16**). Modify the stroke weight, alignment, and style. Press Enter or Return when you're finished.

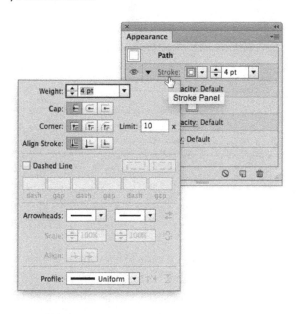

Figure 11.16 *Save a trip to the Stroke panel; just click Stroke in the Appearance panel.*

Multiple Fills and Strokes

This is where the real fun begins. If you've ever needed multiple borders on a shape, chances are you accomplished that by stacking multiple objects. There's a much easier way—the Appearance panel enables you to add

TIP Some Stroke options (such as Stroke alignment) are not available for live type. If you need those options, convert the text to outlines first.

multiple strokes and fills to a single object, allowing you to build very complex looks with just the controls within the panel (**Figure 11.17**). Just choose *Add New Fill* or *Add New Stroke* from the Appearance panel menu. The potential for tacky design is virtually unlimited—please use this only for good, never for evil. You can store the total appearance for future use by choosing *New Graphic Style* from the Graphic Styles panel menu (*Window > Graphic Styles*). You can also drag and drop artwork on to the Graphic Styles panel to create a new style.

Figure 11.17 *The Appearance panel lets you add multiple strokes and fills to a single object. To reuse the cumulative attributes, create a new graphic style from the selected object.*

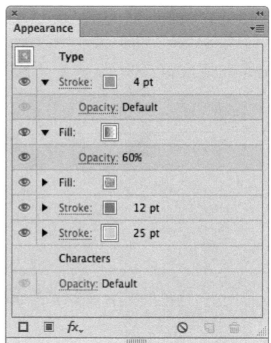

But wait—there's more. Because fill and stroke attributes are distinct components, you can do some very interesting things with them individually. For example, you can change the stacking order of the strokes and fills by dragging them up and down in the Appearance panel. Some strokes could appear in front of fills, some could fall behind.

Beyond that (I just can't stop myself), you can control the opacity and blending mode of each stroke or fill, and you can even apply different effects to each entry (**Figure 11.18**).

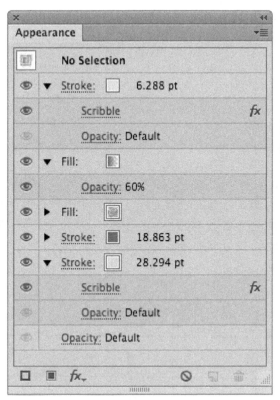

Figure 11.18 *Different Scribble settings have been applied to separate strokes on the heart object. Think of the fun you could have!*

Creating 3D Artwork

If you need an excuse to buy a faster computer, you may find your excuse in the 3D effects in Illustrator. These effects don't rival genuine 3D programs, but they do allow you to add dimensionality to shapes through revolving or extruding operations. As you might expect, such effects can generate very complex files. Because the illusion of dimensionality depends on realistic shading, 3D effects rely on the resolution setting in the Document Raster Effects Settings dialog box to determine the resolution of that shading. To speed up processing and display, use 72 ppi while you're working on the file, then switch to the final resolution when you're finished.

If you perform a 3D operation on a spot-color object, the default setting converts the object to process color; Illustrator subtly warns you in the 3D Revolve Options dialog box in tiny text ("Spot colors will be converted to process") but doesn't emphasize that you have the power to change things. If you click the More Options button, you will discover lighting options and an easy-to-miss check box: Preserve Spot Colors (**Figure 11.19**).

Figure 11.19 *By default, Illustrator's 3D operations will convert spot colors to process. However, you can preserve spot colors by clicking the More Options button to reveal the Preserve Spot Colors option. Note the warning (and advice) under the Preview check box.*

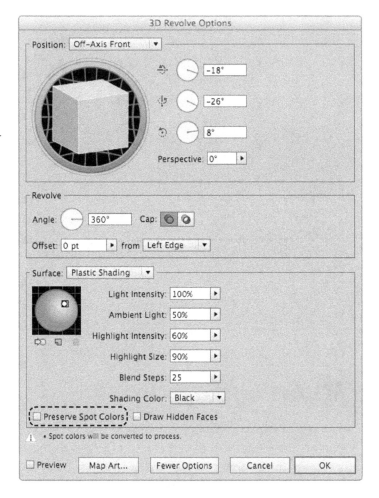

After you check Preserve Spot Colors, Illustrator provides another subtle warning, but this time it adds some guidance: *"Spot colors will be shaded with black overprint. Turn on Overprint Preview to view."* Illustrator renders the 3D spot object as a combination of black and the spot color, and uses overprint to image the 3D effect correctly. At first, it seems that your object has become grayscale, but turn on Overprint Preview (*View > Overprint Preview*) and you'll see that all is well (**Figure 11.20**).

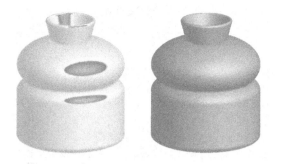

Figure 11.20 *The initial view of a 3D spot-color object is disturbing; it appears mostly grayscale, with some spot-color segments showing through (left). Turn on Overprint Preview to see the artwork as it will print (right).*

To modify any 3D effect, use the controls in the Appearance panel. There's no need to expand such objects unless you want to tweak the results; expanding prevents any further editing to the 3D effect itself—for example, after expanding, you would not be able to rotate an object to show a different side of it. And, as with other effects, expanding does not have any effect on the way the artwork will output and print.

Transparency

The opacity and blending mode options in Illustrator allow you to create interesting visual interactions between objects, but some operations may produce unexpected results when spot colors are involved. Color interactions between objects may change radically if you create them as spot-color objects, apply blending modes or opacity settings to them in Illustrator, and then place the files into another application such as InDesign and output as CMYK. That's why Illustrator provides a warning as you save the file (**Figure 11.21**).

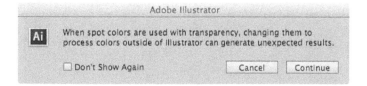

Figure 11.21 *Spot-color objects using transparency may not fare well when other applications render the Illustrator file as CMYK. At least Illustrator warns you. Don't check the Don't Show Again option—it's good to keep this warning in mind.*

Even if you intend to print spot colors as spot, Illustrator's display can mislead you about the final outcome. The blending mode interactions between colors (especially if spot colors are involved) are not correctly shown in normal display mode. Perhaps it's Illustrator's way of speeding up performance, but it can break your heart when the job goes to print (**Figure 11.22**). Find out the true story by activating Overprint Preview (*View > Overprint Preview*).

Figure 11.22 *Illustrator's normal display mode doesn't tell the truth about blending mode color interactions. The circle is PANTONE 2925 (blue) and the rectangle is PANTONE 150 (orange). Use Overprint Preview to find out what's really going on.*

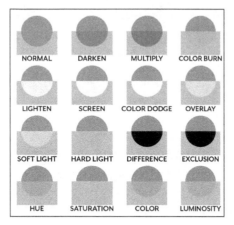

DISPLAY: OVERPRINT PREVIEW OFF   DISPLAY: OVERPRINT PREVIEW ON

Particularly treacherous is the fact that two blending modes—Difference and Exclusion—will cause overlapping spot-color areas to be converted to the document's working color mode, rather than remaining as a spot color (**Figure 11.23**). Not good news on a two-color job.

Figure 11.23 *When the supposedly two-color job is examined in Separations Preview, you'll discover that the Difference and Exclusion modes can only be rendered in process colors.*

For example, the most you can have of any given single ink is 100 percent—solid ink coverage. You can't fill an object with 200 percent of PANTONE Cool Gray 5 unless you're printing a double hit of the color. But if you fill two objects with a solid ink, and then apply a blending mode of Multiply, Illustrator will darken the overlapping area in normal display (**Figure 11.24**).

It's an unfortunate display error. However, if you turn on Overprint Preview, the display is correct. Overprint Preview is a great forensic tool to help you diagnose numerous problems, but it can slow down performance a bit in complex files.

Figure 11.24 *Both the text and rectangle are 100 percent PANTONE Cool Gray 5. The text is set to Multiply. Normal view (top) implies that the overlapping area will be darkened. Overprint Preview (bottom) proves that you can't have 200 percent of the same color.*

Flattening Transparency

If your print service provider is using truly ancient, coal-powered equipment that has not been upgraded in years, they may have difficulty outputting files containing transparency. If this is the case, consider sending your work to a more modern printer with better capabilities.

Effects such as transparency and blending modes enhance the design flexibility of Illustrator, but those effects go beyond the imaging model of Adobe PostScript, which has long been the native language of imagesetters (devices that output film for printing plates), platesetters (which directly output printing plates), and many desktop printers. Although major RIP vendors now market imaging devices that use the Adobe PDF Print Engine, which supports live, unflattened transparency, you may still encounter printers that use older workflows based on PostScript, so you should be aware of the limitations this imposes.

Illustrator, InDesign, and Acrobat all support live, unflattened transparency. If you're creating artwork in Illustrator with the intention of later placing it as a native AI file in InDesign, you don't have to worry about any special handling for transparent objects while you're working in Illustrator; any transparency flattening is deferred until the output from InDesign.

But if your Illustrator file is saved in a file format that doesn't support live transparency, such as PDF/X-1a, you must face the mysteries of transparency flattening. The Illustrator file itself won't be flattened; layers are untouched, your shadows and glows are intact, and everything remains editable. The flattening process affects only output and export, and happens on the fly during export or printing. The purpose is to replace transparent elements with opaque elements, mimicking the colors created in transparent overlaps by creating new colors and invoking PostScript overprint if necessary. The result resembles a jigsaw puzzle, but it's a purely PostScript puzzle that is easily digested by PostScript imaging devices (**Figure 11.25**). It's a fairly impressive engineering feat.

Figure 11.25 *What happens during transparency flattening? The design is rendered in separate opaque objects to accommodate older workflows that don't support native transparency. It looks like the original art when printed.*

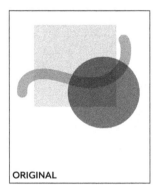
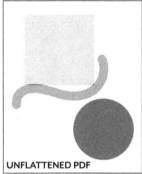

ORIGINAL | UNFLATTENED PDF | FLATTENED PDF

When you save a document in a format such as PDF/X-1a or an ancient version of Illustrator, you will have to specify a transparency flattener preset to handle the conversion of transparent content. If the recipient of your file gives you any guidance, follow that lead. Lacking that, you should create a widely applicable recipe for flattening. Choose *Edit > Transparency Flattener Presets*. Select *High* Resolution, and then click the New icon. In the Custom Transparency Flattener Options dialog box (**Figure 11.26**), set Line Art and Text Resolution to the resolution of the final imaging device. If you don't know that, use 2400 ppi. Use 300 ppi for the Gradient and Mesh Resolution.

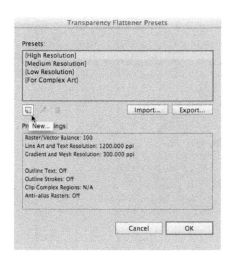 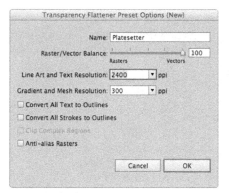

Figure 11.26 *Creating a custom transparency flattener preset. Select High Resolution, and then click New. Ideally, the Line Art and Text Resolution setting should be in keeping with the ultimate device resolution. The Gradient and Mesh Resolution can usually remain at 300 ppi.*

Linked and Embedded Images

Image resolution rules and restrictions still apply to images placed in Illustrator, of course. That is, scaling up or down beyond reasonable limits (roughly 75 to 125 percent) has repercussions in terms of degradation of detail and increased processing time. As in page-layout applications, it's best if the image is the correct final size to begin with and is placed at 100 percent into Illustrator.

When you place raster images in an Illustrator file, you can choose to link or embed those images. Each method has its advantages and disadvantages.

Linking an image results in a smaller Illustrator file than embedding. Additionally, because images are externally stored, they are easily color corrected or retouched. To open an image linked in an Illustrator file, hold down the Option (Mac) or Alt (Windows) key, and then double-click the image. The image opens in Photoshop, where you can make your edits and save the file. When you return to Illustrator, an alert displays, asking if you'd like to update modified images. Click *Yes* to update the image.

Embedding an image increases the Illustrator file size, because the size of the image is added to the file. While embedding makes it easier to keep track of all the components of a file, it complicates image editing. If the original image is still available, you can choose *Relink* from the Links panel menu and then navigate to the external image. If the original image is not available

NOTE When you unembed an image, you have the choice of TIFF or PSD for the extracted image, even if the original image might have been a different format. If the original image was a layered PSD or TIFF, and you've embedded with the Layers to Objects option selected, each layer becomes a single object in Illustrator and must be extracted separately.

Adjustment layers are not maintained even with the Layers to Objects option. Images containing adjustment layers will give an error when you attempt to unembed them.

as a stand-alone file, you can unembed the image by selecting its entry in the Links panel (*Window > Links*), then choosing *Unembed* from the Links panel menu (**Figure 11.27**). Save the unembedded image; Illustrator automatically forges a link to the saved image.

Figure 11.27 *If you need to edit an embedded image, unembed the image and save it as a stand-alone disk file.*

To gather up all the fonts and graphics required by an Illustrator file for submission to a printer (or to archive the job), choose *File > Package*. Generally, you should leave all of the Package options checked (**Figure 11.28**).

NOTE Versions of Illustrator prior to Illustrator CC did not provide options for packaging documents or unembedding images.

Figure 11.28 *Illustrator makes it easy to gather up the fonts (except Chinese, Japanese, Korean, and Typekit fonts) and linked files necessary to output the document.*

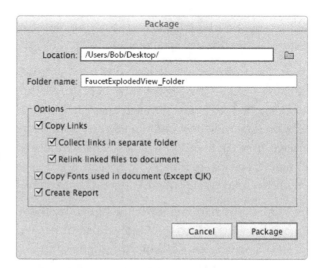

Blended Objects

Illustrator allows you to select two different objects and then use the Blend tool ( ) to create transitional shapes between them. It's an interesting effect, but if the starting objects are filled with spot colors, the intermediate shapes are generated as CMYK objects (**Figure 11.29**). Try this yourself, then use Separations Preview (*Window > Separations Preview*) and turn off the visibility of the spot colors to see what's really happening; the shapes that are still visible are CMYK builds, not spot colors.

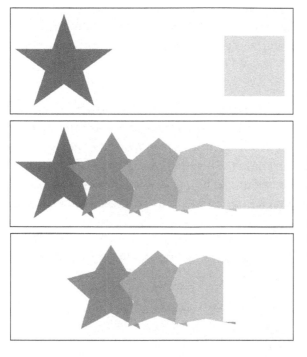

Figure 11.29 *Start with two spot-color objects (top). The Blend tool allows you to create discrete intermediate shapes (middle) or a smooth gradient-like transition between the objects. But there's bad news: Intermediate shapes (bottom) are rendered as CMYK, not spot, which would be incorrect on a two-color job.*

If the blend effect is crucial to your design, and the job must be printed in spot colors, you might create each starting shape as a single process color but let the process color represent a spot color. For example, use cyan in lieu of PANTONE 294 and magenta instead of PANTONE 128. Then inform the print service provider that the cyan plate should be used to print PANTONE 294 and the magenta plate for PANTONE 128. If there are also four-color images in the job, however, this approach won't quite work for you.

Spot Colors

Illustrator CC uses the PANTONE PLUS libraries, which use Lab color values by default to define and display the ink colors. The numbering system is the same as in previous PANTONE libraries (i.e., PANTONE 485 is still the same red), but new colors were added to the basic guide, and the guides are now arranged chromatically rather than numerically.

The spot-to-CMYK conversion values have also changed, reflecting improvements in pigments and sophisticated computerized press controls. This can present an issue if you pick from the new PANTONE PLUS library and then convert to CMYK; this results in different values than previous libraries yielded. If you're working on a project that must match an older project in which a spot-to-process conversion was performed, the new job may not match the old job.

If it's important to replicate the old appearance of ancient artwork, open the old file in the original version of Illustrator and then convert the spot-color swatches to CMYK so they won't be reinterpreted by other applications (**Figure 11.30**). If you don't have the original version of Illustrator, the conversion to CMYK will be based on the newer spot-to-process recipe, so you may have to tweak the CMYK build values to more closely resemble the original printed job.

Figure 11.30 *The Swatch Options dialog box initially displays Book Color for the Color Mode of a spot-color swatch (left). To convert the swatch to process (right), first change the Color Mode to CMYK, then change the Color Type to Process Color.*

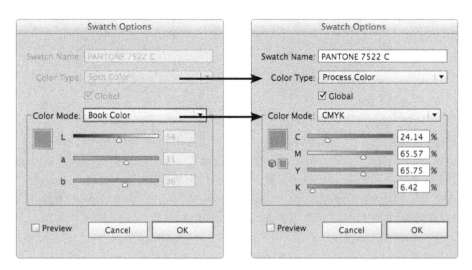

You'll also find that the built-in spot-to-CMYK conversions in Illustrator yield different CMYK values than you'll see displayed in the PANTONE Color Bridge book. My advice? Go with the Adobe conversions; they seem to do a better job of approximating the spot color.

Better yet, don't play this way. If you're working on a job that will print in process colors, pick your colors from a process-color resource, such as the PANTONE CMYK Coated guide.

Too Much of a Good Thing

If you attempt to use the Overprint Preview feature (*View > Overprint Preview*) in an Illustrator file using more than 27 spot colors, you will receive an error (**Figure 11.31**). You'll also see this warning if you try to use the Separations Preview feature (*Window > Separations Preview*), because Overprint Preview is required to correctly display separations. You are also warned if you attempt to print separated output from a file using more than 27 spot colors, which is Illustrator's way of saving paper (and sparing you some embarrassment).

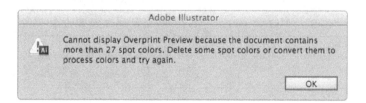

Figure 11.31 *Illustrator will not launch Overprint Preview in a document using more than 27 spot colors. Can you blame it?*

Illustrator doesn't object to you *having* more than 27 spot colors in the Swatches panel; it just balks at more than 27 spot colors actually being *used* by objects.

What About My Old PANTONE Guides?

Your existing PANTONE fanbooks are not truly obsolete: Because the numbers of existing colors have not changed, you can continue to use them as references to specify color unless they're ancient, or have been exposed to UV light for long periods of time, in which case they're faded and thus unreliable. PANTONE encourages users to buy up-to-date fanbooks to ensure color fidelity, and I don't argue with that, especially in light of the expanded choices in the PANTONE PLUS offerings.

Separations Preview

Viewing individual inks allows you to check an Illustrator file for extraneous spot colors. Choose *Window > Separations Preview* to open the Separations Preview panel, and then check the *Overprint Preview* option so you can view all separations (**Figure 11.32**). You can control the visibility of individual printing inks by clicking the eye icons next to ink names. This is much easier (and faster) than printing separated lasers. Think of the trees you'll save.

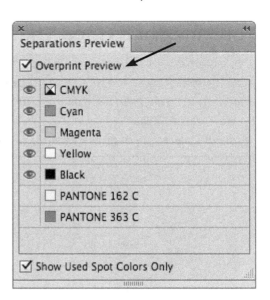

Figure 11.32 *Selectively view individual separations by using the eye icon visibility controls. Note that Overprint Preview must be checked to activate Separations Preview.*

Why All Swatches Should Be Global

When you're creating colors in an Illustrator project, there are two habits you should develop.

- Always save colors as official swatches, rather than just creating and applying a color by using the Color panel (*Window > Color*). While colors created in the Color panel display and print correctly, swatches make it much easier to keep track of the colors you're using.

- Always designate swatches as global swatches. If you change the definition of a global swatch, all objects using that swatch will change.

Although you could use selection options such as *Select > Same > Fill Color* to find and change multiple objects, you can save some time and aggravation by always choosing the Global option when creating swatches.

If you create a swatch without checking the Global option, what happens? If you change the swatch, objects using the swatch will not change unless they're selected when you make the change (**Figure 11.33**).

 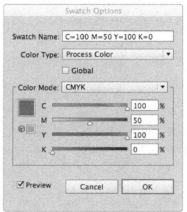

Figure 11.33 *The same swatch is applied to all four rectangles. But changing the recipe for the swatch doesn't affect the objects, because the swatch is not a global swatch.*

It's easy to overlook the Global option because you're usually concentrating on the color values or color type when you're creating a swatch, and the Global option doesn't catch your attention (**Figure 11.34**).

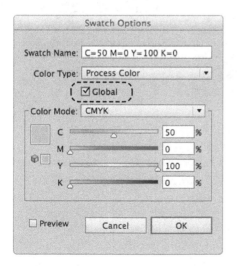

Figure 11.34 *The Global option is hiding in plain sight, nestled in the Swatch Options dialog box. Once you've found it, remember to select the option every time you create a swatch.*

TIP If you forgot to designate a swatch as global, select all the objects using the swatch, then double-click the swatch in the Swatches panel and check the Global option in the Swatch Options dialog box.

Global swatches have a small white triangle on the lower-right corner of the swatch thumbnail (**Figure 11.35**).

Figure 11.35 *If you've wondered why some swatches have white corners, now you know—the white corner identifies Global swatches.*

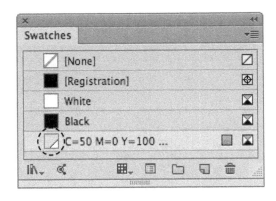

You might think of Global swatches as "brand name" swatches; change the swatch, and those changes are reflected throughout the document (**Figure 11.36**).

Figure 11.36 *No need to select objects; global swatch changes are automatically applied globally.*

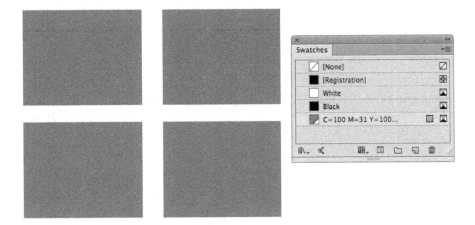

Swatches in Illustrator's built-in swatch libraries, such as Earthtone, Nature, or Art History, are not global swatches. However, swatches that you add from any of the Color Books, such as PANTONE Plus Solid Coated or Toyo Color Finder, are already defined as global swatches.

Because they are global, spot-color swatches sport the white corner as identification. Additionally, because they are spot colors, they have a little...spot in the white corner. It's only about one pixel in size, but it's a quick way to identify spot colors in the Swatches panel (**Figure 11.37**)

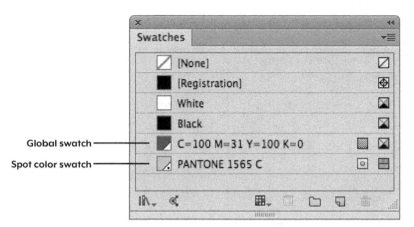

Figure 11.37 *All global swatches display the telltale white corner. Spot swatches have a small dot inside the white corner, identifying them as both global and spot.*

Type and Fonts

Illustrator offers extensive type features, from hanging punctuation to complete OpenType support. For more information about fonts and font licensing, see Chapter 6, "Fonts."

Point Type and Area Type

If you select the Type tool (T), click in the document, and start typing, you're creating *point type*. If you just keep typing without ever hitting Return, that line of type will just keep going on forever (or until you run out of monitor, whichever comes first). If you press Enter or Shift-Enter (soft return), you force a line break. If you select a block of point type and pull on the selection handles, you'll distort the type (**Figure 11.38**). Point type is great for callouts and labels but painful for long flows of text.

Figure 11.38 *Dragging on the handles of a point-type object will distort the type (bottom).*

This is Point Type.

This is Poin

If you click and drag to create a type container, you create *area type*. If you drag the handles of an area-type object to change the dimensions, text rewraps—there is no distortion. Area type is suitable for longer flows of text (i.e., anything longer than a label or callout).

What if you create the wrong species of text—click and drag when you should have just clicked or vice versa? Lucky you; Illustrator lets you change point type to area type and back again (**Figure 11.39**).

Figure 11.39 *Double-click the control to change an area-type object to point type and back again.*

Type on an Open Path

To adhere type to a path, just create a path with the Pen or Pencil tool, then click the path with the *Type on a Path Tool* ( ) To control the behavior of the type, or its orientation with respect to the path, choose *Type > Type on a Path > Type on a Path Options* (**Figure 11.40**).

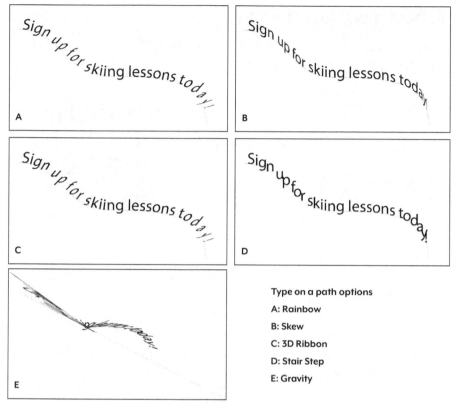

Figure 11.40 *Festive options for type on a path. Personal gripe: I say the Skew and 3D Ribbon names are swapped. What do you think?*

Type on a path options
A: Rainbow
B: Skew
C: 3D Ribbon
D: Stair Step
E: Gravity

You can use alignment controls to left-align, center, or right-align the text. You can also use the options to control the vertical alignment of the text, aligning either the ascender, descender, center, or baseline of the text to the path.

Type on a Closed Path

When you create an area-type container, it's easy to see where the walls are and where the In Port and Out Port are located (**Figure 11.41**).

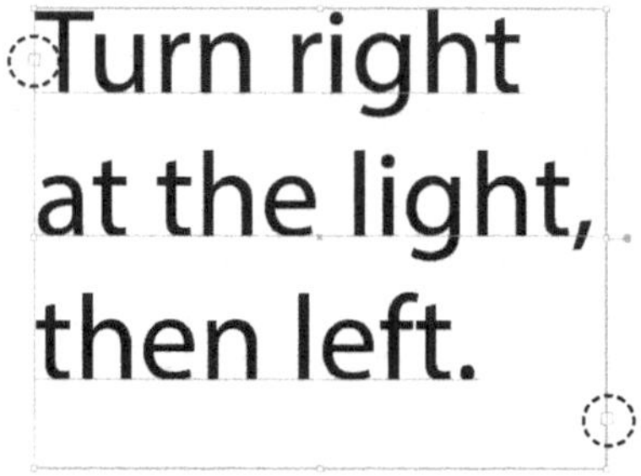

Figure 11.41 *The In Port and Out Port (circled) are easily identifiable on an area-type container.*

Turn right at the light, then left.

Those controls aren't quite so obvious on a closed path (**Figure 11.42**), where they behave more like bookends. The small gap between the start and end lines are intended to give you a hint, but it's a very subtle hint. Use the Selection or Direct Selection tool to move the start and end "bookends" closer to the start and end of the text, and you'll be a happier person. You can also use the center point line to drag the text around on the path.

Figure 11.42 *For easier handling of text on a closed path, such as a circle, use the Direct Selection tool (the white arrow) to move the start and end lines farther apart. Drag the center point to herd the text around the shape.*

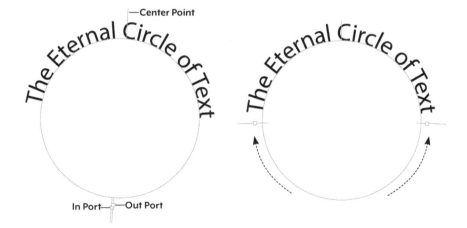

Embedding Fonts

Funny story about Illustrator's native format, AI—under the hood, it's actually based on the PDF language specification. Although an AI file isn't strictly a PDF, it *contains* a PDF 1.5 file. It's like a chocolate-covered cherry—it's really two files in one:

- A native Illustrator CC file, recognized when you open the file in Adobe Illustrator

- Unflattened PDF 1.5 content, perceived by other applications, including Adobe Acrobat

It's this PDF-ish nature that allows fonts to be embedded in Illustrator files *for purposes of display and print*. Read that part again: *display and print*. You can place an Illustrator file into an InDesign layout and it will print and export to PDF correctly, even if you don't have the correct fonts (**Figure 11.43**).

Figure 11.43 *Although the Beyond Wonderland font isn't active on the system, a placed Illustrator file will image correctly—as long as you don't try to edit it.*

However, if you open the file in Illustrator, you will be slapped with a missing fonts alert (**Figure 11.44**).

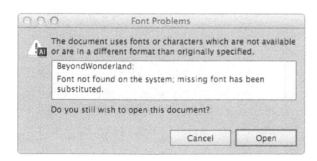

Figure 11.44 *Illustrator displays an alert if you open a file using a font that isn't active on your system.*

NOTE If you open an Illustrator file without the required fonts, no harm is done to the file if you close the file without resaving; the file will still print correctly if placed in InDesign.

Even if you don't edit the text, resaving an Illustrator file with missing fonts will ruin the file—font embedding is lost. You will need to obtain the necessary font, or request that the file creator send you a revised file with outlined text (**Figure 11.45**).

Figure 11.45 *If you edit and resave an Illustrator file for which you don't have the necessary fonts (even if you don't touch the text), the file will not print correctly.*

Don't Miss Our Neighborhood **Hallow- een Party**

Outlining Type

You might want to convert type to outlines for several reasons:

- To modify the shapes of letters; for example, to create a logo

- To prevent problems if the file is edited

- To avoid sending fonts, in compliance with font licensing

Fonts contain a feature called *hinting*, which optimizes the rendering of type at any size onscreen and when printed. When you convert type to outlines, you lose that hinting information. Outlined type should be indistinguishable from live type when output to a high-resolution device (over 600 dpi). But on low-resolution devices, such as a 300 dpi desktop printer (rare these days), it may look a bit rough because of the loss of hinting information.

You can convert both area type and point type to outlines, but you can't convert just selected letters within a flow of type; you can only convert the entire type object to outlines. And, although most foundries' font licensing allows the conversion of type to outlines, it might be worth taking a peek at the End User Licensing Agreement (EULA) for the font before you choose *Type > Create Outlines* to confirm that outlining is allowed for the particular font you're using. Oh, and you might want to check your spelling, too.

Typekit Desktop Fonts

Illustrator, like all the other applications on your computer, is perfectly happy using Typekit desktop fonts. Type can be filled, stroked, outlined, treated with loads of effects, and embedded in PDFs. A native Illustrator AI file using Typekit desktop fonts can be placed into an InDesign layout and the text will display and print correctly because of the dual nature of an AI file; the internally stored PDF of the file contains embedded fonts (see "Embedding Fonts" in this chapter).

The only limitation imposed by Typekit desktop fonts is that they cannot be packaged. If you choose *File > Package*, all conventionally licensed fonts will be included in the Fonts folder in the package, but the Typekit desktop fonts will not. The font files themselves are invisible on your system, so you cannot package them manually.

If you send packaged Illustrator files to a printer who also subscribes to Creative Cloud, they already have access to the same fonts through Typekit, so this will not be an issue.

If you are collaborating with another designer who requires live type, either avoid using Typekit desktop fonts, or advise them to subscribe to Creative Cloud or to the Typekit service (www.typekit.com). Of course, your collaborator can also purchase the necessary fonts conventionally from the font foundry.

Why Versions Matter

Illustrator allows you to save files as older versions, but this process is often a one-way street. For example, a 3D effect created in Illustrator CC will be expanded during a backsave for Illustrator 8, which did not have 3D effects, and the dynamic editability will be lost if you reopen the file in Illustrator CC. If you're working in a mixed environment with users who have multiple vintages of Illustrator, be mindful of these speed bumps. The ideal solution is to move all members of a workgroup to the same version, but that isn't always feasible, especially if you are working with freelancers. In self-defense, keep a current working version of your Illustrator document when it's necessary to save older versions for collaborators, in case something's munged by saving to an earlier version.

Purely vector components survive backsaving and round-tripping but type may not. Illustrator CC provides support for the extended character sets in OpenType fonts and enables fine typographic controls and elegant composition. But because the text composition engine has been revamped through the years to allow these improvements, text in older files undergoes conversion when those files are opened in Illustrator CC.

Text conversion is unavoidable, but at least you're warned when you open a file from Illustrator 10 or earlier (**Figure 11.46**). The yellow triangle of terror is looming behind the Illustrator icon, and you're presented with three confusing options, none of which seems like a safe choice.

Figure 11.46 *When you open a file created by Illustrator 10 or earlier, you're faced with this alert. Don't panic. The correct option is to choose OK.*

- Update will revamp the text according to the newer text composition rules, but you won't be watching while it happens. If there's text reflow, you may not catch it. One could argue that this shouldn't even be an option. Don't choose this.

- Cancel prevents the file from opening. You'll have to face this file eventually, so don't chicken out now.

- OK opens the file without modifying the text. If you're not planning to edit text in the file, this is the correct choice because it leaves the text untouched. And if you are planning to edit text, this ensures that you'll be watching when the text is translated, so you can make the necessary adjustments. It's understandable that this is the default choice. If you press the Enter or Return key out of habit, you've accidentally done the right thing.

When you click OK in the opening alert, you postpone the recomposing of text. As long as the correct fonts are active when you open the file, no harm is done to text by just opening and resaving the file, although resaving does label the file as having been created by the newer version of Illustrator.

Performing edits to other elements of the file won't adversely affect the text. Text is protected until you attempt to edit it (**Figure 11.47**).

Please exit to your left, through the blue double doors.

Form a single line, and turn right as you exit the auditorium.

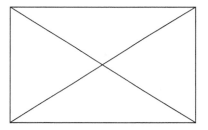

Figure 11.47 *In Outline view, it may appear that the legacy text is being handled as an image, but that's misleading; it's just protected until you edit it.*

When you attempt to edit legacy text, you encounter another alert and another decision (**Figure 11.48**). Choosing Cancel just delays the inevitable. The real choice is between Update and Copy Text Object.

Figure 11.48 *When you begin to edit text in a file from Illustrator 10 or earlier, you face yet another alert. The correct choice is Copy Text Object.*

- As in the opening alert, Update will recompose the text by the newer rules of Illustrator CC. Unless you have hard copy or a photographic memory as reference, you might not notice any resulting text reflow.

- Copy Text Object preserves an unchanged copy of the text as it appeared in the original file, while creating a duplicate block of text that plays by the new rules. Most importantly, you now can compare the two versions, see what really happened, and repair as necessary. This is the preferred choice.

When you click Copy Text Object, Illustrator creates a ghosted replica of the text as it appeared in the original file (**Figure 11.49**). Use the reference text as a guide as you make any edits necessary to match the appearance of the text in the original Illustrator file. You may see a very slight change in the vertical position of a text block, or a slight change in line spacing, but these problems are easy to fix.

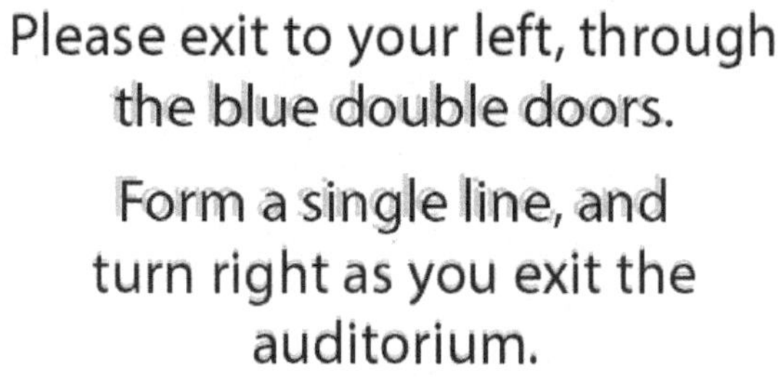

Figure 11.49 *The black text is live text, composed by the rules of Illustrator CC. While the original line breaks are preserved, leading will have to be tweaked to match the legacy line spacing seen in the ghosted reference text.*

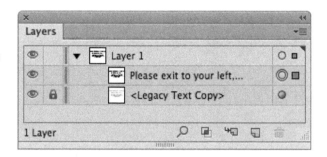

Where is that ghosted reference type? Illustrator automatically generates two objects within the layer—the ghosted legacy text and an unlocked copy of the text block that uses the newer rules in Illustrator CC (**Figure 11.50**). After completing the edits, delete the reference text object.

Figure 11.50 *The legacy text block is locked so it can serve as a reference as you edit the converted type.*

What about backsaving? If you save for Illustrator 10 or earlier, then round-trip the file, you will find that multiline text blocks have become separate clumps of text rather than a continuous flow of text, but the appearance of the text should be maintained. If you reopen the file in CC, the text will still be in separate bunches (**Figure 11.51**).

Figure 11.51 *Backsaving is a one-way trip; the changes imposed on text flow remain when the file is reopened in Illustrator CC.*

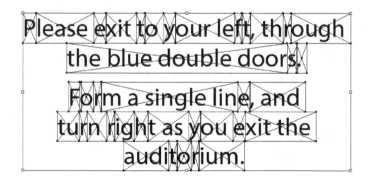

If you inherit a file with those annoying little clumps of type, there is a way to unclump it. It may seem like the long way around, but it's saner than editing broken-up text. You'll need Adobe Acrobat Pro for the job.

1. Save a copy of the Illustrator file as a PDF, because you're only going to use this as a source of text. Your choice of PDF preset isn't important.

2. Open the PDF in Acrobat Pro. Although Acrobat Pro XI provides enhanced text-editing capabilities, including reflowable text, that's not the approach you're going to take. You need to get the text back into Illustrator in an easily edited form.

3. Select the Edit Object tool ( ). In Acrobat Pro XI, it's in the Print Production tools; in Acrobat Pro X, it's in the *Content* tools (the Acrobat team does like to keep us on our toes).

4. Click the text block, then right-click or Control-click and choose *Edit Object* from the contextual menu. The Touch-Up object is opened in Illustrator.

5. In Illustrator, you'll see that the text is intact, but it's in single lines; if you need to perform an edit that requires a reflow, that's still annoying. But don't give up hope. One more step, and you'll be in business.

6. Select all the text with the Selection tool, and copy to the Clipboard.

7. Switch to the Type tool, and click and drag to create an empty area-type container.

8. Paste the copied text into the area-type container and squeal with joy: It is now intact, reflowable text.

9. Whew.

Saving for Other Applications

Whereas the undisputed choice of file format once was EPS, that's no longer the case: There are significant advantages to saving Illustrator files in the native AI format. InDesign fully supports the blending modes and transparency effects in AI files, allowing such attributes to interact with other elements on an InDesign page. The Object Layer Options feature in InDesign allows you to selectively reveal or hide layers of placed Illustrator AI files (this option is not available for EPS). And even though we now have enormous hard drives and tons of RAM, it's nice to know that an AI file is usually smaller than an EPS file.

If you're asked to supply an EPS because of the requirements of a client's workflow, of course, honor the request.

When you save as EPS, you are given the choice of a range of flavors of EPS, from Illustrator CC all the way back to Illustrator 3, and Japanese Illustrator 3 (no, I don't know what makes Japanese Illustrator 3 EPS files different from other Illustrator 3 EPS files). If you save an Illustrator file as an EPS earmarked for versions CS through CC, the resulting EPS is completely editable in Illustrator and still behaves predictably in other applications. Think of the file as an Illustrator native file wearing an EPS disguise for the benefit of placement into other applications that don't recognize native Illustrator files.

However, if you save as an Illustrator 10 or earlier version EPS, the contents of the file may be permanently altered: Shadows become embedded images, effects such as Scribble are expanded to literal vectors, and editing becomes much more complex as a result. This is necessary because file formats have changed substantially since these earlier versions. Reopening such a file in Illustrator CC will not restore effects to full, live editability, so you should keep a CC version of the file as an AI file for full future editability.

Saving Files with Multiple Artboards

If you're planning to place an Illustrator file containing multiple artboards into InDesign, just save the file as a native Illustrator AI file. When you choose *File > Place* in InDesign, hold down the Shift key to temporarily invoke Import Options: A second dialog box allows you to pick which artboard (or range of artboards) you want to place (**Figure 11.52**). You can also specify how the content is cropped; choose from Bounding Box, Art, Crop, Trim, Bleed, or Media.

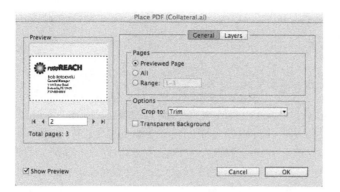

Figure 11.52 *Place an Illustrator file with multiple artboards into InDesign, and choose which pages to place. Notice that the dialog box is called Place PDF, even though the file is an Illustrator AI file.*

Glance at the name of the second dialog box, and you'll realize that InDesign perceives the artboards as individual pages of a multipage PDF. Why is this? Is InDesign confused? No—this is because, under the hood, Illustrator has a bit of PDF-ish flavor.

For this reason, you should always check the Create PDF Compatible File option when saving an Illustrator AI file. This is the default option. If you uncheck the option, you'll see nothing but a tiled pattern of warning text when you place the file in InDesign or attempt to open it in Photoshop (**Figure 11.53**).

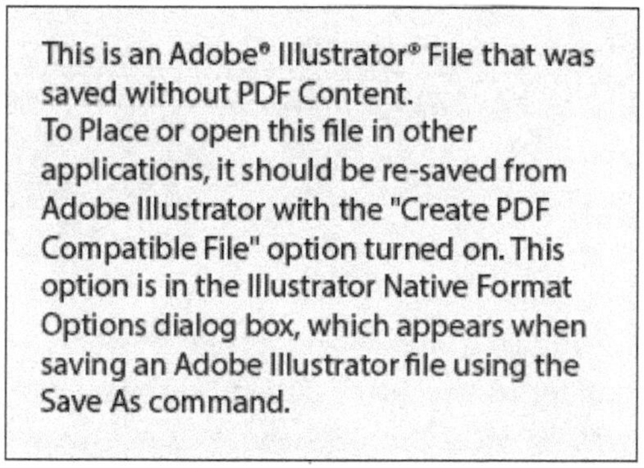

> This is an Adobe® Illustrator® File that was saved without PDF Content.
> To Place or open this file in other applications, it should be re-saved from Adobe Illustrator with the "Create PDF Compatible File" option turned on. This option is in the Illustrator Native Format Options dialog box, which appears when saving an Adobe Illustrator file using the Save As command.

Figure 11.53 *If you uncheck Create PDF Compatible File, this is what you'll see when you place the file in InDesign or open it in Photoshop. At least it tells you what to do.*

Saving Artboards to Older Versions

If you save an Illustrator file containing multiple artboards to an earlier version of Illustrator, you can choose between saving each artboard as a separate Illustrator file or saving all the artwork on the canvas as a single file. While all artwork will be retained, the artboard definitions are lost, and are not restored if you reopen the file in Illustrator CC. Versions of Illustrator older than CS5 do not support multiple artboards.

Saving As EPS

Because the EPS format does not support multiple artboards, Illustrator gives you the option of saving each artboard as a separate EPS or saving the entirety of the artwork as a single EPS. If you choose the Use Artboards option in the Save dialog box, a separate EPS will be created for each artboard. The default filenames are based on the name of the Illustrator file with -01.eps, -02.eps, and so on appended to the filename. You can also specify a new base file-name, which will receive the same numbered addenda.

Including Bleed in Export

If the Illustrator file has been set up with a defined document bleed (*File > Document Setup*), the bleed is included automatically and is recognized by Photoshop and InDesign, whether the file is saved as an AI or EPS. Both applications give you the option to crop the incoming file according to the trim, bleed, or bounding box. When you choose *File > Place* in InDesign, hold down Shift as you click OK in the Place dialog box to display the *Import Options* dialog box, which provides the same crop options for an AI file. You will not see those options when you place an EPS because the bleed is included by default.

Packaging Illustrator Files

Choose *File > Package* to gather up any linked graphics and fonts (except Typekit, Chinese, Japanese, or Korean fonts) necessary if the file is opened on another computer. If you're collaborating with someone who does not have Illustrator CC, recommend that they invest in Scoop (www.worker72a.com), an Illustrator plug-in that enables users of older versions of Illustrator to package files.

Creating PDF Files

Even though most print service providers should have no problem outputting a native Illustrator file, there are some advantages to submitting your Illustrator job as a PDF. Doing so eliminates the need to gather up images and fonts because everything is included in the PDF. It also prevents casual editing (and the resultant errors).

Because Illustrator speaks fluent PDF, creating a PDF is a Save As function, not an export operation. There is rarely a legitimate reason to go the long way around, generating PostScript and cranking up Distiller to create a PDF. Don't feel guilty—do it the easy way.

Saving to PDF

As always, consult the printer or publication for the correct specifications before you submit a PDF file. Make sure you know the version of PDF they will accept and whether they allow live transparency in a PDF, or whether it must be flattened.

If your printer or publication has provided specifications or settings, of course you should use them. But you'll find that some printers and publications still leave it up to you—"just send us a nice PDF"—and then you're on your own.

Choose *File > Save As*, and select Adobe PDF as the format. Provide a filename for the PDF, and then click Save. You'll then see the same PDF creation settings (.joboptions) in Illustrator as you would see in InDesign and Distiller (with the exception of a few extras in Distiller). If you have created or imported custom settings, those will also appear.

The default setting is (naturally) Illustrator Default. The option to Preserve PDF Editing Capabilities ensures that you can safely reopen the PDF in Illustrator. But this option can create very large files, and some prepress workflow software, such as imposition applications, may have difficulty handling such a new-fangled PDF, so this is usually not ideal for job submission.

If the printer or publication has not provided specifications, you can't go wrong by saving as PDF/X-1a:2001. The default PDF/X-1a settings are fine, but you will have to set the bleed value. If you created bleed in the document setup, just check the option to Use Document Bleed Settings on the Marks and Bleed tab.

Opening PDF Files in Illustrator

With the exception of PDFs created from Illustrator with the Preserve PDF Editing Capabilities option selected, it's rarely a good idea to open and edit PDF files in Illustrator. Even though Illustrator is willing to give it a try, you run the risk of causing damage to the file integrity, especially when the PDF has been generated by non-Adobe applications.

If a PDF contains very simple content—say, just a vector logo—you may be successful editing the file in Illustrator. But if you attempt to edit a file containing a font not available on your system, you won't be able to edit any text, and the file will not image correctly because font substitution will take place. If you need to edit graphics or text in a PDF, you will achieve more satisfactory results if you use the TouchUp feature in Adobe Acrobat: Using the *Select Object* tool, select the object, then right-click or Control-click to choose either *Edit Image* or *Edit Object* (depending on the nature of the selected content). Perform the necessary edits in Photoshop or Illustrator, then choose *File > Save* to write the corrected content back into the PDF.

InDesign Production Tips

12

InDesign offers wonderful creative tools and splendid typographical controls. Thanks to its integration with other Adobe applications, it's part of a nearly seamless graphic ecosystem. But like any application, it has some little quirks that can surprise you if you don't know the workarounds.

Graphics

InDesign accepts a wide variety of graphics formats, but that doesn't mean that all those formats are equally well behaved. In addition, while InDesign offers some interesting methods of placing graphics, not all of those methods will yield satisfactory results.

Creating Graphics Frames

Both the *Rectangle Frame* tool ( ) and the plain old *Rectangle* tool ( ) create shapes that can hold graphics (or text). In fact, any enclosed shape—even one drawn by the Pen tool—can hold text or graphics.

It's worth noting some differences in the behavior of the two tools. This would be so much easier to explain if the tools had noticeably different names.

TIP You can modify the Basic Graphics Frame Object Style, which governs the Unassigned Content shapes, so that every shape you draw has the fill and stroke attributes you specify in that style. However, you can't change the Frame tools (the ones with the placeholder "X" through them)—they carry a fill and stroke of None. You can, however, create a frame and then apply an object style to it afterward. Clunky, but it works.

The Frame tools (including the Ellipse Frame and Polygon Frame tools hidden under the Rectangle Frame tool) create shapes with a fill and stroke of None, which is sort of like clear plastic: You can select these shapes by clicking anywhere inside them. This makes it easy to determine where objects are in the stacking order—just click and see what wakes up.

By default, the plain old shape tools (Rectangle, Ellipse, and Polygon) create objects that are basically disembodied floating strokes with no innards. InDesign defines these objects as Unassigned Content (*Object > Content > Unassigned*). You can't select the shape by clicking inside it (because it's utterly empty). You must click on the stroke instead. Until you discover that, you click everywhere, muttering. And until it has content (either a graphic, text, or a fill color), a plain old shape can really get in the way: If you accidentally click in such a frame with a loaded text or graphics cursor (usually intending to target what's behind it), the plain old shape will intercept and take the content.

You get a lot of visual feedback in InDesign, so keep your eye on the cursor's appearance. If your loaded-graphics cursor ( ) develops parentheses, you're about to place your graphic in an existing frame. You've been warned. But even if you slip up, you're not stuck. Just undo once and you're back to a loaded graphics cursor, so you can place the graphic in the correct frame. Changed your mind completely? Click the Selection tool (black arrow) or press the Escape key and you're relieved of the graphic burden, so you can start over again.

Selecting Files to Place

In the Place dialog (*File > Place*), you can select multiple graphics and text files by Shift-clicking, Command-clicking (Mac), or Control-clicking (Windows) multiple filenames. Click OK when you've scooped up all the files you want. If you want to add more files to the pile, choose *File > Place* again, and go shopping in another location, clicking OK when you're finished. InDesign generates small thumbnails of the graphics so you know what you're about to place when you click. You can cycle through the files you're carrying by using keyboard arrows, and you can press Escape to discard a file you've decided not to place.

Part of the fun of InDesign is that you don't have to select—or even create—a frame before placing a graphic. Just choose *File > Place*, select a graphic, and then click anywhere in an empty area of the page. InDesign creates a frame on the fly, snug to the edges of the image. It's a tremendous time-saver.

There's Good Drag and Drop...

Rather than using the *File > Place* command, you can drag and drop from Mini Bridge (**Figure 12.1**). Mini Bridge is just a portal to Bridge; you have to launch Bridge first for Mini Bridge to work. The Mini Bridge window can be positioned wherever you like over the InDesign page and provides high-quality thumbnails of graphics to make it easy to find the correct files.

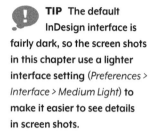

TIP The default InDesign interface is fairly dark, so the screen shots in this chapter use a lighter interface setting (*Preferences > Interface > Medium Light*) to make it easier to see details in screen shots.

Figure 12.1 *Mini Bridge makes it easy to find graphics for placement into an InDesign layout.*

...and There's Bad Drag and Drop

Once you discover drag and drop, it's tempting to try it with everything. However, not all dragging and dropping (or copying and pasting) will produce usable results. For example, it's (unfortunately) possible to drag and drop directly from Adobe Photoshop into InDesign. Neither application prevents you from doing so, and you're given no warning that you might be dissatisfied with the results. But if you drag and drop directly from an open Photoshop file into an InDesign page (or copy image content in Photoshop and paste it into InDesign), there are unpleasant repercussions:

- The size of the image is added to the heft of the InDesign file. If you drag the contents of a 10 MB Photoshop file into an InDesign page, you've added 10 MB to the file size of the InDesign file.

- There is no information about the resolution or color space of the image in the InDesign Info panel.

- A dragged or pasted image has no connection to its Photoshop source. There's no entry in the InDesign Links panel, and no direct editability with the Edit Original options. Basically, it's an orphan. If the image later requires retouching or color correction, the image is not available to work with unless you still have the original somewhere. (In desperation, you can export the page to PDF with no compression or resampling, and then use the TouchUp Object tool in Acrobat to extract the image into Photoshop, but this is no way to live.)

So the time you think you're saving by dragging or pasting directly from Photoshop into InDesign isn't really time saved. Bluntly speaking, don't do it.

As for drag and drop or pasting from Adobe Illustrator, results are more reliable (although not perfect). The addition of dragged vector content doesn't cause a substantial increase in the size of an InDesign file, because of the svelte nature of vector art. But the dragged file is also an orphan, with no link back to the original Illustrator file.

It's important to note that if the Illustrator file contains transparency effects such as opacity settings or blending modes, those effects are *not* honored when artwork is dragged or pasted into InDesign. Shadows are converted to opaque images with no entry in the Links panel (like image content dragged from Photoshop), and any transparency effects and blending modes are lost. In short, the artwork does not faithfully represent the original.

Special circumstances, however, might motivate you to drag and drop from Illustrator into InDesign. If you want to create a complex shape to use as a container in InDesign for text or an image, you may find Illustrator's drawing tools more flexible than those in InDesign. When you copy content in Illustrator and paste it into InDesign, the vector content is fully editable with InDesign's vector tools; you may have to ungroup complex artwork to edit all components.

The File Handling & Clipboard preferences in Illustrator govern how dragged or copied Illustrator content behaves in other applications. The default setting in Illustrator CC and later ensures that Illustrator passes content through the clipboard correctly (**Figure 12.2**).

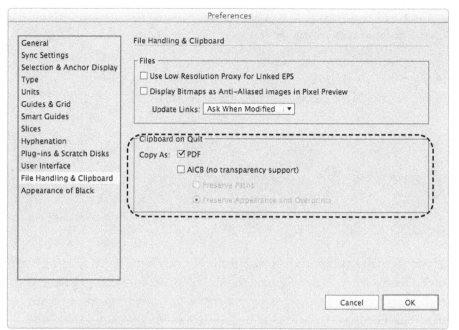

As long as you think of this as just allowing you to draw in Illustrator for ultimate use in InDesign, you won't be too disappointed by the loss of transparency and other attributes.

Embedding and Unembedding Graphics

By default, InDesign links to external files and only stores a proxy representation of the graphic in the page. However, InDesign will allow you to embed graphics in the page-layout file so that they are not externally stored.

Embedding can slow down performance by increasing the size of the InDesign file, and embedded images must be extracted for any color correction or retouching. A change to the original graphic file will have no effect on the embedded version, because it no longer has any relationship with the original. A high wind is not going to blow through your hard drive, peeling graphics out of your InDesign file.

There are points in favor of embedding: If you are collaborating by using InDesign Snippets, embedding graphics will ensure that the image content is also part of an exported Snippet. Otherwise, the Snippet contains only a

TIP An InDesign Snippet is just page geometry, extracted from a document and made portable. You might think of it as a free-range library item. To create a snippet, select a frame, multiple frames, or a group, and choose File > Export. In the Export dialog box, chose InDesign Snippet for the format.

To place a Snippet, just choose File > Place.

reference to a graphic. If your collaborators don't already have the graphic, they'll be faced with a missing link.

To unembed an image for editing, select its name in the Links panel and then choose Unembed File from the Links panel menu. InDesign will ask how you want to handle the unembedding (**Figure 12.3**).

Figure 12.3 *InDesign presents options for unembedding graphics, but the choices may seem confusing at first.*

The choices might not seem quite clear upon first (or second) reading. If you have a copy of the original graphics file, and you want to link to it rather than use the embedded version of the graphic, select Yes (meaning, "Yes, I have a copy of the graphic and I want to link to it rather than embedding it."). If you don't have the file, and you want InDesign to extract the embedded image and put the extracted image in a folder so you can link to it, select No (meaning, "No, I don't want to link to the original file. Well, I want to, but I can't. So please extract it.").

Updating Missing or Modified Graphics

The Links panel (**Figure 12.4**) allows you to see the current status of graphics (I'll explain more about that later) and information about them. If your document is part of an InCopy workflow, assigned stories will be listed in the Links panel. If you have opted to link to placed text or spreadsheet files, they will be listed here, too.

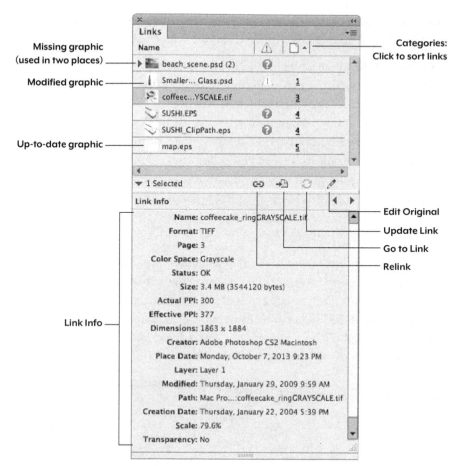

Missing graphic (used in two places)

Modified graphic

Up-to-date graphic

Categories: Click to sort links

Edit Original

Update Link

Go to Link

Relink

Link Info

Figure 12.4 *Click an entry in the top of the Links panel, and the Link Info area below displays everything you'd want to know about that graphic. You can completely customize the information shown in both compartments of the Links panel.*

The Links panel has two sections: The top compartment lists the linked files, followed by the page number where the graphic is used. The page number is blue and underlined, indicating that it's a hyperlink. Click the number to jump directly to that page.

If a graphic is used multiple times in the InDesign document, a triangle appears to the left of the name in the Links list, followed by a number in parentheses indicating how many times the graphic is used. Click the triangle to display the individual instances of the graphic.

The bottom compartment of the Links panel is the Link Info area, which displays extensive information about a selected file, including color space, actual PPI, creation and modification dates, and even the date the file was placed into the InDesign document. The only thing missing is the astrological sign (the selected link in Figure 12.4 is an Aquarius).

You can sort the Links panel list by clicking a category column head, and you can toggle the display in ascending or descending order by clicking a column head again. This can be helpful when you'd like to quickly highlight problems, such as low-resolution images. (Note, however, that InDesign cannot report on the resolution of EPS images, images embedded in or linked to a placed Illustrator file, or placed PDFs.) You can hide the Link Info compartment by clicking the small triangle just above the compartment. By the way, the correct name for this kind of control is "disclosure triangle." You can win points at a geek party by knowing obscure facts like that (or maybe you should go to better parties).

Choose Panel Options from the Links panel menu to customize the behavior of the Links panel. You can choose from Small, Regular, or Large row sizes, and you can select which types of information are displayed in each compartment of the Links panel. By default, only Name, Status, and Page are displayed in the top compartment, but you can expand this into "Too Much Information" mode by selecting additional options (**Figure 12.5**).

Figure 12.5 *You can customize the Links panel display by choosing Panel Options from the panel menu.*

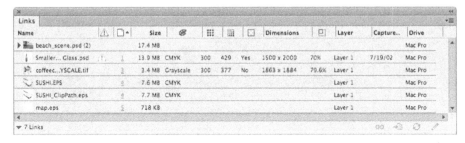

If linked graphics have been moved or renamed, InDesign can't find them and displays a red stop sign icon by the link name in the Links panel list. If a graphic has been modified and resaved with the same name, a yellow alert triangle is displayed by the link name. When you open an InDesign file containing missing or modified links, an alert gives you the option of updating links then (click the Update Links button in the alert) or deferring that until later (click the Don't Update Links button). If you've performed all the work and know the status of all the linked files, feel free to update all links automatically. But if you're collaborating on a file in a workgroup and you aren't familiar with all the bits and pieces, it's a good idea to defer updating so you can watch as graphics are updated. That way, you can make sure that there are no surprises, such as a recropped image or incorrect graphic with the same name.

Finding Missing Graphics

To find a missing graphic, select the link name in the Links panel list, and then choose *Relink* from the Links panel menu, or click the Relink button at the bottom of the panel (⊜ᵊ). Navigate to the graphic file and select it. Can't remember the filename? Just look up in the title bar of the Locate window as you search; it lists the complete directory path InDesign remembers, with the filename at the end of the string.

If you update a missing link, and other missing links are in the same directory, by default InDesign automatically updates all remaining links it finds in that directory (clearly, trying to be helpful). If you want to update one link at a time, glance down at the lower-left corner of the Locate dialog box, and uncheck the Search for Missing Links in This Folder option (**Figure 12.6**). The choice you make is sticky, so if you want to return InDesign to automatic update mode, recheck the option the next time you update missing links.

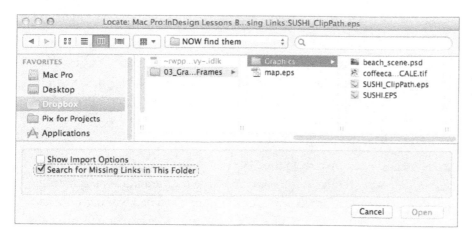

Figure 12.6 *By default, InDesign automatically updates all links in the same folder. Uncheck the Search for Missing Links in This Folder option to disable this behavior.*

Updating Modified Graphics

If you want to update a single modified link, click its entry in the Links panel list, and then select Update Link from the Links panel menu or click the Update Link button at the bottom of the Links panel (↻) to kick off the hunt. Only that link will be updated. If you want to update all modified links, Option-click (Mac) or Alt-click (Windows) the Update Link button.

Replacing Current Graphics

The Relink button is good for more than just finding missing graphics. It's also an easy way to replace an existing graphic with a new one (as opposed to starting over with *File > Place*). For example, if you've applied a special effect to an image in Photoshop and saved the enhanced image as an alternate version, you don't have to hide the previous image to convince InDesign to take the new one. Just click the Relink button and navigate to the replacement image. InDesign will update the image while retaining any transformations (such as cropping, scaling, or rotation) applied to the previous image.

Editing Graphics in Other Applications

InDesign offers several quick methods for opening graphics in their originating applications for editing. You can select the graphic in the Links panel and then click the Edit Original button ( ) at the bottom of the panel. Or you can select the graphic on the page and right-click (Control-click on the Mac) to display the context menu. The easiest route is to press the Alt key (PC) or the Option key (Mac) while double-clicking the graphic in the page. Regardless of the method you choose, InDesign awakens the original application and opens the graphic.

If you'd like to manually select the application to edit the graphic, right-click (Control-click on the Mac) on the graphic in the page and then choose Edit With from the context menu, and select the application from the Edit With menu. You can also select the link name in the Links panel and choose Edit With from the Links panel menu.

Make the necessary changes to the file in the original application, and then choose *File > Save*. Return to InDesign and the edited graphic is automatically updated, without so much as a click of a button. If you had manually opened the artwork, edited it, and then saved it, you'd also have to manually update the graphic through InDesign's Links panel. The Edit Original approach is a great time-saver.

Why Is My Graphic Opened by Mac OS X Preview?

The first time you choose Edit Original on the Mac, an image or vector graphic may be opened in Apple's Preview application rather than Photoshop or Illustrator. This is because the default file associations under OS X are set to open graphics in Preview.

The fix? You have to educate the operating system. Select a Photoshop native file (PSD) in any directory, then choose *File > Get Info*. From the *Open with* list (initially set to Preview), select Adobe Photoshop instead (**Figure 12.7**). If you have several versions of Photoshop installed, go for the newest version.

NOTE: You must click the Change All button for this to take effect for all Photoshop images. You'll also have to do this for all the popular graphics formats that you intend to open with Photoshop, including TIFF and JPEG. Find an AI file and connect it to Illustrator. And fix your PDF files so they'll be opened by Acrobat rather than by Preview.

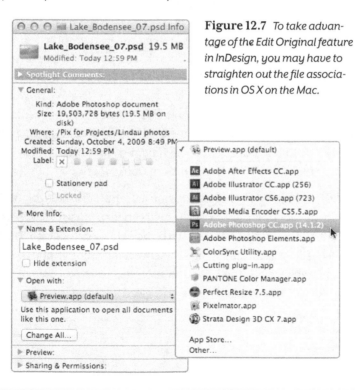

Figure 12.7 *To take advantage of the Edit Original feature in InDesign, you may have to straighten out the file associations in OS X on the Mac.*

Transforming Frames

There are multiple ways to scale frames containing graphics in InDesign. Select the frame with the Selection tool ( ). Then you can use the Free Transform tool ( ) to scale the frame and its contents. Or you can enter percentage values in the scale fields in the Control panel (**Figure 12.8**). You can also scale interactively by pressing Control+Shift (Windows) or Command+Shift (Mac) and then dragging on a corner of the frame.

Figure 12.8 *The Scale Percentage fields in the Control panel are linked. Type a value in the top field, press the Return or Enter key, and the bottom field is automatically populated with the proportional value.*

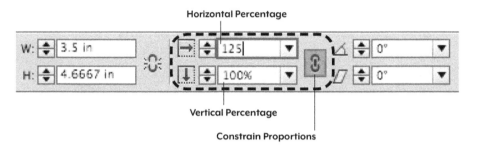

You may be surprised to learn that if you'd like to scale a graphic frame to a dimension and don't care to do the math, you can just enter the desired dimension in the Scale field. Really. For example, if you'd like to resize a 6.125-inch wide frame to 4 inches wide, just enter "4 in" in the Horizontal Percentage field. Because the horizontal and vertical Scale Percentage fields are, by default, linked together (unless you've unlinked them), press the Return (Mac) or Enter (PC) key and the height of the frame will also be scaled in proportion. It's much more fun than doing math.

Regardless of the method you employ to scale a graphic frame, you might be confused by the fact that the X/Y scale fields cheerily insist that the scale factor is still 100 percent when selected with the Selection tool ( ). However, if you select the graphic itself with the Direct Selection tool ( ) or click on the Content Grabber with the Selection tool, the Scale Percentage fields tell the whole story (**Figure 12.9**). What's going on?

Figure 12.9 *If the graphic is selected, the scale factor for the graphic (not the frame) is displayed in the Scale Percentage fields.*

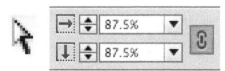

Scaling Graphics

It's important to realize that InDesign perceives a graphic and its frame as two distinct entities. When you select a frame with the Selection tool (🔺), you're addressing the whole shebang—frame and graphic together. When you select a graphic with the Direct Selection tool (🔺) or by using the Content Grabber (◎), you're speaking directly to the graphic itself. This is the only way to find the true scale factor of a graphic in the Control panel. But if you scale the whole shebang, why don't the X/Y scale fields reflect the new size? Why do they bounce back to 100 percent? I suppose it's InDesign's way of saying, "This is your new 100 percent." You'll just have to laugh it off, and ignore the scale fields unless you're using the Direct Selection tool.

If this drives you nuts (and it will), modify the Links panel options so that the Scale info appears in the Links panel, and just look there instead, while muttering under your breath.

If you wonder about the scale factor of an image because you're concerned about its resolution, just check the Effective Resolution entry in the bottom half of the Links panel. Then you don't have to worry about the scale factor; just keep an eye on the Effective Resolution value.

Using Native Files

InDesign extends its flexibility and efficiency by allowing you to use Photoshop (PSD), Illustrator (AI), and Acrobat (PDF) files as artwork. There's certainly nothing wrong with using old-fashioned TIFF and EPS files, but there are advantages to using native files, including the ability to maintain live transparency and manage layer visibility.

Photoshop Native Files (PSD)

It's not necessary to flatten Photoshop layered files before placing them in an InDesign page. In fact, unless a Photoshop file has reached an unwieldy size, there are compelling reasons *not* to flatten it because of the flexibility and editability you sacrifice when you flatten. Maintaining live layers means simplified housekeeping because there's no need to keep a separate working image file. But there are some situations that present challenges.

TIP The Content Grabber is meant to make it easier to select a graphic inside a frame, without requiring you to switch to the Direct Selection tool. But in very small frames, it can cause you to inadvertently move the graphic when you intend to move the frame. If you want to disable the Content Grabber, choose View > Extras > Hide Content Grabber.

There's still an easy way to select a graphic: double-click with the Selection tool to select the graphic. Double-click again to select the frame again.

TIP Be sure to save Photoshop PSD files with Maximum Compatibility turned on, both for compatibility with older (and future) versions of Photoshop, and for better performance in InDesign. This is the default setting.

Drop That Shadow

Photoshop, Illustrator, and InDesign make it easy to add drop shadows to objects, which is why you see shadows under everything these days. Tastefulness aside, InDesign and Illustrator create perfectly nice drop shadows that interact correctly with other elements in an InDesign page (**Figure 12.10**). As long as you want a simple concentric drop shadow, it's just one click away.

Figure 12.10 *If you just need a simple drop shadow, InDesign creates perfectly nice ones.*

NOTE A *drop shadow* is concentric to a shape. A *cast shadow* simulates a more realistic shadow being cast on another surface.

However, in some cases you may want to create a custom shadow in Photoshop, for a more realistic cast shadow effect. The one-click built-in shadow effects in Photoshop essentially repeat the shape of the parent object. But if you want to create the illusion of a shadow cast on another surface, you'll have to create a new layer, paint a shadow, and then set the shadow layer to Multiply so the shadow realistically darkens underlying content. As long as the shadow is interacting with other layers in Photoshop, this works fine.

But there's a limitation in the way InDesign handles shadows from Photoshop. As mentioned in Chapter 10, "Photoshop Production Tips," Photoshop's blending modes are ignored by InDesign. If the shadow falls on empty space, this doesn't matter. However, if the shadow needs to realistically darken other content beneath it in InDesign, it will require some special handling.

When you place a Photoshop image containing a custom shadow on top of other content already in InDesign (**Figure 12.11**), you'll have to use a workaround to allow the shadow to interact correctly with underlying elements. Because the Multiply blend mode applied to the shadow in Photoshop is not honored by InDesign, the Photoshop shadow is opaque, and it hides (rather than darkens) underlying elements in the page.

Figure 12.11 *Custom shadows created in Photoshop (left) need special handling when placed in an InDesign document, or they will not interact correctly with underlying elements in the page (right).*

Fortunately, InDesign provides a nifty workaround for this shadow shortfall: Object Layer Options. In the next section, you'll see how to solve this common dilemma.

Object Layer Options

The Object Layer Options dialog box (*Object > Object Layer Options*) allows you to selectively hide or display layers within a placed Photoshop file, native Illustrator file, placed InDesign file, or layered PDF, with nice possibilities for versioning and design flexibility. A layered file can be placed multiple times in an InDesign document, displaying a different combinations of layers.

You can choose to invoke Object Layer Options either when you import a graphic or after it's placed in the page. To invoke Object Layer Options on a placed graphic, select the object, and then choose *Object > Object Layer Options*. In the dialog box, you'll see a list of all the layers in the graphic; select which layers you want to display (**Figure 12.12**). If you've used Layer Comps in Photoshop, you can also select a Layer Comp state to display.

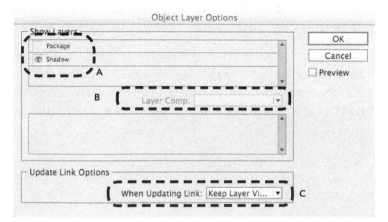

Figure 12.12 *Object Layer Options allow you to selectively show or hide layers within a Photoshop or PDF file (A). f you use Layer Comps in Photoshop, InDesign allows you to select them by name (B). The Update Link Options (C) determine what happens if you edit the image in Photoshop after placement.*

To correctly handle a manually created shadow like the example in **Figure 12.13**, you'll still have to duplicate the frame—one for the shadow and one for the silhouetted subject. But at least you only have to keep track of one image on disk with this method. Here's the recipe:

1. Place the image, and then copy the frame to the Clipboard.

2. With the frame still selected, choose *Object > Object Layer Options*. This frame will serve as the shadow. Turn off the visibility of all layers except the shadow layer. Set the blending mode of this frame to Multiply.

3. Choose *Edit > Paste in Place* to paste the Clipboard copy of the frame so the pasted copy lines up with the original.

4. With the newly pasted frame still selected, open Object Layer Options again. Hide the shadow layer. You may find it easier to deal with these two frames by dragging the sides of the topmost frame in a bit, so it's clear which is which. It's also a good idea to group the two related frames.

Figure 12.13 *Think of this process as creating a shadow sandwich. Start with a background (A). Then place the shadow image (B) and set its frame to Multiply in InDesign. Top it off with the silhouetted object (C) and you have the finished assembly (D).*

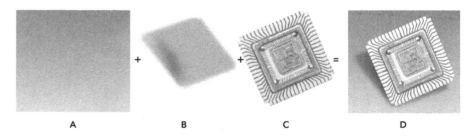

A   B   C   D

You can choose whether to keep InDesign's layer visibility overrides or start over when updating. The default is to retain the overrides you've applied in InDesign.

If you add, delete, or rename layers in the original file, InDesign starts over when you update, resetting the layer visibility to reflect the updated file's state. You receive an alert (**Figure 12.14**), and you have to reopen Object Layer Options to restore the custom visibility you previously set.

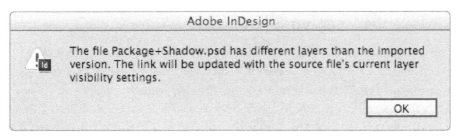

By default, InDesign does not provide hints in the Links panel that Object Layer Options have been used on a graphic. However, you can use the Links panel options to turn on the Layer Overrides category (**Figure 12.15**). InDesign displays "Yes" in that category for objects affected by Object Layer Options, followed by a number indicating how many layers are involved.

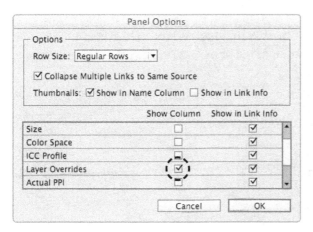

Figure 12.15 *Check the Layer Overrides category in the Links Panel Options dialog box and you'll be able to quickly determine which graphics are affected by Object Layer Options.*

To take advantage of InDesign's Object Layer Options feature, you have to save graphics files appropriately from other applications:

- Photoshop files must be saved as PSD files. Layers in TIFF files or Photoshop PDF files aren't recognized by InDesign.

- Illustrator files must be saved as native AI files; EPS files can't play.

- InDesign files are fine just as they are.

- PDF files must be saved with Acrobat 6 or later compatibility to contain layers. The layers are created from layers in the originating application, such as InDesign or Illustrator.

Illustrator Native Files (AI)

Transparency and blending modes in Illustrator AI files are fully honored by InDesign. Drop shadows created in Illustrator with the *Effect > Stylize > Drop Shadow* method will interact correctly with underlying elements in an InDesign page—unlike Photoshop's drop shadows. Illustrator objects with blending modes such as Multiply, Screen, or Darken will affect InDesign elements as expected: InDesign and Illustrator speak the same dialect when it comes to blending modes. You can also invoke Object Layer Options for an AI file. A native file can also be a somewhat smaller file than an EPS version of the same file, with no loss of data. Remember to leave the default Create PDF Compatible File option checked so the Illustrator file can be placed in InDesign (see Chapter 11, "Illustrator Production Tips").

If you add a drop shadow to a truly ancient EPS (say, Illustrator 8 or earlier), you may encounter a bug in the way the shadow is created (**Figure 12.16**). The fix is to resave the graphic as an AI file or as an EPS file with a TIFF preview.

Figure 12.16 *Drop shadows created for old EPS files have an unfortunate bug. If you add a drop shadow, it will display and print as if the shadow is following the containing frame (right). The answer? Resave the graphic as a native AI file—then the shadow displays and prints correctly.*

InDesign Files as Graphics

You can place one InDesign file into another as artwork. For example, ads submitted as InDesign files can be placed just as you'd place AI or PDF files. Just choose *File > Place* and import the InDesign file. Move it, scale it, and crop it as you would any artwork. The Links panel lists the InDesign file, along with any artwork linked to it (**Figure 12.17**). The artwork names are indented under the placed InDesign file-name to indicate their relationship.

Figure 12.17 *The Links panel lists any support art linked to a placed InDesign file. It's sort of like Russian nesting dolls.*

If you need to make changes, just right-click (Control-click on the Mac) on the placed InDesign file and choose Edit Original. The original InDesign file opens, you can make your edits and resave, and the placed file will be updated. If you need to edit artwork linked to (nested inside) the placed InDesign file, it takes an extra step; you can't Edit Original for artwork in a placed file. Instead, open the placed InDesign file via Edit Original, and then select the artwork within that file for editing. Save the modified artwork, update that InDesign file, and save. Return to the "parent" InDesign file and update the placed file. It sounds more complicated than it is in practice. Just think of it as double bagging.

When you package the job, all the bits and pieces will be gathered up, including the parent InDesign file and all its artwork and fonts, as well as the placed InDesign files and all their fonts and artwork; there's no need to package the placed files separately.

TIP You can't place the same InDesign file into itself. Think about it: If you changed the file, you'd invalidate the placed version, which would in turn invalidate the parent file, and so on. If you watch any science fiction at all, you already know this just wouldn't work. If you need to do this, use PDFs of the final InDesign pages instead.

PDF Files as Artwork

In general, you'll use PSD, AI, and TIFF files as graphic content, but there are times when a PDF is appropriate. For example, Photoshop PDFs contain transparency and true vector art (including text), whereas vector components in a PSD are rasterized when placed in InDesign (see Chapter 10, "Photoshop Production Tips").

Multipage PDFs can be placed one page at a time. Select Show Import Options when placing a PDF, and you can page through preview thumbnails to choose a single page, specify a range of pages, or choose the entire multipage PDF. If you choose multiple pages, your placement cursor changes appearance (⌐▨⌐), and each mouse click deposits a separate page of the PDF. To stop placing pages at any time, just click the Selection tool. You can click and drag to scale any page of the PDF as you place it.

As an alternative, you can use the PlaceMultipagePDF script (*Window > Utilities > Scripts*; the script is inside the Samples group), which automatically places each page of a PDF on a separate InDesign page. You can specify a starting page, but then all remaining pages of the PDF are placed at 100 percent, positioned in the upper-left corner of each target page. It's quite a time-saver if you need to pour in all the pages of a PDF.

Swatches

It may seem redundant that InDesign has a Color panel as well as a Swatches panel, but they serve different functions. Think of the Color panel as an informal mixing bowl for creating a color you'll apply only to a selected object. Colors created in the Color panel are not automatically stored in the Swatches panel—they evaporate. You can specify only CMYK, RGB, or Lab colors in the Colors panel. However, if you select an existing object colored with a spot color, the Colors panel does offer a quick method of creating a tint of the spot color.

In practice, it's best to create swatches rather than informal colors. In addition to allowing you to select from popular swatchbooks, the Swatches panel ensures that you have global control. Change the recipe for a swatch, and you change every object filled or stroked with the swatch. For information on the PANTONE PLUS system, see Chapter 2, "Ink on Paper," and Chapter 11, "Illustrator Production Tips."

If you've applied colors with the Color panel, you can easily turn those colors into official swatches without even hunting for the objects to which those colors have been applied. In the Swatches panel menu, choose *Add Unnamed Colors*, and InDesign finds them and adds them to the Swatches panel.

The Swatches panel can be a bit confusing (**Figure 12.18**). The colorful semaphore flags in the right column do not indicate whether a swatch is spot or process. Instead, those icons merely indicate the color mode used to generate the onscreen appearance of the swatch. It's the column with the dull gray icons that answers the question "spot or not?". A gray square indicates a process color (a swatch that will image in CMYK), regardless of the swatch name or the color mode indicated in the far-right column. A white square containing a gray circle—a spot—indicates a spot color.

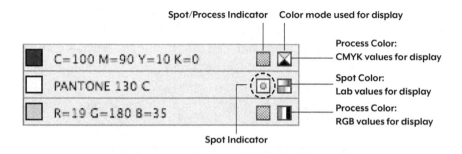

Figure 12.18 *The indicators in the Swatches panel can be confusing. Here's a decoder ring.*

RGB colors may drastically change appearance when converted to CMYK. If you're in a color-managed workflow, you may want to retain your RGB swatches but preview their conversion to CMYK. To do this, choose the appropriate color profiles in InDesign by choosing *Edit > Color Settings*. Choose *View > Proof Colors* to display content using the applied color profile.

If you're not in a color-managed workflow, and the print service provider requests that there be no RGB content, double-click the name of an RGB swatch, and then change its color mode to CMYK. Keep in mind that this conversion is governed by your current color settings, so use a color setting recommended (or provided) by your printer. Lacking that, use North America Prepress 2 and hope for the best.

NOTE You can use Adobe Bridge (available in the Apps & Services section Downloads of Creative Cloud) to synchronize the color settings across all your Creative Cloud applications. Just choose *Edit > Color Settings* in Bridge, choose the desired color setting, and click Apply.

What to Do About All Those Extra Swatches

Does this sound familiar? You're working on a job that should consist of CMYK plus one spot color, PANTONE 130. After importing duotone images created by your team's retouchers and placing the vector art provided by another designer, you realize that there are three spot colors in the Swatches panel—PANTONE 130 C, PMS 130 CVC, and something named Harvest Gold. Although we easily recognize that *PMS 130 CVC* and *PANTONE 130 C* refer to the same color (and we suspect that *Harvest Gold* does, too), a RIP sees the different names as indicating different inks and faithfully outputs them separately. Consequently, you need to take measures to ensure that only one spot-color plate — PANTONE 130 — is output. And you'll have to perform some detective work to find the culprits responsible for the extra spot colors.

To determine which artwork uses each spot color, you could print out separated prints if your desktop printer supports that feature (some non-PostScript devices don't). But this would require you to endure the printing process, waste half a tree, and get out of your chair and walk over to the printer. You could export to PDF and then use the Output Preview feature in Acrobat XI Professional, but that's an extra step. There's a much more efficient way to determine where the spot colors are being used. You can use the Separations Preview feature in InDesign. Choose *Window > Output Preview > Separations Preview*.

Initially, the Separations Preview panel (**Figure 12.19**) doesn't do anything special, until you choose Separations from its View menu. When you do, InDesign assumes you want to know as much as possible about your document, so it activates Overprint Preview, which in turn displays all graphics at high resolution. Consequently, in a document containing extensive graphics, you may experience slower performance.

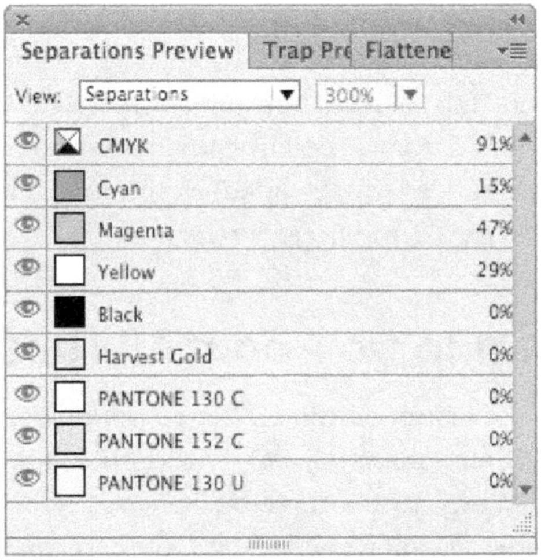

NOTE If you close the Separations Preview panel while it's set to Separations view or Ink Limit display, Overprint Preview and High Resolution Display remain in effect, which slows things down a bit. Before closing the Separations Preview panel, choose Off from the View menu. This turns off Overprint Preview and returns display performance to the setting in effect before you activated Separations Preview.

Figure 12.19 *The Separations Preview panel lets you selectively display individual or multiple printing plates. As you move your mouse over the page, the percentage value of each ink color is displayed in the right column. There's bad news here: It's a five-color job, so you'll have to resolve those three extra spot colors.*

Using the visibility controls in the left column of the Separations Preview panel, you can hide and display individual plates or combinations of plates. As you move your mouse over the document, the right column displays the percentage values of each ink. You can also view areas in excess of a total ink limit value by choosing the Ink Limit option from the Separations Preview panel menu. Enter the appropriate value (ask your print service provider) and InDesign highlights areas in violation of the specified value.

The Separations Preview feature may show you where most color problems are, but it can't *fix* the problems. To correct the problem, you could open all the images and vector artwork containing the incorrect color components and change them to use the correct inks. If you're under a tight deadline, you could instruct the print service provider to resolve the problem during output. Or you could be a hero and fix it in seconds by using the Ink Manager.

Ink Manager

The primary purpose of the Ink Manager (**Figure 12.20**) is to fix spot-color errors by remapping extraneous colors to correct inks. In this example, the job should only have one spot color, PANTONE 130 C. So the Ink Manager is used to remap the two problematic colors— PMS 130 CVC and Harvest Gold—to the correct PANTONE 130 C plate for output.

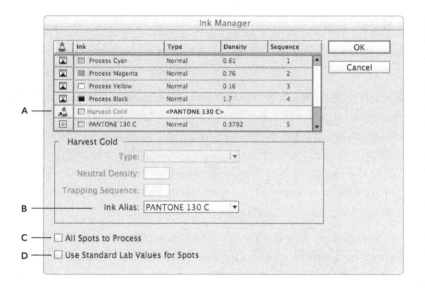

Figure 12.20 *The Ink Manager can remap an incorrect spot color (A) to the correct ink (B) by using what InDesign calls Ink Aliasing. With one click, you can designate all spot colors to image as CMYK builds (C). Selecting the Lab option (D) may provide more accurate onscreen approximation of spot colors. In a color-managed workflow, this option may provide more accurate rendering of spot colors in CMYK. However, this may not match output from previous versions of InDesign.*

You can launch the Ink Manager in several locations:

- Separations Preview panel menu

- Swatches panel menu

- Print dialog box (under Output)

- Export dialog boxes for both EPS (under Advanced) and Adobe PDF (under Output)

To map one spot color to another spot color (or to a process color) with the Ink Manager, select the spot color you want to remap. The dialog comes to life, offering you the Ink Alias list. Choose the correct color in the Ink Alias list and you're done. You can even remap a spot color to a single process plate—output the Harvest Gold on the magenta plate, for example. You cannot, however, map a process color to a spot color. But you can convert all spot colors to process with one click, by selecting the All Spots to Process check box in the Ink Manager dialog box.

The remapping function is nondestructive—the remapping takes place in the output stream as the file is printed or exported to another format such as EPS or PDF. It doesn't actually change placed graphics or any content created in the InDesign file, so it's easy to undo at any time if you make the wrong choices. Just turn off the Ink Alias for an ink, or deselect the Spots to Process option in the Ink Manager dialog box.

Changes made in the Ink Manager are not reflected in the Swatches panel, which may unnerve you. But there's a certain logic to this. Because you haven't actually changed content, the Swatches panel doesn't feel compelled to change its display. But rest assured that any output, whether it's an export to EPS or PDF, or the results of *File > Print*, will contain only the correct inks. You can confirm this by reopening the Separations Preview panel for a correct view of all process and spot-color usage.

If you're sending native InDesign files to the print service provider rather than submitting PDF files, it's a good idea to inform them that you have already rectified the spot-color issues with the Ink Manager, lest they freak out unnecessarily ("Is this a 15-color job?!").

Colorizing Images

InDesign allows you to colorize grayscale and bi-level (black and white, with no shades of gray) TIFF and PSD files to create simplistic monotone effects. Colorizing is a quick-and-dirty way to apply color to images with the ability to change your mind late in the game.

There are two ways to colorize images in InDesign. Select the image by clicking with the Direct Selection tool ( ), and then choose the swatch. Alternatively, you can just drag a swatch on top of the image (but, counter-intuitively, the frame must *not* be selected first), and then release the mouse button. The swatch is then applied to the image, not the frame.

If you want to create a true duotone, it's preferable to use Photoshop, where you have complete control over the mixing of inks. But if you're in a hurry or don't care about the refined controls in Photoshop, InDesign allows you to create what's often called a *fake duotone*. First, colorize the image using one of the methods above, and then apply another swatch to the frame itself. The frame color will show through the lighter areas of the image in the frame. (Warning—this has the potential to be truly ugly.) For somewhat more duotone-like results, select the image with the Direct Selection tool ( ) and then, using the controls in the Transparency panel, apply the Multiply blend mode to the image itself. This offers the advantage of allowing you to change the applied color quickly without having to rework the image in Photoshop and update it in InDesign.

Note that grayscale TIFF and PSD files with transparency on the bottom layer cannot be colorized by InDesign. All other layers can contain transparency, but the bottom layer cannot. InDesign does not give you any warning or explanation when you try to colorize such an image—it just doesn't do anything.

Alternate Layouts

Although the Alternate Layouts feature in InDesign CC is geared toward the creation of digital layouts for tablet devices such as the Apple iPad, it's a life-saver if you have to create print documents at multiple sizes—for example, a letter-size piece for use in the United States and an A4 version for European distribution.

Liquid Layout Tools

The true engine of the alternate-layout process is a set of options called the Liquid Layout tools (**Figure 12.21**), available under *Window > Interactive*.

Figure 12.21 *The Liquid Layout tools govern the rules used by InDesign when you create an alternate layout.*

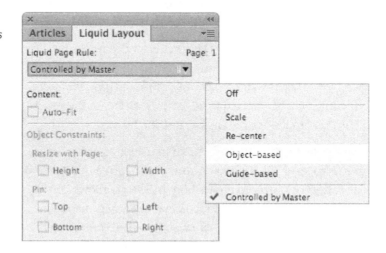

TIP Liquid Layout controls aren't just for alternate layouts. If you need to resize a document, use the Liquid Layout rules to control how page content will respond, then change the dimensions of the document by choosing *File > Document Setup*. Although you will probably have to fine-tune the results, it's more fun than starting from scratch.

The Liquid Layout rules are specified on a spread-by-spread basis (unless you elect to set a Liquid Layout option for the master page and invoke that):

- **Scale:** Page content scales in an attempt to match the new dimensions of the layout.

- **Re-center:** Page content is centered on the new layout without scaling.

- **Object-based:** Scaling and pinning are specified for each object.

- **Guide-based:** Special guides allow the objects they touch to resize horizontally, vertically, or both.

The most granular (and thus most tedious) approach is to use the Object-based Liquid Page Rule (**Figure 12.22**).

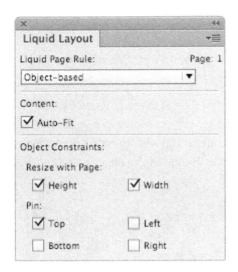

Figure 12.22 *The Object-based Liquid Page Rule allows you to specify object behavior when a new layout is created. You can control whether graphics will scale and how their frames will relate to the page edge.*

Generating the Alternate Layout

After you have established the Liquid Layout rules to be used, create the alternate layout by selecting *Create Alternate Layout* from the Pages panel menu. In the dialog box that follows, specify the dimensions of the new layout (**Figure 12.23**).

NOTE You're not limited to just one alternate layout—InDesign allows you to create as many as you want.

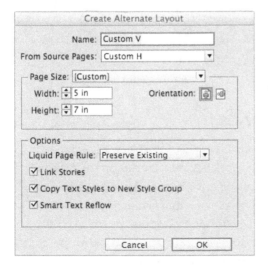

Figure 12.23 *In the Create Alternate Layout dialog box, specify the dimensions of the new layout, the Liquid Page Rules, and whether to link stories from the original layout.*

If the initial layout is vertical (for example, a portrait orientation letter page), InDesign assumes that you intend to create a horizontal alternate layout.

NOTE If you've ever used Section Starts for page numbering control (for example, numbering front matter with lowercase Roman numerals while using Arabic numerals for the remainder of the document), just know that alternate layouts are actually a type of section. All the pages are still part of the same document.

This is because the Alternate Layout feature's origins lie in converting documents for digital publishing devices, such as a rotating tablet display. Of course, you can enter any dimensions you wish, up to InDesign's maximum page size, which is a whopping 18 feet by 18 feet.

The new layout is displayed in the Pages panel next to the original layout (**Figure 12.24**). Here's a little secret: These two layouts happily coexist in the same file because they're actually just layout sections of the same document. But InDesign displays alternate layouts side by side in the Pages panel to represent the way you tend to think of them.

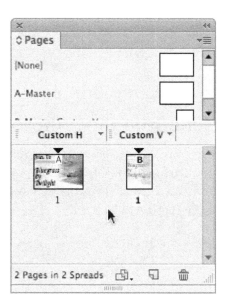

Figure 12.24   *The alternate layout, Custom V, is displayed next to the original layout, Custom H. InDesign is also kind enough to generate a new master page to govern the new layout.*

Managing Linked Stories

TIP Those tiny yellow triangles can be hard to see in the layout, so you may find it easier to track and update modified text by using the Links panel. If you don't want to see the yellow warning icons, turn them off under View > Extras > Hide Link Badge.

Because the individual layouts are related parts of a project, InDesign is polite enough to automatically form a link between stories on the original "parent" layout and their descendants on any alternate layouts. This is especially helpful when you change text on the original layout; instead of having to manually update text on all the subsidiary layouts, you can rely on InDesign to treat them in much the same way it treats modified graphics. A yellow triangle appears on any related text frames in alternate layouts, indicating that the original text has changed (**Figure 12.25**).

Figure 12.25 *The yellow triangle on the text frame in an alternate layout indicates that the text in the "parent" frame on the original layout has changed. You can update the text by clicking the triangle.*

Click the yellow indicator to update the text, and the layouts are now in sync (**Figure 12.26**).

Figure 12.26 *There's no need to manually track text updates across the layouts—let InDesign do the heavy lifting for you.*

Miscellaneous Document Tips

These short topics are just little factoids that you need to know about; they're not all pitfalls—some, like Automatic Recovery, are actually good news.

IDLK Files

When you have an open InDesign document, there is an additional file with a similar name that magically appears in the same location as the file you have open. For example, if you have opened a file named *Chapter_1.indd*, you'll see a companion file named *~chapter_1~p965so.idlk* in the same location. The tilde (~) in front of the name and the file extension .idlk tell you that this is an InDesign lock file. Its purpose is to prevent multiple users from simultaneously opening an InDesign file across a network. Instead, they'll see an alert informing them that they do not have permission to open the document.

Don't delete .idlk files—InDesign cleans up after itself. The files will evaporate when you save and close the file. If InDesign should crash while a document is open, it won't have time to delete the .idlk file, but just leave it anyway. InDesign will take care of the housekeeping the next time you open, save, and then close the file.

Automatic Recovery

As you work, InDesign keeps track of what you're doing; without impeding performance, it keeps a private version of your working file. This is the same mechanism that gives you unlimited undo capability, which can really be quite a lifesaver.

If your system crashes for any reason—power outage, system crash—let InDesign recover as much of your document as it can. Resist the panicked urge to reopen your original file. Instead, relaunch InDesign and marvel as your document reappears. You may lose the last few things you did, but you won't lose everything you did in that session. That's because InDesign keeps your most recent operations stored so you can quickly undo, and it may not have time to write those to disk as it crashes. But it's better than losing the whole shebang. You can't turn off Automatic Recovery—and why would you want to? You can change where InDesign keeps the recovery information by choosing *Preferences > File Handling* and selecting a directory.

Going Back in Time

If you need to save an InDesign CC document for use in InDesign CS4 or later, you must export or save an InDesign Markup Language file (.idml).

It's not ideal to collaborate with someone who isn't using the same version of software that you are, but sometimes it's unavoidable; this caveat is not limited to InDesign.

- Some content created in InDesign CC, such as alternate layouts, won't have an equivalent in CS4.

- If the file is saved in CS4 and then reopened in CC, special features are not reinstated. If your document contains such features, consider the IDML procedure as a one-way trip.

- It's not a bad idea to include a PDF of the document with the IDML file so that your recipient can double-check the content.

Reducing File Size

InDesign files are fluffy by nature; it's just a fact of life. But you can economize a bit by performing a *File > Save As* at the end of the job. When you just choose *File > Save*, InDesign appends any new data to the existing file on disk. It's faster than rewriting the entire contents of the file, but it results in a larger file size. However, when you choose *File > Save As*, InDesign completely rewrites the file and does a bit of housecleaning. As a result, you should see a reduction in file size, especially in a document with a lot of large graphics. For example, the file for this chapter had ballooned to 13.4 MB. Performing a Save As reduced that to 8.4 MB. Enormous disk capacities have made us lax about taking up space — (I have a 1 TB hard drive. Why should I ever throw anything away?), but you may find that document performance improves as a result of using Save As instead of Save.

Let It Bleed

When you create a new InDesign document, you're given the option to create a dedicated bleed zone. In the New Document dialog box, click the triangle to the left of Bleed and Slug (**Figure 12.27**). Entering a value in the Bleed fields does more than just provide spiffy red bleed guides. It earmarks a special bleed area so you can easily invoke it with one click when you print or export the file.

Figure 12.27 *Click the triangle next to Bleed and Slug to set these parameters. Creating a dedicated bleed area in this manner makes it easy to invoke bleed as you print or export.*

If you forgot to designate the official bleed area when you created the document, you can still do so at any time by choosing *File > Document Setup*. When the Use Document Bleed Settings check box is selected and you've extended page elements into the bleed area, you will get the desired result during output.

It's important to note that InDesign makes a distinction between this *official* bleed area and any bleed you *manually* create by extending frames beyond the trim edge of the page, and this fact can bite you. During print or output, if you select *Use Document Bleed Settings*, InDesign looks for the dedicated bleed value entered in the Bleed options fields of the Document Setup dialog box. If you haven't entered values in these fields, InDesign sees a zero value and obligingly gives you zero bleed. So keep an eye on the bleed value fields; don't just blindly click the Use Document Bleed option.

Checking Out of the Library

InDesign libraries are a great way to have a ready repository of commonly used elements, including text, graphics, and page geometry. These elements can then be quickly dragged into a page without having to re-create them each time. Libraries can be stored locally or on a server (although they must be locked on a server for multiple users to have access).

If you're missing graphics that are required by the library content, you get no warning when you open the library. For example, if you place an image in a page and then drag the image frame to the library, the library entry represents the geometry of the frame and the directory path of the image in the frame at the time it was placed in the library. If you subsequently delete that image from your hard drive or server, the library doesn't warn you that it contains obsolete content.

However, when you drag an obsolete library item onto a page, it appears as a gray frame with no graphic content, which is your hint that there's nobody home. One workaround for this dilemma is to embed the graphic in InDesign before dragging it to the library. In the Links panel, select the link name, and then select Embed File from the Links panel menu. Then you can safely drag the graphic or a group containing it to the Library panel. When you drag the library item onto another page, the embedding is maintained, and there's no need to hunt for the original artwork. One caveat: Embedding is most appropriate for small artwork because embedding increases the InDesign file size by the amount of the graphic. Embed a 2 MB image in an InDesign file and you have increased the InDesign document size by 2 MB. Do this for 20 images in a document and—well, you get the idea.

Getting Smart

Neatness counts in page layout; that's why we have ruler guides and measurement readouts to four decimal places in the Control panel. But with Smart Guides, you may find that you can forget about creating ruler guides but still keep your ducks (well, objects) in a row.

Smart Guides

The gray "flag" containing measurement information appears when you create a frame (**Figure 12.28**). At first it may seem annoying, but you quickly learn to ignore it if you don't need its information. When you create a frame near an existing frame, Smart Guides really shine: Subtle green arrows indicate when you've matched the height and width of a nearby frame. It's more intuitive than it sounds, and you'll soon grow fond of the guidance system.

Figure 12.28 *Smart Guides display width and height values, as well as subtle dimension hints to tell you when you've created a new object that aligns with an existing object. They even indicate when you've created an object of the same height and width as a nearby object.*

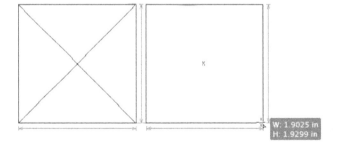

As you're positioning objects in the page, subtle Smart Guides appear to let you know when you've arrived at the center of the page, or when the center of the object you're dragging aligns with the center of a nearby object. The Smart Guides aren't overwhelming; they're polite, not pushy.

Smart Guides can even help you rotate a frame to match the angle of an adjacent frame: Angle indicators appear in both frames when you've hit the mark (**Figure 12.29**).

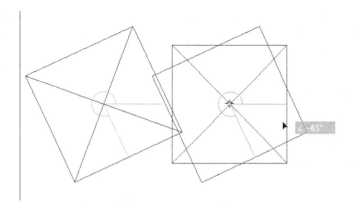

Figure 12.29 *Smart Guides indicate when you've rotated an object to the same angle as a nearby object.*

Smart Spacing

As you position objects near other objects, the Smart Spacing indicators kick in. If you want to position objects in a row so they are equal distances apart, of course, you can use the Distribute controls in the Align panel (*Window > Object & Layout > Align*). But the Smart Spacing indicators are more fun because they appear while you are positioning objects: When they show that the object is properly positioned, release the mouse button (**Figure 12.30**).

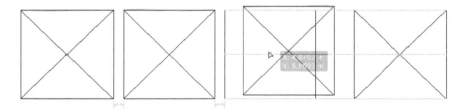

Figure 12.30 *Smart Spacing indicators let you know when you've positioned an object so that its distance from an adjacent object is equal to spacing between nearby objects. This can actually be entertaining.*

Smart Guide Preferences

To turn Smart Guides on or off, choose *View > Grids & Guides > Smart Guides*. A check by Smart Guides means they're turned on; choose it again to toggle Smart Guides off. You can control the behavior and appearance of Smart Guides in Preferences, under Guides & Pasteboard. By default, the Smart Guide indicators are Grid Green, but you can change the color of Smart Guides, selecting from a list that includes Lipstick and Cute Teal (who says software engineers don't have a sense of humor?).

You can also turn on or off the Align to Object Center, Align to Object Edge, Smart Dimensions, and Smart Spacing options, although you may want to leave these options on.

Smart Text Reflow

While it isn't part of the Smart Guide arsenal, Smart Text Reflow is, well, smart. It allows InDesign to add new pages when a threaded story is threatened with overset text. By default, Smart Text Reflow only works with text frames based on master page text frames, but you can change that in *Preferences > Type*. For Smart Text Reflow to become activated, your last text frame must be threaded to at least one other text frame (on a preceding page). If you're working in a long document, it might take a few seconds for the new page to be created and the text to be threaded to a new frame on the page. For those few seconds, you may see an error in the Preflight status indicator at the lower-left corner of the document window, but be patient; that will pass.

NOTE When transparency was first introduced way back in InDesign 2.0, it was challenging for printers to process. Those days are long gone; modern workflows have no issue with transparent content.

Transparency

InDesign's ability to create transparency effects has great appeal for designers. It's easy to make objects translucent, feather the edges of vector components, and add drop shadows to anything. But the introduction of transparency in InDesign 2.0 caused printers to grumble. The short story is that transparency effects, such as blend modes and opacity settings, use an imaging model that goes beyond what PostScript understands. And because PostScript has long been the native tongue of imagesetters, platesetters, and many of our desktop printers, this presents a challenge.

Although the increasing use of the Adobe PDF Print Engine and other RIP engines that support transparency in output devices solves transparency issues, not all devices are using the PDF Print Engine yet. Large commercial printers stay up to date on technology, but if you're sending your work to a smaller shop or to a printer in another country, you may be asked to submit a PDF with *flattened transparency*. In the flattening process, InDesign converts new-fangled transparency content to a form that can be correctly handled by PostScript devices.

Flattening occurs during any of the following procedures:

- Choosing *File > Print* and then selecting a desktop printer or PostScript file as the target.

- Choosing *File > Export* and then selecting the EPS format.

- Choosing *File > Export* to create a PDF and then selecting Acrobat 4 (PDF 1.3) compatibility.

Transparency Flattening

Nothing within InDesign is flattened by Transparency Flattening. Your layers remain intact, and all transparency effects are still live. Instead, it's the output stream that is flattened. Content is cut apart, re-created, and reassembled in a form acceptable to crotchety old PostScript devices (**Figure 12.31**). And this jigsaw puzzle will image as you expect—if you provide the correct ingredients and the right recipe.

Figure 12.31 *During print or export, InDesign deconstructs transparent objects, creating opaque stunt doubles (right) that look like the original effect. Note where the glass cup interacts with text: A text-shaped clipping path is created, which contains a generated image to portray the color interaction of the cup with the text.*

Taking some relatively simple precautions when you build a document containing transparency will ensure that it produces predictable results when flattened and processed by a PostScript RIP. And there are some changes that print service providers must make to correctly handle transparent content. The following sections present some best practices for handling transparency as you create documents.

Put Text on Top

When text and vector elements fall beneath transparent elements in InDesign, those elements may be rasterized or converted to outlines during printing or exporting. Bring text and vector elements to the top of the pile and they'll be safe from rasterization (well, until they hit the RIP). Putting such elements at the top of the stacking order within a layer should be sufficient. But it's not a bad idea to think in layers, just as a reminder of the issue (**Figure 12.32**).

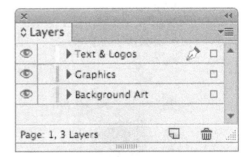

Figure 12.32 *Placing text and vector art on a topmost layer ensures that such content will not be rasterized as a result of interaction with transparent content.*

Choose the Appropriate Transparency Blend Space

As InDesign flattens transparent overlapping objects, it must create new objects to replace the overlap area (**Figure 12.33**). While this may sound like extra work, it's necessary as part of creating an output file that PostScript understands. To create the most faithful color in the replacement area, InDesign looks to the Transparency Blend Space setting to determine how it should do the color math. To control the Transparency Blend Space settings, choose *Edit > Transparency Blend Space*.

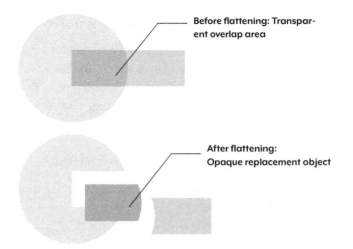

Before flattening: Transparent overlap area

After flattening:
Opaque replacement object

Figure 12.33 *It's easy to create interesting effects using opacity settings and blend modes (top, before flattening). During the transparency-flattening process, InDesign creates replacement objects for overlapping areas (bottom, after flattening).*

The default setting for Transparency Blend Space is CMYK, and you should leave it that way for print. When generating a PDF for the Web or an onscreen presentation, you can reduce file size by choosing a PDF preset such as Smallest File Size, which uses the RGB color space. In that situation, change the Transparency Blend Space to RGB in keeping with the fact that content will become RGB in the outgoing PDF. This will result in a more satisfactory rendering of the color in overlapped areas in the resulting PDF.

Is Flattening Required?

Because modern imaging workflows intelligently handle transparency effects, it's likely that you will *not* be asked to provide a PDF with flattened transparency: the Great Transparency War of 2001 is over. Enlightened printers can accept the PDF/X-4 format, which allows both RGB content and live transparency (we live in wonderful times).

But don't assume—always ask the printer for the preferred PDF presets to ensure that your job will be correctly handled.

Choose the Appropriate Transparency Flattener Preset

As InDesign performs flattening, it needs a recipe for generating two important components—rasterized text and vector art, and soft-edged effects. That recipe is contained in the Transparency Flattener Preset (**Figure 12.34**). Before we discuss appropriate flattener settings, it's helpful to consider some of the functions that take place during flattening.

Figure 12.34 *Transparency flattener presets are invoked during output or export to govern the generation of shadows and feathered effects. They also govern any necessary rasterizing of text and vector art. The default flattener presets in InDesign are only a starting point. Custom presets are necessary for proper imaging.*

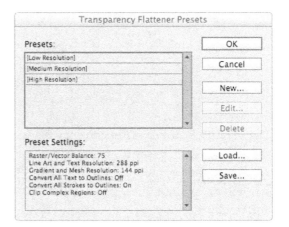

Rasterizing Text and Vector Content

The interaction of transparent images with text and vector art is one of the most challenging combinations to image. Text and vector content must sometimes be rasterized during export or output to satisfy PostScript requirements. While it may be disturbing to hear the words rasterize and text in the same sentence, rasterizing text is not inherently a bad thing (you are no doubt gasping in distaste as you read this). In truth, this rarely happens in InDesign documents during export or print currently, but it's still helpful to know the rules.

But consider this: Your text and vector content will be rasterized eventually when it is processed by a RIP—a raster image processor. The RIP ultimately converts everything to pixels but at such a high resolution that pixels are not apparent in the output. So it isn't the rasterization process itself that's problematic. It's the choice of incorrect resolution during rasterization that can lead to undesirable results.

Similarly, when you scan signatures, maps, or drawings, you set the scanning resolution to a high value, such as 1200 ppi, to smoothly render drawn lines. Pixels are not apparent in the final artwork because of the high resolution. See? Pixels aren't a problem, as long as the resolution of an image is sufficient to fool the eye into seeing a smooth line.

Generating Shadows and Feathered Edges

All those festive drop shadows you're tempted to create in InDesign must be expressed in pixels. Similarly, feathering effects (*Object > Effects > Basic Feather*) applied to InDesign objects and placed artwork are also accomplished with pixels. The feather and drop shadow aren't literal pixels until you export or print—they're just live effects for display until output makes them real. And the resolution of those effects is determined by the flattener preset chosen at the moment of export or print.

Appropriate Flattener Settings

To create and edit flattener presets, choose *Edit > Transparency Flattener Presets*. The dialog box offers three default flattener presets, but because you're creating content for print, the Low and Medium Resolution settings are fairly useless. To create a worthwhile flattener preset for print, select the High Resolution option as a starting point, and then click New.

The two key values in the Transparency Flattener Preset Options dialog box are Line Art and Text Resolution, and Gradient and Mesh Resolution. There isn't a one-size-fits-all transparency flattener setting. The settings should be dictated by the resolution of the output device.

The Line Art and Text Resolution option governs the rasterization of text and vector content. It should equal the resolution of the output device. For example, if you're printing to a desktop printer with a resolution of 600 ppi, set the Line Art Resolution to 600 ppi. On the other hand, a prepress technician preparing to generate PostScript for a 2400 ppi imagesetter would choose 2400 ppi, and so on. If you're creating PDF/X-1a files to send to a print service provider, ask them to give you specific instructions for creating a flattener preset. Be concerned if your contact responds, "Oh, I don't know. Just make a PDF." Push your way past that person and ask to speak to a prepress technician for guidance.

The Gradient and Mesh Resolution value governs the generation of drop shadows and soft feathered edges created in InDesign. A prepress technician would usually choose 300 ppi for general output, although lower resolutions might be sufficient for low line-screen jobs such as newspaper work.

If you're printing to your 600 ppi desktop printer, 150 ppi is probably a sufficient gradient setting for printing comps. By the way, this setting has no effect on the resolution of placed images—only on the shadows and feathered edges generated by InDesign (**Figure 12.35**).

Figure 12.35 *Flattener options should be in keeping with the resolution of the output device. For output on an imagesetter or platesetter, a typical setting might be 2400 ppi for line art and 300 ppi for gradients.*

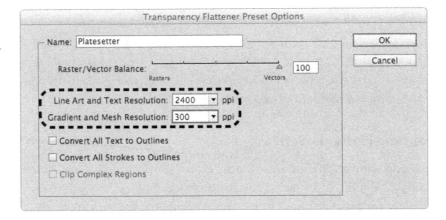

For a desktop printer with an imaging resolution of 600 ppi, the line-art resolution should be 600. Setting the gradient resolution to 150 may save a little time in the printing process.

Invoking Transparency Flattener Presets

Although you may have created custom flattener presets, they don't actually do anything until you invoke them during print or export. You'll need to pick the proper flattener preset when you print, export an EPS, or generate a PDF with Acrobat 4 compatibility (**Figure 12.36**). Flattener presets are located in the Advanced section of Print and Export dialog boxes.

Figure 12.36 *When exporting a PDF with Acrobat 4 compatibility, such as PDF/X-1a, select the appropriate flattener preset in the Advanced section of the Print and Export dialog boxes.*

Chances are, you'll be invoking flattener presets in one of two situations—printing to your desktop printer or generating PDFs for submission to the print service provider. Revisit Figure 12.35 to see suggested settings for both of those situations: Your actual settings will depend on output resolution. We'll wait here while you look up your desktop printer resolution or while you're on hold, waiting to talk to a technician in the print service provider's prepress department so you can inquire about their RIP resolution.

Special Case: Spot Color Content

In addition to performing the jigsaw trickery of flattening during output or export, InDesign instructs some components to *overprint* in order to output objects using blending modes such as Multiply.

What is overprint? Here's a simple example: Create a solid yellow square, and then place a solid cyan circle on top of the yellow square. The cyan circle knocks out (covers up) the portion of the yellow square underneath it, because shapes are usually opaque in graphics programs (and PostScript reality). Like pieces of construction paper, they completely cover up anything underneath them.

However, if you set the cyan circle to *overprint*, it's no longer opaque. It allows the yellow square underneath to show through, and the overlap area becomes green (cyan plus yellow, as shown in **Figure 12.37**).

Figure 12.37 *By default, opaque shapes knock out everything underneath (left). Overprinting allows a shape to intermix with everything underneath (right).*

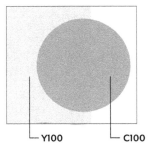
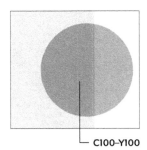

Overprint is not a complicated concept, and it's been part of PostScript forever. InDesign counts on the RIP and other applications to understand overprint in order to properly image transparency effects. If you display a flattened PDF containing a drop shadow (or other transparency effects) on top of spot-color areas in Acrobat, you'll be alarmed to see that the shadow has disappeared. Don't panic: Just turn on Overprint Preview in Acrobat and the display will be correct.

Yucky Discolored Box Syndrome (YDBS)

When you print a file containing transparency effects to your desktop printer, even something as seemingly innocent as a simple drop shadow can cause what I've come to call Yucky Discolored Box Syndrome. Where the area of the shadow overlaps underlying content, a rectangular discolored area mars the output (**Figure 12.38**).

Figure 12.38 *The area around the white circle (left) should contain only the shadow and the underlying darker rectangle. The square discolored area (right) results from the fact that some desktop printers (and even some larger digital devices) handle the color rendering of image content and vector content differently.*

Apparently, this occurs because as the content is RIPped, the image content and vector content are color managed differently. High-end RIPs (such as those for platesetters) don't have this issue. The solution is to rasterize everything, so the same color, management treatment is applied to all content. Here's the easy way to do it in InDesign.

First, create a custom Transparency Flattener preset. Then, for print, follow these steps:

1. Choose *Edit > Transparency Flattener Presets*, click on High Resolution as a starting point, and then click New.

2. In the ensuing dialog box, drag the raster/vector slider all the way to the left. Set the linework resolution to the printer's resolution (for example, 600), and set the Gradient and Mesh Resolution to 150.

3. Save as a new flattener preset.

4. Choose *Edit > Transparency Blend Space*, and choose CMYK for most toner-based printers. Choose RGB for most inkjet printers.

5. Choose *File > Print*, and under Output, choose Composite CMYK (or RGB, depending on document content).

6. Check Simulate Overprint.

7. Under Advanced, select your new all-raster flattener preset.

Note that since you're printing Composite, spot colors are converted to CMYK (but this is for a desktop printer anyway).

For export to PDF (when you know the PDF will be printed on an in-house device that is prone to YDBS):

1. Export to PDF/X-1a using that new flattener preset. Spot colors remain spot.

2. Print from Acrobat, and no Yucky Discolored Box. In Acrobat, you can see what's going on by turning Simulate Overprint off and on; it's all in puzzle pieces, using overprint to maintain correct appearance.

Drop Shadows: The Sun Never Moves

In the real world, if you rotate a box sitting on a table, the shadow doesn't rotate with the box because the light source remains stationary. The same rules apply in InDesign; its imaginary sun doesn't move either. If you rotate objects, their shadows do not rotate with them. In home-brewed imposition, a shadow's relationship with its parent object will change. In **Figure 12.39**, the SmithcoMatic logo is supposed to have a drop shadow that's positioned down and to the right of the logo. However, rotating the art 180 degrees causes the shadow to be positioned up and to the left of the art. This is because, while the object rotates, the shadow doesn't rotate.

Figure 12.39 *This looks fine, doesn't it? Try standing on your head and you'll see what's wrong with this picture: The shadow's relationship with the logos is incorrect in the rotated artwork.*

The only cure is to manually change the position of the shadow by choosing *Object > Drop Shadow*, and then entering a new value for the shadow position (**Figure 12.40**). In the example, the correct shadow position is 0.0972 inch for both X and Y offsets. To correct for the rotation, the shadow for the rotated artwork is set to -0.0972 inch for both X and Y offsets (that's a minus sign in front of the number, indicating a negative value).

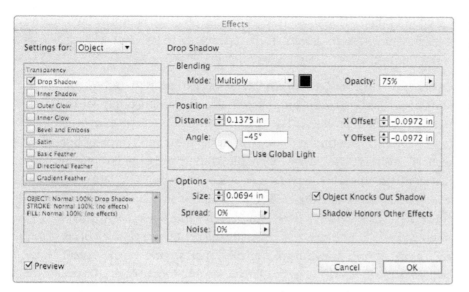

Figure 12.40 *To compensate for InDesign's single-sun approach to drop shadows, you may have to alter the X and Y Offset values for rotated objects (for example, during manual imposition).*

Finding and Fixing Problems

InDesign provides a number of tools that are useful when you're playing "What's wrong with this picture?" before you send your job to the print service provider. Several tools help you spot problems visually, and the new Live Preflight feature can alert you to problems the instant they arise.

Forensic Tools

However careful you might be while you're creating an InDesign document, it's easy to develop blind spots when you're trying to find mistakes. Let InDesign help you find problems that are easy to overlook.

Preview Mode (*View > Screen Mode > Preview*) simplifies your view of the document, hiding any nonprinting objects such as guides, frame edges, and hidden text characters so that you can concentrate on content and design. You can toggle the Preview mode among four states: Normal, Preview, Bleed, and Slug. But you can easily toggle between the two most common states, Normal and Preview, just by pressing the W key on your keyboard. In addition to simplifying your view, Preview mode will hide any images or other elements that have been assigned a nonprinting attribute in the Attributes panel

(*Window > Output > Attributes*). If you've set an object to Nonprinting while you experiment with your design, its disappearance in Preview mode serves as a reminder to change the attribute or delete the object.

Overprint Preview (*View > Overprint Preview*) can be used to confirm that you've set objects to overprint. But perhaps more importantly, you can use it to catch common problems. For example, white objects set to overprint will disappear during output and they'll disappear during Overprint Preview as well. Why is this? The color white in illustration and page-layout applications just signifies "this is blank paper—no ink prints here." The rare exception would be a literal white ink created for printing on metallic surfaces or clear substrates. What kind of a fiend would set a white object to overprint? Oh, nobody does it intentionally. It's usually the result of creating a black object, such as a logo, in a drawing program and then setting it to overprint. Subsequently changing the object's fill to white does not turn off the overprint attribute. When you're working in Illustrator, a tiny yellow alert triangle appears in the Attributes panel if you change an overprinting object to white, but it's easily overlooked, and InDesign doesn't provide the same warning.

Overprint Preview also provides a more realistic representation of blending modes applied to spot-color objects. The default view mode in InDesign doesn't always correctly represent the effect of blending modes (**Figure 12.41**).

Activating Overprint Preview also turns on High Resolution Display, so you may experience slower performance in a graphics-heavy document. When you're finished using Overprint Preview, you may want to turn it off to speed up performance.

Figure 12.41 *It's impossible to have 200 percent of a single ink without a second printing plate. But if you create two objects with the same 100 percent spot fill, and then apply the Multiply blending mode (top), InDesign's display implies that the overlapping area will be darker. But turn on Overprint Preview (bottom) and the display tells the true story.*

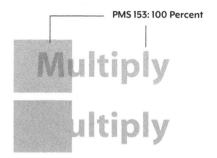

PMS 153: 100 Percent

Flattener Preview (*Window > Output > Flattener Preview*) uses red highlighting for text and vector content that may be rasterized during the output process (**Figure 12.42**). Notice the word *may*. During printing or a direct export to

PDF, InDesign performs engineering feats to avoid rasterizing such content. However, some workflows that break imaging files into separate linework and image components, such as Scitex or some systems, may treat text areas as image content if the text interacts with transparency effects.

Figure 12.42 *The Flattener Preview uses red highlighting (here, represented by black) to indicate potential text and vector rasterization.*

The Component Information dialog box (**Figure 12.43**) provides a peek under the hood of your copy of InDesign as well as a glimpse of a document's life story. In Windows, hold down the Control key as you choose About InDesign from the Help menu. On the Macintosh, hold down the Command key and choose About InDesign from the InDesign menu.

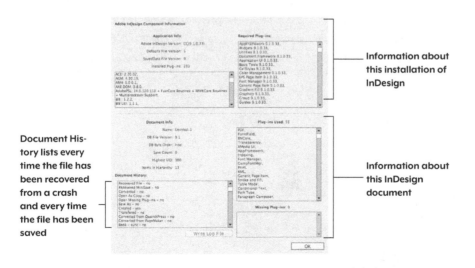

Figure 12.43 *The Component Information dialog box provides details about the application itself as well as the currently active open document.*

The top part of the dialog box shows information about the current version of InDesign (Figure 12.43 shows version 9.1.0.33) and the active plug-ins. This may be useful if you need help from Adobe tech support, because you'll need to provide the current version and other environmental information when you call.

The bottom part of the dialog box displays information about the active InDesign document, including the very useful Document History, which constitutes a personal diary of the document. You'll see whether the document was converted from QuarkXPress or PageMaker, whether it's been recovered after a crash, and how many times it's been saved (including the versions and platforms in effect during the saves). Would you ever be this nosy about a file? Well, if it's neurotic—crashing frequently or just plain acting strange—take a look at the Document History. If the file has had a traumatic childhood, it may be worth exporting it to InDesign Markup (IDML) as a purification ritual. Then, open the IDML file in InDesign CC and make a new start.

Live Preflight

The Live Preflight feature constantly monitors the state of the document, checking it against a set of user-specified preflight rules. InDesign ships with a basic, bare-bones preflight profile, but you might want to create a more ambitious custom profile. If your print service provider or a publication gives you a custom preflight profile, use that profile to ensure that you're meeting their requirements.

Because preflight is dynamic, you can fix problems as soon as they occur if you train yourself to keep an eye on the constantly updated Preflight status in the lower-left corner of the document window (**Figure 12.44**).

Figure 12.44 *Keep an eye on the Preflight status in the lower-left corner of the document window; it's trying to help you.*

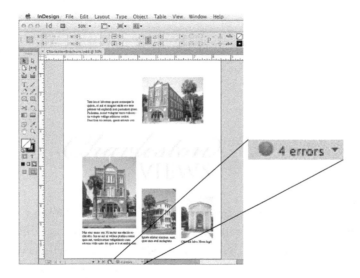

Most people only pay attention to what's going on in the center of the screen, but it's worth developing the habit of glancing down to make sure the light's still green. If the light turns red, stop working and check the report in the Preflight panel. You can double-click the status area in the corner of the document window, or choose *Window > Output > Preflight*.

The Preflight panel (**Figure 12.45**) details all violations of the current preflight profile. Click a hyperlinked page number to jump to the error in the document.

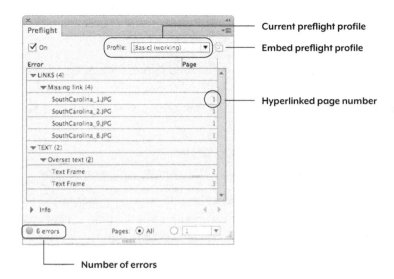

Current preflight profile

Embed preflight profile

Hyperlinked page number

Number of errors

Figure 12.27 *The Preflight panel lists all conditions that violate the currently active preflight profile. Double-click an entry or click a hyper-linked page number to jump to the offending frame.*

Creating a Custom Preflight Profile

The basic preflight profile is sort of anemic: It only checks for missing or modified links, missing fonts, and overset text. You can't modify the default basic profile, so if you want to customize the preflight options (and you should), you have to create a custom profile.

Open the Preflight panel (*Window > Output > Preflight*), and then choose Define Profiles from the panel menu. Click the plus icon under the left column of the dialog box, name the new profile, and begin modifying the settings (**Figure 12.46**).

Figure 12.46 *Click the New Preflight Profile button (the plus sign) to create and edit a new custom preflight profile.*

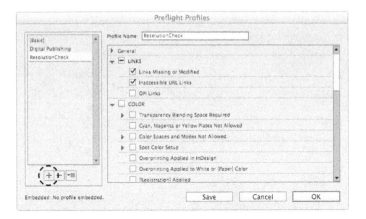

The extensive preflight options allow you to be granular when creating the preflight recipe. Explore the options to familiarize yourself with the possibilities and determine what's appropriate for your document. The options include:

- **General:** Enter a description for the profile.

- **Links:** Check for missing or modified links and OPI links.

- **Color:** Check for transparency blending space, plates not allowed, color spaces not allowed, overprinting in InDesign, overprinting white objects, warn if Registration color has been used.

- **Images and Objects:** Check for incorrect image resolution based on thresholds you specify (color, grayscale, and 1-bit images), nonproportional scaling layer visibility overrides, bleed/trim hazard.

- **Text:** Check for style overrides, dynamic spelling errors, non-proportional type scaling, minimum type size, out-of-date cross-references, conditional, text indicators set to print.

- **Document:** Check for page size/orientation, blank page status, bleed and slug setup. Note, however, that you will not be warned if an object has insufficient bleed; you're only warned if no bleed is defined for the document.

Once you've set up the preflight options, click OK to save the profile. Then, in the main Preflight panel, choose the new profile from the Profile panel menu to make it the active profile. You can even embed a profile in a document to ensure that the recipient is playing by the correct rules. To do this, choose Embed Profile from the Preflight panel menu. To delete a preflight profile, choose Define Profiles from the Preflight panel menu, select the profile name, and click the Delete Preflight Profile button (the minus sign) underneath the list of profiles.

Choose Preflight Options from the Preflight panel menu to specify whether to use the prevailing profile or the embedded profile when opening a document; whether Preflight should check all layers, just visible layers, or just visible and printable layers; and whether nonprinting objects should be included.

Importing and Sharing a Preflight Profile

If your print service provider sends a custom profile, import it and use it as your working preflight profile. You might want to supply a custom profile to collaborators or contributors to help them submit healthy files (or at least to remove any excuse for not doing so). To import a new preflight profile, choose Define Profiles from the Preflight Profiles panel menu, choose Load Profile from the easy-to-overlook tiny menu beneath the list of profiles, and navigate to the new profile; look for a file with the extension .idpp. To export a preflight profile, select the profile name in the list and choose Export Profile from the menu. You can also choose Embed Profile to embed the selected preflight profile in the current document (**Figure 12.47**).

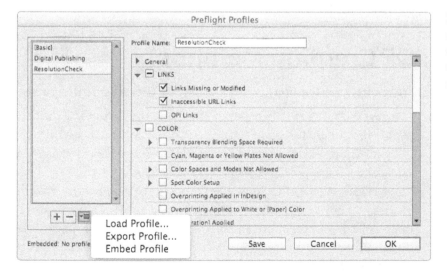

Figure 12.45 *To import or export a preflight profile, choose Load or Export from the small menu underneath the list of profiles.*

Packaging the File

InDesign's Package function (*File > Package*) copies all necessary fonts and linked files into a folder for job submission—under most circumstances. You're warned in the Package dialog that InDesign will not package CJK (Chinese, Japanese, Korean) fonts, or any Typekit desktop fonts.

If you've created any text layers in Photoshop and placed the image as a native PSD into InDesign, fonts will not be packaged. It's preferable to save such images as Photoshop PDF files anyway, because fonts can be embedded, and vector edges remain sharp.

It's a good idea to check the Preflight status of the document before you package. Once you've cleaned house, launch the Package function. InDesign copies fonts and artwork rather than moving them. Depending on the options you select, the package folder contains:

- A new copy of the InDesign file.

- A Fonts folder containing the necessary fonts (with the above Multiple Master, CJK, and Photoshop exceptions).

- A Links folder containing all linked files.

- An Instructions text file that lists the contents of the Links and Fonts folders.

PDF Creation Methods

There are multiple methods for generating PDF files from InDesign files.

- **Export to PDF:** You'll be happy to know that the easy way is the best way—how often does that happen? A PDF file generated via InDesign's direct export (*File > Export* with Adobe PDF as the export format) is as digestible as one created by distilling PostScript. And, most important, there's less chance of vector and text content being rasterized during a direct export. Like Illustrator and Photoshop, InDesign contains the necessary resources to create PDF files without invoking Acrobat Distiller. Unless your recipient instructs you otherwise, use *File > Export*, and then choose the PDF/X-1a setting.

- **Print to Adobe PDF:** By default, this approach uses Distiller as the target printer, following the PDF job options last used by Distiller. There's rarely a reason to use this method to create a PDF: Transparency is flattened, and it's the long way around.

- **Acrobat Distiller:** Another long way around. Generate PostScript by selecting *File > Print* and then selecting PostScript File for the printer. For PPD (PostScript Printer Definition), choose Adobe PDF unless instructed otherwise by a print service provider. Use Acrobat Distiller to convert the PostScript to PDF. Whereas this long-winded approach was previously recommended to minimize CID (Character ID) font encoding, you'll achieve equivalent results by exporting from InDesign. You may still encounter instances of CID font encoding in a directly exported or distilled PDF because some glyphs must be CID-encoded regardless of the method of PDF creation. Current RIPs shouldn't have any difficulty with the fully compliant PDFs created using *File > Export*.

- **Save As PDF (Mac only):** The Macintosh operating system offers a built-in approach to creating PDF files. You'll encounter a Save As PDF option in Print dialog boxes in OS X 10.3.9 and earlier. In 10.4 and later, you'll see just a PDF button. While this method is acceptable for PDF files intended for a quick-and-dirty email attachment, it does not offer appropriate controls for making a print-ready PDF file.

To sum up, direct export from InDesign is the preferred method unless the file recipient specifically instructs you otherwise. And it's worth asking "Why?" if you are asked to go the PostScript-and-Distiller route. You may find that they're open to changing their old-fashioned thinking once they discover that their systems fully support directly exported PDFs.

PDF Creation Settings

It's important to know that the P in PDF stands for *portable*, not for perfect. It's possible to make a bad PDF, so barring any specific guidance, it's good to know that InDesign provides reliable recipes for common circumstances:

- **Smallest File Size** is appropriate for PDFs that are to be emailed or posted online. This setting resamples raster images to 100 ppi, applies aggressive compression, and converts all images to RGB while retaining spot colors. This generates a file that is inappropriate for commercial printing and results in color shifts that may adversely alter the appearance of the PDF onscreen. The PDF is compatible with Acrobat 5.0—meaning that transparency is not flattened.

- **High Quality Print** is meant for printing on a desktop printer. Images are downsampled to 300 ppi and compressed at Maximum quality. RGB images are not converted to CMYK, but existing CMYK and spot-color content is maintained, and the PDF is compatible with Acrobat 5.0.

- **Press Quality** is similar to High Quality Print, but it uses InDesign's current color-management settings to convert any RGB content to CMYK on the fly, while retaining any spot content. While this setting generates a healthy PDF, its compatibility with Acrobat 5.0 may cause some problems with older devices. It places you at the mercy of someone else's approach to transparency flattening.

- **PDF/X-1a:2001** is your best choice when you're given no specifications for PDF file creation. RGB content is converted to CMYK during PDF generation, spot colors are maintained, transparency is flattened, and the compatibility with Acrobat 4.0 ensures compatibility with a wide variety of devices.

- **PDF/X-3:2002** is for use in a color-managed workflow. Color profiles are embedded in the PDF, and RGB content is not converted to CMYK. These PDF files are compatible with Acrobat 4.0—any transparency content is flattened in the process of generating the PDF. The same specs apply to PDF/X-3:2002 (Japan).

- **PDF/X-4:2008** is intended for use in a color-managed workflow that supports live, unflattened transparency. If the print service provider is using RIPs that implement the Adobe PDF Print Engine, they should support this flavor of PDF. Going forward, you can expect more service providers to accept this more modern format. When you choose this option, you'll see that the Standard menu reads PDF/X-4:2010; this just reflects a few tweaks to the standard in 2010.

- **MAGAZINE Ad 2006 (Japan)** is equivalent to PDF/X-3:2002.

By the way, if you're curious why PDF/X-2 isn't listed, that's because the X-2 spec was never published.

Acrobat
Production Tips

13

In 1991, Dr. John Warnock, one of the cofounders of Adobe Systems, proposed Project Camelot, in which he suggested using the graphics and imaging operators of PostScript to create portable documents that could be displayed and printed on any computer, regardless of the originating application. These documents would contain all the resources necessary to represent the original document for display and printing. Images and vector art would be crisp. Regardless of operating system or computer platform, fonts would be embedded, ensuring that text would be readable and line breaks would be preserved—even if recipients didn't have the same fonts as the document's creator. Sound familiar?

Thus, what came to be known as Adobe Acrobat was intended to create what might be called digital carbon copies for office document interchange and storage. But a funny thing happened in the graphic arts world. We discovered that converting stubborn documents to Portable Document Format (PDF) files often made them more manageable as print jobs. For example, while Microsoft Word allows you to add festive clip art and other decorative bits such as Word Art to documents, it's really intended for word processing. Turning a Word file into something suitable for printing in two spot colors might require that you generate a PDF, then open that PDF in Adobe Acrobat Professional and use the PitStop plug-in from Enfocus (www.enfocus.com) to deconstruct the artwork, fix the things that fell apart during the conversion, and then assign the correct printing colors. It may seem like the long way around, but at least you'd have something that could actually be printed as intended.

Fast-forward to current day. Many publications and print service providers request that you submit your jobs as PDF files to eliminate the need to send a combination of page-layout files, linked artwork files, and the necessary fonts. While this simplifies job submission, it also shifts the responsibility for more of the job's quality control to the person making the PDF file.

That would be you.

Acrobat Product Line

Currently, the Acrobat family consists of four products, each having a specific target audience:

TIP Adobe Reader XI allows users to add comments to a PDF and to save a filled form. However, older versions of Reader don't have this functionality. If you have no guarantee that recipients have Reader XI, it's a good idea to save as a Reader Extended PDF and include the rights to comment and save filled forms.

- Acrobat XI Standard is intended primarily for creating PDFs from office applications. Consequently, it lacks the print-oriented preflighting and repair tools found in the professional product. However, it does allow users to participate in comment-and-review processes and allows users to rights-enable PDFs for commenting and form-filling by users of older versions of Adobe Reader. Acrobat Standard also includes Acrobat Distiller for converting PostScript to PDFs.

- Acrobat XI Pro provides extensive tools for creating PDF files from images, text files, Microsoft Office files, and Web pages. When you install Acrobat XI Pro, it adds PDF export functionality to Microsoft Office applications, so you can create PDF files from within an open Microsoft Word file, for example. Acrobat XI Pro enables you to initiate and participate in comment and review cycles, and contains tools for creating forms and adding interactivity to PDF files. The print production tools make it valuable in design and prepress environments. It's the most popular and widely used version of Acrobat. Acrobat XI Pro also includes Acrobat Distiller for converting PostScript to PDFs.

- Adobe Reader XI is the free PDF viewer. Reader users can participate in comment–and–review processes and save filled-out Acrobat forms if a PDF has been specially rights-enabled from within Acrobat XI Pro. Reader cannot create PDF files.

Don't be confused by the selections in the Acrobat family. For those of us in the graphic arts who need to manipulate PDF files, the appropriate version to use is Acrobat XI Pro.

Where Do PDFs Come From?

Acrobat isn't like drawing or page-layout applications; it's purely intended for modifying PDFs. PDF files begin life somewhere else, outside of Acrobat. While Acrobat enables you to create PDFs from a scanner, an existing image, or a Web page, they're often exported from other applications such as Adobe InDesign or Illustrator.

Although Adobe Systems originated the PDF concept and its specifications, anyone is allowed to use the information in the publicly available PDF Reference to write software that creates, reads, or edits PDF files. Given that the PDF Reference is in excess of 1000 pages, it's clearly not a trivial undertaking.

All PDF-creation solutions are not the same. Some third-party implementations of the PDF specifications, such as those used to generate PDF files from non-Adobe applications, may not fully utilize all the features possible in a PDF file. This is not to imply that non-Adobe methods of creating PDFs are inferior. On the contrary, some commonly used PDF creation tools create perfectly good PDF files. But non-Adobe applications may have slightly different controls or options, which makes it challenging to generalize about how, exactly, to go about making a PDF file. For that matter, not all Adobe applications use the same approach when making PDFs, although they all share the common PDF Library.

Creating PDF Files

The chapters on Illustrator, InDesign, and Photoshop have offered some suggested PDF-creation settings, but it may be helpful to consider what's important regardless of the tool you're using to create PDF files.

Determining Which Type of PDF You Should Create

To use a very basic definition, a document consists of images, text, lines, and color areas on a page of a certain size. The purpose of creating a PDF is to retain all of these components of the document across multiple operating systems and to ensure that it can be printed as intended. It all sounds so simple, doesn't it? However, there isn't a single, one-size-fits-all recipe for creating PDF files. Broadly speaking, there are several types of PDF files you're likely to create.

- PDF files to be submitted to a print service provider should be generated from page-layout or drawing applications after carefully checking content and job requirements. Images need to be high resolution, which can result in large file sizes. Fonts must be embedded correctly, and it's important to properly define your colors as CMYK, color-managed RGB, or spot color. Think of this as a hermetically sealed, final job file, and don't count on editing it to perfection later.

- PDFs for email (for example, for commenting and review) will require that you sacrifice image quality in the interest of smaller files, but font embedding must still be handled correctly to ensure accurate display and printing.

- PDF files that will be posted online need to be small enough for downloading, but documents such as product brochures or instructional manuals should contain enough image detail to make them satisfactory resources. You'll have to reach a compromise between desired image quality and reasonable file size. You might consider breaking larger documents into smaller chapters and then hyperlinking the files together to aid the end user in finding their way.

- PDF files intended for distribution on CD/DVD can be larger files since downloading isn't an issue, so you don't have to compromise image quality. You might even consider adding multimedia content and extensive hyperlinking to enrich the files. While such features take you beyond a purely print environment, you can easily start with print-ready PDF files and bring them to life with Acrobat's built-in multimedia capabilities.

Table 13.1 *PDF creation settings*

Setting	PDF Version	Downsample/ Threshold[1]	Compression Image Quality	Color Policy	Purpose
Smallest File Size	5.0	100/150	Low	Convert to sRGB	Onscreen display and email
Standard	5.0	150/225	Med	Convert to sRGB	Viewing and printing business documents
High Quality Print	5.0	300/450	Max	Leave Unchanged	Viewing and printing design documents
Press Quality	5.0	300/450	Max	Convert to CMYK	For prepress
PDF/X-1a:2001	4.0	300/450	Max	Convert to CMYK	For prepress. Defines TrimBox[2], BleedBox[3]
PDF/X-3:2002	4.0	300/450	Max	Leave Unchanged	Use in color-managed workflows
PDF/X-4:2008	5.0	300/450	Max	Leave Unchanged	Use in color-managed workflows Retains live transparency
PDF/A-1b:2005 (RGB)	5.0	300/450	Max	Convert to sRGB	For archive
PDF/A-1b:2005 (CMYK)	5.0	300/450	Max	Convert to CMYK	For archive
Oversized Pages	7.0	150/225	Med	Convert to sRGB	Supports engineering drawings larger than 200" by 200"
Illustrator Default	6.0	None	ZIP	Leave Unchanged	Maintains layers; can round-trip to Illustrator

[1]Downsampling reduces image resolution. Threshold is the resolution above which Distiller will downsample image content.
[2]TrimBox is the trim edge of the document, based on the originating file.
[3]BleedBox is the edge of defined bleed, based on information in the originating file.

PDF Settings and Some Important Standards

The default PDF-creation settings available in the Creative Cloud applications include a wide spectrum of presets for generating PDF files (**Table 13.1**). Settings such as Standard, Smallest File Size, and Press Quality give some hint of what kind of PDF file they're intended to create. The PDF/X and PDF/A settings are based on standards intended to ensure that a PDF behaves as expected. The X in PDF/X-1a stands for "exchange," signifying that a PDF complying with one of the PDF/X standards can be exchanged between the PDF's originator and recipients with some assurance the recipient will get a usable file. The PDF/A settings are based on standards geared toward long-term archiving and retrieval of electronic files (hence the "A").

A core set of PDF settings is stored in a common repository and shared among all Adobe Creative Cloud applications: A new PDF setting created in InDesign will also be available in Illustrator, Photoshop, and Distiller automatically. But a few settings are available only to a single application, such as Illustrator's Default setting or Distiller's Oversized Pages setting.

The Digital Distribution of Advertising for Publications (DDAP) association established requirements for print-ready PDFs for advertisement submission, which were then implemented by the Committee for Graphic Arts Technologies Standards (CGATS) as the basis of the PDF/X standards. (Was that enough acronyms for you?) With the constant increase in the number of PDF files submitted for advertising, the PDF/X standards are intended to streamline file submission.

The most commonly requested PDF format for print in the United States is PDF/X-1a. (The 2001 appellation you see after PDF/X variations in Acrobat XI Pro is added because PDF/X is an evolving standard.) To comply with the PDF/X-1a specification, a PDF file must meet the following requirements:

- Images must be CMYK or spot color (no RGB or Lab images).

- Fonts must be embedded and subset. Subsetting embeds only the characters needed in the PDF file and assigns a special name to the font content so that an output device will not substitute another font for it.

- The trim edges of pages must be explicitly defined. Internally, a PDF file refers to this information as TrimBox.

- The bleed limits must be explicitly defined. Internally, this is called BleedBox.

The PDF/X-3 is a specification intended for use in a color-managed workflow. The stipulations are similar to those for PDF/X-1a, with the exception that image content can be RGB or Lab tagged with color profiles. Unless you and your print service provider are using color management, you're unlikely to be asked to submit PDF/X-3 files. PDF/X-4 allows color-managed RGB content and retains live transparency: This type of PDF would be appropriate in a workflow that is based on the Adobe PDF Print Engine. And PDF/A-1b indicates an emerging PDF standard for archiving documents for reference long into the future. The A represents "archive."

Export vs. Distiller

Because all of the Creative Cloud applications speak fluent PDF, it's possible to directly export PDF files from InDesign, Illustrator, and Photoshop without using Distiller. If you want to retain layers, live transparency, or interactivity, you have to export rather than use Distiller. Although it's rare these days, occasionally a print service provider or publication may insist that you take the Distiller route, but that sentiment is largely built on old wive's tales about creating PDFs. Because exporting is faster and easier than using Distiller, it's worth having a conversation with file recipients to find out why you're being asked to take the long way around. Ask them to test an exported PDF created to their specifications, and then you'll both know what really works.

All the Creative Cloud applications offer PDF/X presets. But if the PDF export function in a non-Adobe application doesn't offer named versions of PDF settings, how can you create a PDF that is compliant with the PDF/X-1a specification? It's not difficult, but you need to stick to some basics:

- Set compatibility to Acrobat 4.0. The PDF/X-1a specification stipulates Acrobat 4.0 compatibility (which may seem old-fashioned given that Acrobat at this writing is version 11). This is to accommodate the capabilities of older RIPs, many of which prefer Acrobat 4.0–flavored PDF files. Because Acrobat 4.0-compatible PDF files don't contain live transparency, there's less chance that a RIP that is not PDF based will incorrectly process the file.

- Set image resolution to 300 ppi for typical 150-line screen work, and to 200 ppi for 133-line screen jobs (more about image handling in a moment). Consult with your print service provider to find out the line screen that will be used on your job. If you don't know, you're safe using 300 ppi.

- Set image compression to Automatic (JPEG).

- Ensure that all image content is CMYK or spot or some combination thereof. Convert any RGB content to CMYK.

- Set font embedding to embed fonts. Enable subsetting, and set the subsetting threshold to 100 percent.

Handling Image Content

The primary cause of a PDF file's size is image content, so if you want to make a smaller PDF, that's where you have to squeeze. It's a bit of a juggling act. You have to balance the size of the PDF with the results of compressing and resampling images and decide whether to compromise image appearance to create a more petite file. When making decisions about image compression and resampling, you have to consider the nature of image content as well as the intended use for the PDF file. If the document's text is the most important content and images are just incidental accents (such as gauzy, out-of-focus photographs of soft clouds), then you can be more liberal when compressing images. However, when the images are key elements—for example, in a technical manual in which it's crucial to differentiate between small details—you'll have to be willing to accept a larger PDF so you can maintain important detail.

Image compression and resampling options can look overwhelming in Distiller and other applications' PDF-creation dialog boxes. There are so many fields and menu choices. But in most cases, you're just being asked the same question about different types of image content. What should happen to color images? How should it handle grayscale images? And what about bitmap images (also called bilevel—black and white with no shades of gray)? Being able to control the fates of color, grayscale, and bitmap images separately gives you some flexibility. For example, you might want to maintain higher resolution in color images but not mind reducing the resolution of less-important grayscale images. Separate controls allow you to do that.

Resolution Settings

If you want to more aggressively reduce the file size of a PDF, you can set the base resolution and downsampling threshold to the same value (**Figure 13.1**). Downsampling is the process of reducing the number of pixels in an image. An image downsampled from 300 ppi to 72 ppi is much smaller because it consists of smaller, coarser pixels. The downsampling threshold is the resolution above which Distiller will downsample image content. A setting that downsamples images to 300 ppi if they're above 450 ppi ignores images whose resolution falls between 300 and 450 ppi, leaving their resolution unchanged. Setting both downsampling and the threshold to the same value forces images between 300 and 450 ppi to also be downsampled. You're discarding pixels, but at this level, it shouldn't result in an obvious loss of detail.

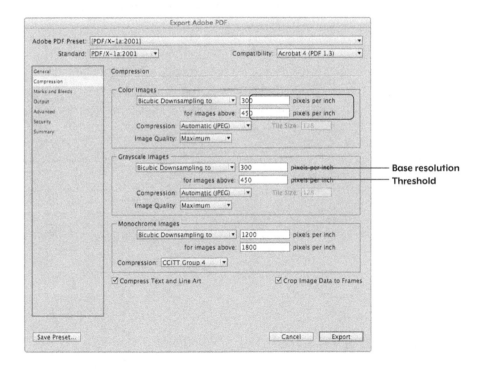

Figure 13.1 *Want to shave a bit more size off a PDF? Make the downsampling threshold value the same as the base resolution. Every little bit helps.*

Compression Settings

Besides allowing you to resample image content to economize PDF size, Distiller and some other PDF-creation processes provide options for compression. Compression involves methods of re-expressing the image content in a more economical way, usually by eliminating redundant information. Overly aggressive JPEG compression, however, can cause a noticeable erosion of an image, resulting in effects such as rectangular artifacts. But don't be terrified of the JPEG compression option in Distiller. Careful compression levels can reduce image size without visibly degrading the image.

Acrobat Distiller and most other PDF-creation applications use both ZIP and JPEG methods of compression. ZIP compression is lossless, meaning that it does not discard image information—it just describes the image in a more compact way. ZIP can reduce the size of flat-color image content such as cartoons or maps. JPEG compression achieves better file-size reduction with photographic image content, because photographs can contain a wide range of colors with smooth transitions. The correct choice of a compression method will reduce the size of the resulting PDF file without unnecessarily impairing its appearance.

What do you do if you have both kinds of content? Good news—choose the Automatic (JPEG) option in Distiller or other Creative Cloud applications, and each type of content is handled appropriately (**Figure 13.2**). It's worth noting that, since ZIP compression is lossless, it's also perfectly appropriate for photographic images, but it will not produce as small a file as JPEG compression can.

Figure 13.2 *Choose the Automatic (JPEG) compression option to allow the application to optimize the compression choice based on content. Use the Image Quality option to control the degree of compression.*

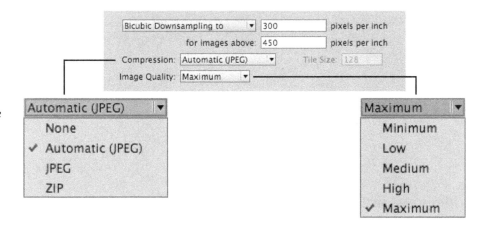

Font Embedding

The purpose of embedding fonts is to ensure that the PDF file looks and prints like the original document. Keep in mind that you're allowed to embed fonts only if the font vendor's End User License Agreement (EULA) allows you to do so—see Chapter 6, "Fonts," for more on font licensing EULAs. It's fairly rare to encounter fonts that prevent embedding.

If you embed a font in a PDF, things can still go awry once the file leaves your hands. If you just embed a font (without subsetting), font substitution can still take place if the RIP is already using a font of the same name. Imagine a RIP thinking, "Why should I bother to pry open this PDF to get its Helvetica Bold, when I already have one warmed up?" It sounds harmless, just substituting one Helvetica Bold for another. But not all Helvetica Bold versions are the same. There may be subtle differences in font metrics that can result in loss of fidelity to the original file. Additionally, fully embedding larger fonts such as OpenType fonts (which can have more than 65,000 glyphs) can add to the size of the PDF file.

> **NOTE** Adobe Creative Cloud applications always embed and subset fonts with the appropriate embedding permissions.

One solution to these issues is to subset font information. Subsetting embeds only the characters used in the document, which reduces file size. If your PDF consists of one line of text reading "ABC123," only the characters A, B, C, 1, 2, and 3 are embedded, rather than packing up the entire font. By default, both Illustrator and InDesign embed and subset fonts.

Editing PDF Files

Because one of the primary purposes of the Portable Document Format is to maintain document integrity, you shouldn't be surprised that the ability to edit PDF files in Acrobat is rather limited. That's not an accident—we're not supposed to pick at PDF files once they're created. They're supposed to be finished files, ready to ship.

Of course, little things happen—a missing comma, a blemish in an image, the wrong spot color—and desperation drives you to start prying at the corners of a PDF file. Although it's best to return to the original document, make the repairs, and generate a new, healthy PDF, you don't always have that luxury.

Acrobat XI introduced a versatile new editing tool, the Edit Text & Images tool (**Figure 13.3**). If you have attempted to edit text in previous versions of Acrobat, you'll relish the improvements that accompany this tool.

Figure 13.3 *The Edit Text & Images tool, as the name implies, allows you to select and edit graphic and text content in a PDF.*

Editing Text

To edit text (or attempt to), select the Edit Text & Images tool. Outlines appear around text areas; you can then highlight text and change it. It's important to note that the purpose of font embedding is to ensure that a PDF file displays correctly and prints as intended. The fonts embedded in the PDF are not available for you to use in any other way—and that includes editing text. Consequently, if you attempt to edit text using an unavailable font, you'll receive a warning alert (**Figure 13.4**).

Figure 13.4 *If the necessary font is not active on your system, you will not be able to correctly edit text in a PDF.*

Even if you do have the correct font, you may encounter problems if the font does not allow editing and re-embedding. Fonts from different foundries may carry different internal flagged permissions, and those permissions are retained when the fonts are embedded in a PDF. This is why text editing can be an inconsistent experience (it's nature's way of saying "get it right the first time!").

Acrobat XI Pro recognizes groups of text and attempts to keep paragraphs together as reflowable text. You may find that a story (or a long paragraph) is broken up into separate containers, requiring you to perform some massaging if you're doing extensive editing. Still, it's a huge improvement over older versions of Acrobat, which saw each line as a separate object; text editing could be a frustrating nightmare.

You can change the font used by selected text to any font active on your system, and even change the color. However, you can't assign spot colors, and although you can create a CMYK color on the Mac OS, you're limited to choosing RGB values on Windows.

Are you starting to take all this bad news as a sign that you're not supposed to tinker with text in PDF files? Good. Hold that thought. It will keep you out of all kinds of trouble.

Editing Graphics

You may be surprised to discover how easy it is to edit most graphics (both vector and raster) in a PDF. When you install Acrobat, it searches for the locations of the newest versions of Photoshop and Illustrator on your computer and opens them when you embark on an edit. Choose the Edit Text & Images tool, select the desired graphic content in the PDF, and then right-click (Control-click on the Mac) to view the context menu. In the context menu, select *Edit Using* and then select Adobe Photoshop or Adobe Illustrator, depending on the type of content you've selected (**Figure 13.5**). The appropriate external application will launch and open a temporary file of the graphic for editing. The title bar of content being edited in Photoshop or Illustrator displays a name such as *Acro1143710152.pdf*, indicating that it's a special file with a relationship to the PDF from which it was extracted.

Figure 13.5 *Select an image with the Edit Text & Images tool, and then right-click (Control-click on the Mac) to select Edit Using. Make the changes, choose File > Save, and the corrected image is written back into the PDF.*

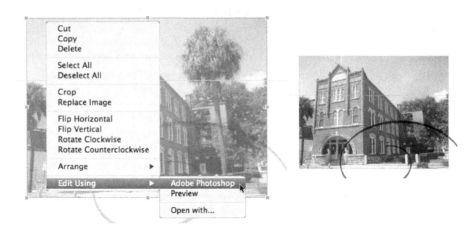

You can add layers in Photoshop to accomplish edits and still write an image back into the PDF. However, the image is flattened as it's written back into the PDF. You can fix blemishes, change color modes—even convert to a duo-tone. When you're done, choose *File > Save* in Photoshop, and the corrected image is saved back into the PDF file.

Using the Edit Text & Images tool to select vector content opens Illustrator to modify the selected content. As with images, you can make your edits and then choose *File > Save* to write the vector content back into the PDF file. You can add layers and even rotate and scale content in Illustrator. When you choose *File > Save*, Illustrator communicates the changes back to Acrobat and modifies the PDF file accordingly.

While the Edit Text & Images tool may bail you out of problems as deadlines loom, it's often safer to go back to the original file to make corrections, if you can. Sometimes PDF files just fall apart during editing (nature's way of saying don't mess with them). You should watch carefully for shifted content or unwanted changes. If you're required to frequently edit PDF files because your customers send you PDFs with problems, you should consider adding the dedicated editor Enfocus PitStop to your Acrobat arsenal.

TIP Need to extract an image or vector component from a PDF file for use in another job? Use the TouchUp tool to extract the content. When you have a TouchUp image or vector object open in Photoshop or Illustrator, choose File > Save As and select a format, such as PSD for images or AI for vector objects, to save as a file rather than writing back into the PDF file. This is a great way to extract artwork from a PDF file if the original artwork is not available.

Comment and Review

When you collaborate with other content creators, you may find it saner to send PDF files for them to review, rather than clogging their in-boxes with

InDesign, Photoshop, or Illustrator files. And rather than suffer through faxing marked-up copy ("Is that a blob or a comma?") or the cost of couriers, you can streamline the collaborative process by using the commenting and review features built into Acrobat.

Acrobat XI Standard and Pro both provide extensive markup tools, which mimic real-life markup tools such as sticky notes, highlighters, and markers. Just click Comment at the upper-right corner of the Acrobat window in any open file to reveal the commenting tools (**Figure 13.6**).

NOTE A right-click (Mac: Control-click) can save you a lot of time during the comment and review process. Right-click any Annotation or Drawing Markups tool and set the default properties, add the tool to the Quick Tools bar, and keep the tool selected for quick markups.

Figure 13.6 *Click the disclosure triangle next to each segment of the Comments panel to reveal all the markup options.*

Here's an overview of the tools:

- **Sticky Notes:** Click to "stick" a note to the PDF; type your comments in the note-like area that appears. Right-click on the note icon and choose Properties to change the note icon, select a new color for the note and its icon, or change the author name. To reposition the note icon, just drag

TIP On the Mac, a two-button mouse works the same as it does on Windows. But if you don't have a two-button mouse on your Mac, hold down the Control key as you click to mimic having a right mouse button.

it. By default, the open note appears at the edge of the document page, but you can drag it anywhere in the page.

- **Text Edit tools:** Despite the name, the Text Edit tools don't change text in the PDF; they just indicate desired changes. To indicate a text change or deletion, pretend you're typing: For example, select the main Text Edits tool, click and drag across text you'd like to delete, and press the Delete or Backspace key on the keyboard. A strikethrough appears throughout the text. To indicate replacement text, highlight a range of text, and then type the replacement text. The existing text is struck through and a pop-up note appears, containing the new text you've typed. You'll find that you most often use the Text Edits tool this way, and you'll rarely use the other options hidden in the menu available under the Text Edits button.

- **Stamps:** The Dynamic stamps pick up the user name and, in some cases, the date from the system. The Sign Here stamps are like those little stick-on guides you've seen on contracts. The Standard Business stamps include Void, Confidential, Draft, and the one you'll rarely see in the wild: Approved. You can also create your own custom stamps from Illustrator AI files, PDFs, or JPEGs. To apply a stamp, either click in the page or click and drag to size the stamp as you apply it.

- **Highlight Text tool:** Click and drag across text to highlight it. Right-click on the highlighted area and choose Properties to select a new color or open a pop-up note.

- **Callout tool:** This creates a type-in "balloon" anchored to an arrow. Click where you'd like to anchor the arrow (for example, at the corner of a photograph on which you want to comment), and then drag to where you'd like the rectangular balloon to appear. When you release the mouse button, you can begin typing text in the balloon; as you type, the balloon expands vertically. Right-click to open the context menu; you can spell check selected text in the balloon, or select from text styles such as Bold, Italic, and Underline. You can also change the color, style, and weight of the callout balloon outline.

- **Text Box tool:** Click or click and drag to create a text area, and then type or paste content into the container. As with the Callout tool, you can spell check and apply limited formatting.

- **Cloud tool:** Click (don't drag) in a connect-the-dots fashion to create a polygonal cloud. When you've closed the shape, you can right-click to change the properties or open the pop-up note.

- **Arrow and Line tools:** These two tools are fairly intuitive: The arrow appears where you first click, and the line continues from that first point. As with most of the other markup tools, right-click to change the properties or open the pop-up note.

- **Rectangle, Polygon, and Oval tools:** Click and drag to create these geometric shapes; hold down the Shift key to constrain the shape to a circle or square. By now, you know the right-click drill.

- **Pencil tool:** Draw as you would with a real pencil or marker. Right-click to change properties.

- **Eraser:** Erase part of a drawing markup.

You'll probably find that the Sticky Notes, Text Edit tools, and Pencil tool are the most intuitive and easy to use. All markups except the Callout and Text Box markups can have a pop-up note attached; just right-click on a markup icon in the document to choose Open Pop-Up Note from the context menu.

To delete a comment, select it with the Hand tool and press the Delete key. To customize the properties of future markups of a certain type, or to modify the properties of an existing markup, select a comment, and then right-click and choose Make Current Properties Default.

Reader Users Can Play, Too

While markup features have been available since Acrobat 3.0 (when they were called Annotations), potential collaborators had to purchase a retail copy of Acrobat to participate. But that changed when Acrobat 7.0 Professional added the ability to enable a PDF so that users of the free Reader application could create, import, and export comments and markups. Acrobat 8.0 added the option to enable Reader users to save filled-out forms (previously, form data would vaporize when a Reader user saved a filled form—very frustrating).

The "enable for Reader" feature has changed names and menu locations over the years, bouncing between the Documents, Comments, and Advanced menus. Now it's landed in the File menu.

Users of Adobe Reader XI can add comments to a PDF; however, users of older versions of Reader cannot. To enable a PDF in Acrobat XI for Reader users to comment, choose *File > Save As Other > Reader Extended PDF > Enable Commenting and Measuring*. If you are creating Acrobat forms, choose *File > Save As Other > Reader Extended PDF > Enable More Tools (includes Form Fill-in and Save)*. However, enabling these features for Reader users actually disables some functions for you as the originator of the file: You can no longer edit text or graphic content, nor can you insert or delete pages. So be sure to save a copy of the PDF before you enable it for Reader users.

Collaborating with Others

Now that everyone can mark up your PDF, what do you do next? You have to disseminate the PDF to multiple reviewers and figure out a way to retrieve their comments and view them in context so you know what corrections to make to the original file. Of course, there's a chance that everyone will just use the Approved stamp and leave it at that. In your dreams.

Email-based Reviews

It's easy to email the PDF to recipients, instruct them to add their markups, and then ask them to send the marked-up PDF (or just the comments) back to you. Reviewers can't see each other's markups, so there may be some redundancy or conflict between their requests. The originator of the review (that would be you) will probably want to combine all the harvested mark-ups on a single PDF to see them all at once.

To initiate an email-based review, click Comments to open the Comments pane, then click the triangle by Review and choose *Send for Email Review*. Acrobat launches a setup wizard that walks you through the process. You can select the currently open document or another file and then choose participants by entering their email addresses manually or selecting them from your address book. The wizard generates an email message instructing recipients how to participate, but you can customize the message. Users with Acrobat 6 or later, or version 7 and later of the free Reader, can participate in the review.

Shared Reviews

To start a shared review, choose Comments at the right side of the screen, then, under Review, click Send for Shared Review. You're then given the choice of using Adobe's online service or collecting comments on your own internal server.

If you elect to use your own network server, Acrobat gets you started setting things up. If you choose Adobe's online service, you're asked to sign in with your Adobe ID and password.

The Shared Review wizard will walk you through the remaining steps, regardless of your choice (**Figure 13.7**). Once you've set things in motion, the recipients you choose will receive an email with a link to the URL so they can download the PDF for reviewing. If you're using Adobe's online service, participants will have to create a login before starting their reviews (it's free). A copy of the PDF will automatically be created on their computer with "_review.pdf" appended to the name.

Figure 13.7 *When you begin a shared review, Acrobat guides you through the required steps.*

When the PDF is opened, a yellow bar appears across the top with instructions to add comments and publish them. Participants can comment with Reader or Acrobat and then click the Publish Comments button in the yellow bar to upload their comments. They can check for other reviewers' comments by clicking the Check for New Comments button in the yellow bar. This makes it possible for all reviewers to see each other's markups and perhaps avoid redundancy (**Figure 13.8**).

Figure 13.8 *Participants in a shared review publish their comments and can download other reviewers' comments. It's a great way to solicit feedback from multiple contributors while minimizing redundancy.*

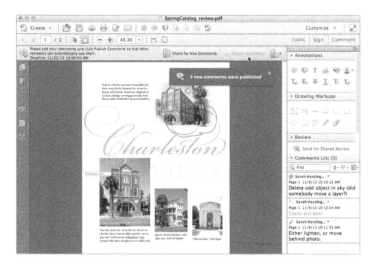

As the initiator of the shared review, you can limit access to the PDF, invite new reviewers, and set (or extend) the review deadline.

Collecting and Summarizing Comments

When it's time to gather everyone's markups into one place, you can use one of several methods, depending on how you've initiated the review.

Shared Review

In the shared review approach, you can just open your review copy of the PDF (that's the one with "_review.pdf" appended to the filename) and click the Check for New Comments button in the yellow bar to download and apply everyone's markups. It couldn't be easier. In fact, once you've used a shared review, you'll likely abandon the comparatively clunky approach of attaching a PDF to an email to solicit reviews.

Exporting Comments

If you have sent the PDF as an email attachment to reviewers, you could have them send back their marked-up PDFs. But if you're dealing with large, multipage PDFs, this could clog your in-box; paging through multiple copies of a long document to make note of all the markups would be time-consuming and tedious. So, rather than ask reviewers to send back the complete PDF, have them just send the markups: It's sort of like having them peel up all the sticky notes and send them. Instruct Acrobat users to open the Comments List, then click the tiny Options icon at the upper right of the list, and choose *Export All to Data File*. Reader users have the same options. Once the markup data file is created, your recipients can just email that much smaller file (usually just a few kilobytes) to you.

Importing Comments

Once you've received all the reviewers' markups, open your original PDF in Acrobat XI Standard or XI Pro, choose *Comments > Import Comments*, and navigate to the data file sent by a reviewer. To speed things up, you can select multiple data files and import them simultaneously. The comment data file has an .fdf (Forms Data Format) file extension. Since the reviewers made comments on a copy of your original PDF, you may see an alert as you import the data files, warning you that the comments are from a different version of the document. Just ignore the warning. And remember that you don't have to import comments if you've used a shared review; they're automatically added to the PDF as they're published.

Summarizing Comments

Once you have received all the comments from a shared review, or imported manually submitted comments, it can be confusing and aggravating to try to sort through all those markups. Make it easy on yourself: In the Comments list options, choose *Create Comment Summary*. The Summarize Options dialog gives you options for layout (my favorite: *Document and comments with connector lines on single pages*), font size (even if you choose *Large*, the text is still rather small), and the color of connector lines (**Figure 13.9**).

Figure 13.9 *Choose a layout for the comments summary, as well as font size and connector line color, and then click Create Comment Summary.*

The summary is generated as a PDF. The "single pages" option yields a thumbnail of the document, with a list of comments labeled by name and type of markup along with the text of all pop-up notes (**Figure 13.10**). It can serve as a great roadmap as you perform the requested alterations.

Figure 13.10 *The comment summary provides a roadmap for performing corrections as well as a helpful record of markups.*

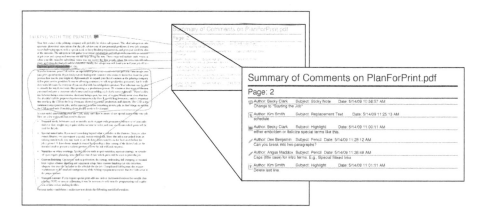

The summary PDF exists only in computer memory until you save it. Then, it's like any other PDF: You can view and print it, and even put comments on it (although that somehow seems wrong).

Print Production Tools

If you receive PDFs to be used as production artwork (for example, ads submitted for publication), it's important to find problems early and fix them if possible. You can accomplish quite a bit just by using Acrobat's built-in tools, but if it's necessary to perform any major surgery, you'll still need to repair the original file and create a new PDF or use a dedicated tool such as Enfocus PitStop to perform the corrections.

To find the Print Production tools, click *Tools*, then click the infinitesimal *Show or Hide Panels* icon in the upper-right corner of the Tools panel (could it possibly be any smaller?) and choose *Print Production* from the list of available tools (**Figure 13.11**).

Figure 13.11 *To reveal additional tool panels, including the Print Production tools, put on your reading glasses and click the Show or Hide Panels icon.*

The Print Production tools include forensic tools to help you find problem areas in a PDF file and repair tools enabling you to fix problems (**Figure 13.12**).

Figure 13.12 *Preflight, Output Preview, and Flattener Preview allow you to find problems. Most of the remaining tools perform repairs, except Acrobat Distiller, which seems strangely out of place.*

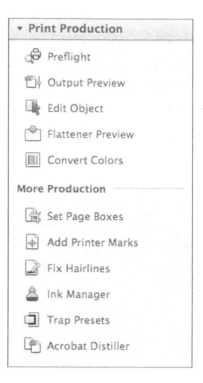

Forensic Tools: What's Wrong with This PDF?

The primary forensic tools, *Preflight* and *Output Preview*, take different approaches. Output Preview uses a visual approach, selectively displaying content according to parameters you choose. You can highlight such elements as RGB images, spot color content, overprinting elements, and rich black areas.

Some problems aren't so easily found visually, which is where the Preflight tool comes in. The Preflight tool tests a PDF file against a preflight profile to ferret out problems and then generates a report to tell you what's wrong. A preflight profile can determine such things as whether a PDF file complies with the PDF/X-1a standard and can check for such problems as insufficient image resolution, incorrect page size, font embedding issues, and much more, based on the rules of the preflight profile used.

Output Preview

Select Output Preview, and then use the controls to show and hide objects in the PDF by various criteria. You'll see a list of inks used in the PDF file, and you can selectively show and hide individual plates to easily see where the inks are used in the page. As you move your cursor over the document, the Output Preview panel displays percentage values for each ink as well as a total area coverage value for the current cursor location. You can choose a cursor sample size ranging from point sample (do you really care about a single pixel?) to 5 x 5 average.

Choose the option to highlight Total Area Coverage, pick a highlight color, enter a value for the maximum ink value, and areas in violation of the value are highlighted in the page. The appropriate value depends on the printing press, ink, and stock being used; you'll have to ask your print service provider to tell you what's correct for your job. If you have large areas carrying more ink than your print service provider recommends for your job, you'll have to go back upstream and alter image content and other artwork so the job will print acceptably. If you're doing your own conversions of RGB images to CMYK, you can factor in this value in your color separation setup.

As you view the PDF, use the check boxes next to ink names to view and hide individual plates, so you can check for incorrect or extraneous inks (**Figure 13.13**).

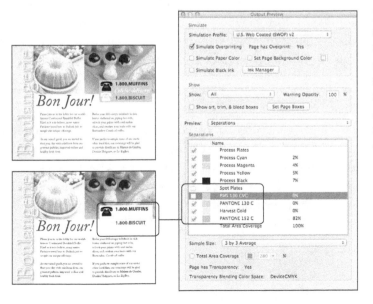

Figure 13.13 *Use the Separations controls in the Output Preview dialog to toggle plates on and off. Here, one rectangle uses an ink named PMS 130 CVC (right). But there's another spot color named PANTONE 130 C, and another named Harvest Gold. That can't be right.*

Select *Show* in the Output Preview dialog to view options for isolating RGB content (**Figure 13.14**) and other types of color space such as grayscale, CMYK, and spot color.

Figure 13.14 *From the Show list, choose RGB, and any RGB objects are displayed while everything else is hidden. It's a quick way to identify content using the wrong color space.*

As with all the Output Preview options, it's up to you to pay attention and take note of what's displayed. In Figure 13.14, one image is displayed when the *Show > RGB* option is selected. Now we've discovered that we have one problem image, which must be converted to CMYK for output. Fortunately, this is a problem you can fix in Acrobat.

Object Inspector

One of the most useful tools within Output Preview is hidden in the Preview pulldown menu. The Object Inspector doesn't select objects for interrogation; it just displays everything that's true where you click in the PDF. Think of it as sort of a core sample that reveals everything underneath. The Object Inspector reports on color space, color values, image resolution, overprint attributes, font information, and more (**Figure 13.15**).

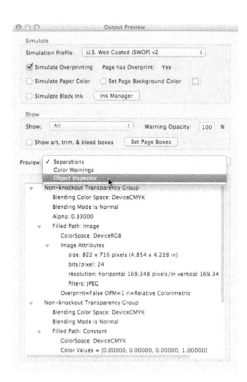

Figure 13.15 *Need to know the color space or resolution of an image in a PDF? The Object Inspector can tell you that, and much more.*

Preflight

While we tend to associate the term "preflight" with just finding problems, preflight profiles in Acrobat can also include repair procedures), called *fixups*. You can check for problems such as image resolution, spot colors, font embedding, or compliance with a standard such as PDF/X-1a. Depending on the rules that constitute the profile you select (and there's quite a variety of preflight profiles supplied with the program), Acrobat can display an error, provide information, fix a problem, or just ignore the results.

To view preflight options, choose *Preflight* from the Print Production toolbar. Be patient; it takes a moment for the Preflight dialog to appear. The Preflight dialog (**Figure 13.16**) consists of four tabs across the top (Profiles, Results, Standards, and Options) and the main options window beneath them. Profiles are organized in groups such as PDF analysis, PDF standards compliance, and so on. Click the triangle next to a group name to display the profiles within that group.

Figure 13.16 *Acrobat XI Pro ships with a wide variety of preflight checks and fixups. The Single Checks and Single Fixups are geared toward quick checks and repairs of common problems.*

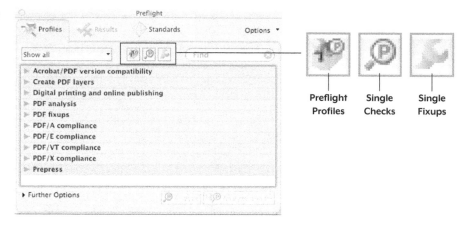

The three icons above the groups of profiles allow you to choose from the group list (Preflight Profiles), Single Checks, or Single Fixups. Single Checks are preset checks that look for a single common problem, such as RGB content or fonts that aren't embedded. Single Fixups can repair a single common problem by performing repairs such as RGB to CMYK conversion.

Once you've selected the preflight profile to run, click the *Analyze* button below the list of profiles. If there's a long list of problems in the preflight report, Acrobat offers a quick way to find the problem visually. Select the item in the preflight report window and then click the Show button next to the report entry; Acrobat displays a dashed red line around the object in question. For a more definitive indicator, select the line in the report, then click the *Show in Snap* button (**Figure 13.17**). The item is displayed in a floating window so you can identify it. Why is it called *Snap*? As your mother would say, "Well, it just is."

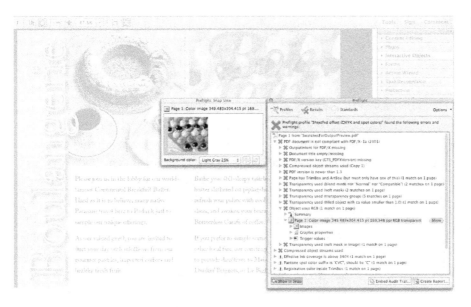

Figure 13.17 *Click the Show in Snap button to display a thumbnail of problem content.*

While Acrobat ships with an extensive set of prefabricated preflight profiles, you may still want to create a custom profile for your needs. The easiest way to do this is to select an existing profile, duplicate it, and then modify it to suit your needs. Select a profile that gives you a good start, and then choose Duplicate Preflight Profile from the Options drop-down menu. Name the new profile, and then modify its settings (**Figure 13.18**).

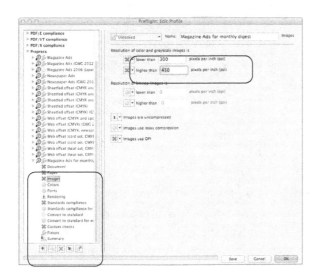

Figure 13.18 *To edit a custom profile, choose a topic from the profile's list of tests, modify the parameters to fit your needs, and then save as a new profile.*

If you need to preflight multiple files with the same profile, you can automate the process by creating a Preflight Droplet. In the main Preflight dialog, select a profile, and then choose *Create Preflight Droplet* from the Options menu.

In the Droplet Setup dialog, you can designate Success and Error folders, allowing Acrobat to sort the preflighted PDF files into separate folders so you can quickly determine which ones passed the preflight criteria (**Figure 13.19**). Acrobat creates a Droplet icon to represent the batch process. To start the process, shift-click to select multiple PDF files, and then drag the whole bunch on top of the Droplet. The preflight-and-sort process doesn't change the PDF files to Acrobat XI files. It just peeks inside the files and sorts them according to the assigned preflight profile without resaving the PDF.

Magazine Ads

Figure 13.19 *To set up a Preflight Droplet, choose a profile and then specify handling for PDFs that pass and those that fail. Here, the Droplet will move the passing PDFs to the MagazinePreflight_PASS folder, and the failing PDFs will go in the MagazinePreflight_FAIL folder. Click the Save button, and Acrobat creates a Droplet wherever you specify.*

Repair Tools

Once you've found all the problems with a PDF file, how do you fix them? Some problems—such as missing fonts, text reflow, and low-resolution images—are best fixed in the originating application. But you can still fix some common problems without leaving Acrobat by using the built-in repair tools (and the fixup functions in the preflight profiles).

Ink Manager

If the Output Preview display has shown that the PDF file contains extraneous spot colors, rather than return to the original application, you can repair the problem with the Ink Manager module of the Print Production tools. Choose an incorrect spot ink in the list, and then select the correct spot ink from the Ink Alias list at the bottom of the dialog. This re-maps all content that is in the wrong spot color so that it will be output on the correct plate (**Figure 13.20**).

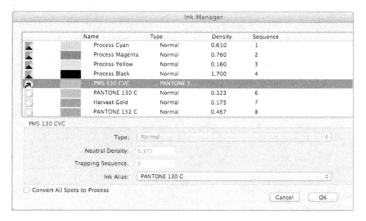

Figure 13.20 *Use the Ink Manager to map one spot color to another spot color. Select the errant spot color in the list, and then use the Ink Alias list to choose the target ink. You can also convert all spot colors to process with one click, or map a spot ink to a process ink.*

There is a bug in the Ink Manager display on the Mac: Spot colors are displayed as blank areas rather than colorful approximations of the actual inks (the display is correct on Windows). It's just One of Those Things; the Ink Manager works correctly despite the visual shortfall (**Figure 13.21**).

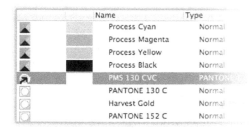

Figure 13.21 *A display bug in Acrobat X and XI on the Mac results in blank spot colors in the Ink Manager. You'll learn to ignore it.*

But there's a catch: Ink Manager settings only affect the PDF temporarily. If you were to output the job directly from Acrobat (which is rare), the output would correctly reflect the Ink Manager settings. But if you save, close, and then reopen the file, you'll be appalled to see that the extraneous spot colors, like zombies in cheap B-movies, have returned. There's good news, though: You can make Ink Manager settings permanent in a PDF by using the Convert Colors tool.

Convert Colors

If you've discovered that you have RGB images in a PDF, and you have no access to the original file to generate a PDF, you can select the Convert Colors tool on the Print Production toolbar to convert RGB content to CMYK. You can specify a document profile as well as a destination space to ensure an appropriate conversion (**Figure 13.22**). Also, the Convert Colors function can make Ink Manager choices permanent. When you click OK in the Convert Colors dialog, you are warned that the changes cannot be undone. But the file is not automatically saved—just choose *File > Revert* to start over.

Figure 13.22 *Select Convert Colors to make color-space changes such as RGB to CMYK, CMYK to grayscale, and so on. This also makes any Ink Manager choice permanent in the file.*

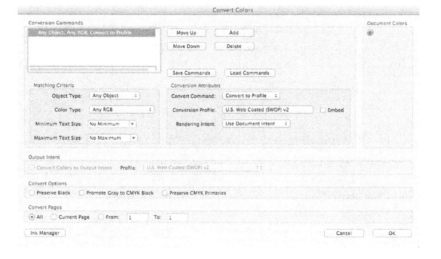

Add Printer Marks

If you need to add trim and crop marks to a PDF file, you can specify trim and bleed marks, as well as color bars and page information, by using the Add Printer Marks tool. You can also select from several styles of printer marks, comparable to the ones generated by InDesign and Illustrator. For the position of such marks to be correct, the PDF file must contain properly defined TrimBox and BleedBox information from the originating application (**Figure 13.23**).

Figure 13.23 *Acrobat allows you to add printer marks based on the internally defined trim and bleed information. But there's a secret to making this work.*

When you click OK in the Printer Marks dialog box, Acrobat alerts you that this operation cannot be undone and asks if you want to proceed. Bravely click OK.

When you add marks, they will initially fall outside the visible edge of the page, which will make you think you've done something wrong—you haven't. You just have to follow up by expanding the document's dimensions so the marks show. The notification that follows the addition of printer marks is unnecessarily confusing (**Figure 13.24**): It implies that the marks are over-lapping the artwork when in fact they fall completely outside the page. The notification also advises you to use the Crop dialog to fix the problem but doesn't tell you how to find the Crop dialog; that sort of "helpfulness" is just part of Acrobat's rustic charm.

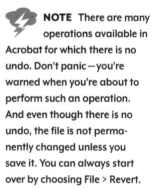 **NOTE** There are many operations available in Acrobat for which there is no undo. Don't panic—you're warned when you're about to perform such an operation. And even though there is no undo, the file is not perma-nently changed unless you save it. You can always start over by choosing File > Revert.

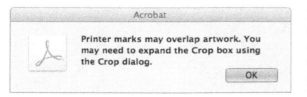

Figure 13.24 *The alert is actually trying to tell you that the page size is too small to reveal the printer marks you've added.*

Set Page Boxes

The Set Page Boxes dialog box allows you to crop a PDF or increase its canvas. If you've used the Printer Marks tool, the Set Page Boxes dialog box is your logical next stop. You'll need to add sufficient new material on the page to allow the marks to be visible. Adding one inch in both directions will usually do the trick. For example, if you've added marks to a page that's currently 10.25 by 8.25 inches, set the new page dimensions to 11.25 by 9.25 inches. Then the newly added printer marks will be visible (**Figure 13.25**).

Figure 13.25 *Printer marks won't be visible until you increase the page size in the Set Page Boxes dialog box.*

There are two paths to the Set Page Boxes dialog box (**Figure 13.26**): Under the Pages tools, select the Crop tool, click and drag in the page, then press Enter/Return to open the dialog box, or just choose Set Page Boxes in the Print Production tools.

View Controls

Crop Margins

Change Page Size

Page Range

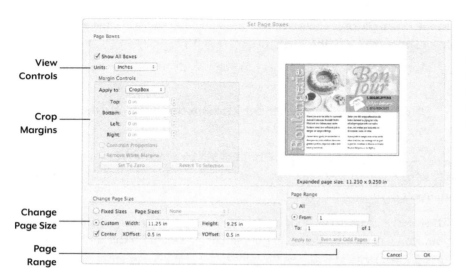

Figure 13.26 *Use the controls in the Set Page Boxes dialog box to view the TrimBox and BleedBox indicators, visually crop a PDF, or expand the page size to accommodate added printer marks.*

While increasing the page size actually changes the dimensions of the PDF page, cropping with the Margin Controls just visually masks out the area outside the margin dimensions. Page content still exists—it just doesn't show. That's why cropped PDF files show no reduction in file size. Everything is still there, lurking. Since cropping isn't final, you may find that some other applications ignore cropping instructions and show the original full content.

Try it: open a PDF and under the Pages tools, select the Crop tool, drag in the page to create an arbitrary crop, press Enter/Return to open the Set Page Boxes dialog box, then click OK. It appears that you have cropped the PDF.

Save and close the file, then reopen it and return to the Set Page Boxes dialog box. Under Margin Controls, press the *Set To Zero* button and you'll see that nothing has truly been eliminated.

But don't despair: There *is* a way to kill the zombie. Usually, that requires a head shot, but in Acrobat, your weapon of choice is a Preflight Fixup. If you're lucky, and you're trying to just shave the bleed off a PDF made from Illustrator or InDesign, both of which explicitly define the trim and bleed boxes in PDFs, it's a fairly easy fix. Launch *Preflight* in the Print Production tools, then select the Select Single Fixups icon ( ).

From the Options menu at the upper right, choose *Create New Preflight Fixup*. In the Create Fixup dialog, name the new fixup, and choose the *Pages* option in the Fixup Category column. On the right, choose *Set page geometry boxes*. In the bottom half of the panel, use these settings:

- **Set pagebox:** MediaBox (meaning "get ready to change the imaginary piece of paper")

- **Dimension based on:** Relative to TrimBox (meaning "use the dimensions of the TrimBox")

Click OK to return to the main Preflight panel. Select your new fixup, then click the *Fix* button. Acrobat asks you to save the new PDF; name and save it, then click OK.

The bleed appears to be gone, but if you're paranoid (printing will do that to you), you will feel compelled to double-check. Relaunch the Set Page Boxes function and squeal with joy: It really is gone—at least as far as Acrobat and most other applications are concerned.

Fix Hairlines

Thin lines can come from CAD artwork or from vector art that's been greatly reduced in a page layout. While direct-to-plate imaging and newer press controls provide the ability to retain and print small details that might have eroded on press 20 years ago, a line of extremely thin width can sometimes benefit from a little fluffing up to ensure imaging.

The Fix Hairlines tool allows you to increase the weight of stroked lines using a threshold value (**Figure 13.27**). It also offers options for padding Type 3 fonts (which can contain patterned or gray components) or pattern fills. A pattern fill could contain hundreds (or thousands) of lines, which would have to be modified during the hairline fixing process. But in a typical PDF file, the hairline fixing should just take a few seconds.

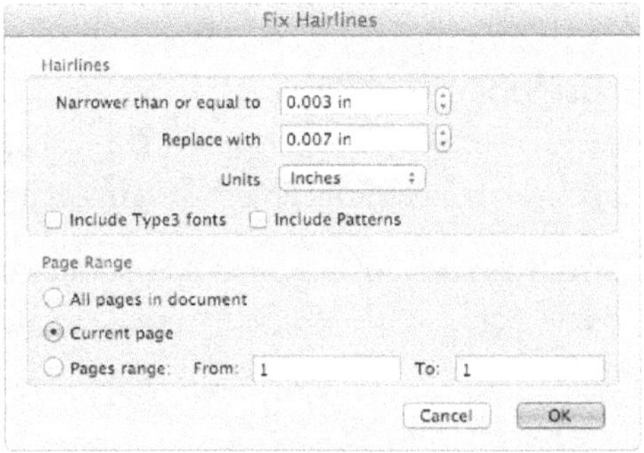

Figure 13.27 *The Fix Hairlines tool adds weight to thin strokes. You may never need this capability, but it's nice to know it's available.*

Transparency Flattener Preview

If your print service provider can't accept PDF files containing live transparency, such as PDF/X-4 files generated by InDesign or Illustrator, you can use Acrobat's Transparency Flattening controls to manage the flattening process (**Figure 13.28**). It's best to return to the originating application and generate a new PDF in keeping with the printer's desired specs, but if you've inherited a PDF that must be flattened before submitting to print, Acrobat gives you full control over the process.

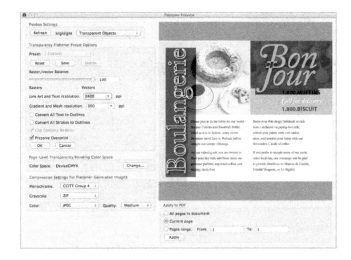

Figure 13.28 *The Transparency Flattening options enable you to see what areas will be affected by flattening.*

Drag the Raster/Vector Balance slider all the way to the right. You should see 100 in the Raster/Vector value. Use the resolution of the print service provider's RIP for the Line Art and Text resolution value, and set the Gradient and Mesh resolution to an appropriate image resolution, such as 300 ppi. Don't select the options for converting text or strokes to outlines, so you can avoid any thickening of text or rules. Click the Apply button to flatten the PDF; Acrobat notifies you that there is no undo for this operation.

PDF Optimizer

To make a lower-resolution PDF from an existing PDF file, or to save for a previous version of Acrobat, use PDF Optimizer if you have no access to the original application file. If you frequently have to create low-resolution PDFs from high-resolution PDFs, consider purchasing a dedicated solution that can streamline that process. Both **PDF Enhancer** and **PDF Shrink** from

Apago, Inc. (www.apagoinc.com) can accomplish surprising reductions in PDF file size while retaining reasonable appearance quality.

Trap Presets

NOTE Trapping is a complicated undertaking that's best left to the knowledgeable folks at the print service provider. In modern workflows, trapping is performed in the RIP, using the RIP vendor's proprietary built-in trapping solution. At this point, you may be wondering why Acrobat includes trapping features. I'm right there with you.

The Trap Presets feature in Acrobat doesn't actually create traps within the PDF file: It lets you specify trap settings that are used as instructions by a RIP that uses the Adobe In-RIP Trapping engine, but only if you print directly out of Acrobat (not common). The trap presets you create are available in Acrobat for future use.

Using External PDF Editors

PDFs are much more complex than they look. Under the hood, they're a spaghetti-like network of things such as XObjects, Arrays, Page Tree Nodes, and Optional Content Groups. That's why some edits can't be undone in Acrobat.

Even if you're using some of the excellent third-party add-ons for Acrobat to perform edits, it's advisable to work on a copy of your file just in case things fall apart.

As for using Adobe Illustrator to edit PDF files...don't. We all have, ah, friends who have done this in desperation in the olden days before PitStop and other PDF editing software. There was no viable alternative back then, and deadlines will drive you to do such unseemly things. But opening a PDF file in Illustrator without the necessary fonts available will wreck font embedding, and manipulating objects may cause unexpected loss of content. It's OK to edit PDFs saved directly from Illustrator, however. They're special files: The original Illustrator file is contained within the PDF, and that's what you'd actually be editing, provided you use the default option to retain Illustrator editing capabilities. But you're risking the possibility of file damage when you use Illustrator to edit PDF files created by other applications. It's preferable to return to the originating application to make edits. Then create a new PDF file and go on with your life.

Print Production Resources

14

When you enjoy what you do for a living, your education never stops. And if your education never stops, there's a good chance that you'll get more enjoyment out of what you do for a living. I once worked with a guy who didn't understand my fondness for learning new software. He once said to me, "If you learn that, they'll just make you do it all the time." Understandably, he couldn't fathom why I'd go to trade shows and conferences for fun. I'm sure he was really disturbed by the fact that I referred to the now-defunct Seybold Seminars in Boston as "Spring Break."

If you consider yourself an avid lifelong learner, and you'd like to add to your arsenal of printing knowledge, I hope you'll find the resources in this appendix useful. I've included information about organizations, online resources, books, and publications, and even some print-related tourist destinations. Really.

Organizations

Organizations related to the graphic arts industry vary in structure and offerings. Some are small, loosely knit, informal user groups that meet for snacks and presentations (not necessarily in that order of importance). Some larger organizations are more like corporations with regional chapters, and they often hold annual international conferences that include extensive seminar offerings, exhibit booths, and awards banquets.

Some organizations consist only of a Web presence and perhaps online forums. Regardless of the type of group that appeals to you, it's helpful to join organizations in order to see how other people approach design and print. Meeting other professionals in the industry, and seeing their work, is inspirational as well as educational.

User Groups

Unlike groups geared toward general design or printing industry members, user groups are usually devoted to a single software program or a suite of programs. The Adobe Acrobat and InDesign user groups hold chapter meetings in various cities around the world. While these two groups are supported by Adobe, they are funded and run by the group members themselves. A typical user group meeting might include demonstrations of software features, opportunities to have questions answered and technical issues solved by expert users or guest speakers, and a chance to win software, books, and other door prizes. And don't forget those snacks.

- **Adobe Acrobat User Community**   www.acrobatusers.com
  Started in 2006, the Acrobat User Community is growing rapidly. The Web site offers links to the individual chapters as well as tips, tutorials, and video presentations.

- **Adobe InDesign User Group**   www.indesignusergroup.com
  The InDesign User Group Web site is a rich portal to all things InDesign, including chapter information, useful plug-ins, and tutorials. It's also an easy doorway to the Adobe forums and the great InDesign Secrets site. Also, check out the InDesign Secrets podcast!

Online Communities and Forums

Joining online communities and forums is sort of like raising your hand and having the entire world answer you. Post a question in an online forum and the answers arrive in your in-box. Strong emotions and priceless information make the online communities like lively little villages, including the inevitable family squabbles.

Some forums (fora? forii?) are sponsored by software vendors and feature the expected product announcements and sales pitches in addition to useful resources. Some forums are maintained strictly by enthusiasts and are free of any corporate influence.

- **Adobe Forums**   www.adobe.com/support/forums
  Adobe forums are available for all Adobe products. While the forums are predominantly user-to-user in nature, they are moderated for civility, and Adobe staff are frequent contributors. The topics are a mix of general software issues and printing issues. When I can't solve a problem through a combination of the scientific method and banging my head on the desk, this is where I go.

- **National Association of Photoshop Professionals**
  www.photoshopuser.com
  The National Association of Photoshop Professionals (NAPP) is a national organization that provides online tutorials, publishes a bimonthly magazine, and hosts regional seminar events, in addition to its yearly Photoshop World conference. Members are also eligible for discounts on software and hardware.

- **Planet PDF**   www.planetpdf.com
  Planet PDF is a service of Debenu Software, a software development company devoted to Acrobat solutions. The searchable Planet PDF store offers a huge variety of plug-ins and software related to Acrobat. The online content also includes tips, tricks, and PDF-themed articles about a wide spectrum of industry uses for Acrobat.

- **PrintPlanet**   www.printplanet.com
  Created and maintained by Dave Mainwaring, the PrintPlanet forums are some of the most lively and most useful printing resources on the Web. Forums are devoted to individual topics, including prepress, digital printing, print technology, packaging, and fonts.

- **Typographica**   http://typographica.org
  Typographica is home to lively discussions on font designs and readability issues, as well as tutorials on font creation, which should give you some deep respect for the efforts of font designers.

Printing Industry Organizations

You may consider yourself to be purely a designer, with no interest in pursuing the technical end of the printing trade. But the online educational resources provided by these printing industry organizations can be very helpful when you want to understand more about printing processes.

- **IDEAlliance (International Digital Enterprise Alliance)**
  www.idealliance.org
  IDEAlliance offers seminars (including some that are available online) on highly technical topics such as XML. IDEAlliance now incorporates members of the International Prepress Association.

- **Printing Industries of America**   www.printing.org
  A result of the consolidation of PIA and GATF, Printing Industries of America hosts two specialty Centers of Excellence—the Center for Technology & Research (formerly GATF) and the Center for Digital Printing Excellence. State chapters serve members at a local/regional level.

Packaging Organizations

Packaging adds another dimension to the printing process, both literally and figuratively. These packaging organizations offer extensive educational resources.

- **Institute of Packaging Professionals**   www.iopp.org
  The IOPP Web site provides access to an extensive bookstore, comprehensive links to industry resources, and information on packaging conferences and training events.

- **Paperboard Packaging Council**   www.ppcnet.org
  Devoted to the folding-carton industry, the PPC Web site provides numerous informational pieces in PDF format, as well as links to publications and industry events. Additional, premium content is available to PPC members.

Technical Education Organizations

A number of organizations are devoted to providing education and reference materials to the printing industry.

- **Graphic Arts Educational and Research Foundation** www.gaerf.org
  GAERF was created by the National Association for Printing Leadership (NAPL); the Association for Suppliers of Printing, Publishing and Converting Technologies (known as NPES for some ancestral reason); and the Printing Industries of America, Inc. (PIA). These three associations own the Graphic Arts Show Company (GASC), which is responsible for a number of industry trade shows, including the huge annual GRAPH EXPO event in Chicago. GAERF finances educational programs and provides information about these programs on its Web site.

- **Specialty Graphic Imaging Association** www.sgia.org
  The SGIA focus is on printing processes that fall outside of offset printing. It offers coverage of a diverse range of imaging and printing processes, including screen printing, large-format inkjet printing, and textile printing.

Conferences and Trade Shows

Perhaps because the Internet has become such a rich source of information, some graphic arts and printing conferences have evaporated. It's no longer necessary to make a pilgrimage to a trade show for the sole purpose of cornering someone in a booth to get answers to questions about equipment or software. Instead, it's easy to go to a vendor Web site and scroll through posted information. The venerable Seybold Seminars—a victim of declining attendance—became a casualty of this shift in recent years. However, there's still a market for the large shows such as DRUPA and On Demand Expo, which feature running presses printing live jobs and finishing equipment spewing out pocket folders.

Printing Industry Events

In addition to featuring fully operational equipment, most printing exhibitions, conferences, and trade shows offer seminars on printing issues. Some exhibitors provide hands-on educational demos. And don't forget to fill up your bag with all those cute tchotchkes such as promotional light-up pens, squeezable software mascots, and company T-shirts.

- **DRUPA**   www.drupa.com (English-language site); www.drupa.de (German-language site)
  Held every even-numbered year, DRUPA is enormous. That's why it's a two-week event. Featuring nearly 2,000 vendors and welcoming nearly 400,000 attendees, DRUPA is a truly international print show. Attendees can see everything from software vendors to bookbinding machines.

- **Graphics of the Americas**   http://goaexpo.com
  This Florida-based trade show is oriented toward Latin American printing consumers. Many exhibitors speak Spanish, and many of the educational sessions are presented in Spanish.

- **IPEX**   www.ipex.org
  Held in England, IPEX is very much an international print show, with large attendance from the United States and Europe.

- **PRINT/GRAPHEXPO/CONVERTING EXPO**   www.gasc.org
  The GRAPH EXPO shows in Chicago occur annually, but every four years (2013, 2017, and so on), they kick it up a notch and present the even larger PRINT show. The PRINT shows include actual operating printing and finishing equipment and occupy the massive McCormick Place convention center from the floors to the rafters. Wear comfortable shoes.

Design Conferences

Many design-oriented conferences are worth attending for the hands-on training sessions that are presented by software sponsors or training consultants. Don't forget to leave extra space in your suitcase for those tempting paper samples, too.

- **AIGA National Conference**   www.aiga.org
  Because the AIGA partners closely with Adobe and Aquent, conferences often include training sessions.

- **HOW Design Conference**   www.howconference.com
  Software companies such as Adobe, Quark, and Extensis are sponsors
  and exhibitors at the HOW Design Conference. Take advantage of their
  hands-on training sessions as well as the software demonstrations in
  exhibit booths.

- **MogoMedia Conferences**   www.mogo-media.com
  The informal atmosphere encourages real-world questions and the
  opportunity to network. Periodic smaller regional seminars comple-
  ment the larger conference offerings.

- **PePcon: Print+ePublishing Conference**   www.pepconference.com
  Devoted to ebooks, print, tablets, interactive documents, and more.

- **Photoshop World Conference and Expo**   www.photoshopworld.com
  Fill your brain with seminars from the best photographers, instructors,
  and authors on the art of capturing and manipulating images. Rest up
  first, though.

Design and Printing Books

I know. We can read PDF files onscreen. But there is still no substitute for
the tactile joys of ink on paper. Maybe I'm just old-fashioned, but I still feel
that books are the most portable, shareable, tangible way to store information. Besides, how could you fill all those bookshelves with the impressive,
leather-bound spines of PDFs?

Desktop Publishing

- **Desktop Publishing for Prepress Production, Second Edition**, by
  Hal Hinderliter (ArtFlow Publishing, 2013)

- **Exploring Digital PrePress: The Art and Technology of Preparing
  Electronic Files for Printing**, by Reid Anderson (Delmar Learning, 2013)

- **From Design Into Print: Preparing Graphics and Text for Professional
  Printing**, by Sandee Cohen (Peachpit Press, 2009)
  A great sequel to *The Non-Designer's Scan and Print Book*, it's updated to
  reflect changes in technology and printing processes, and it's now in
  full color.

- **Inside the Publishing Revolution: The Adobe Story**, by Pamela Pfiffner (Adobe Press, 2002)
  This book is a rousing account of the huge upheavals in design and printing that have sprung from Adobe Systems. It introduces you to Adobe cofounders John Warnock and Charles Geschke and many of the inspired Adobe minds, and provides a fascinating timeline for the developments in software and technology that made desktop publishing possible.

General Design

While there are hundreds of books on all aspects of design, from color to type to visual concepts, three books stand out for capturing important basics. No fluff, just concise and effective information that illuminates concepts, making you think differently about aspects of design that are easily taken for granted.

- **Before & After**, by John McWade (Peachpit Press, 2003)
  John McWade makes design and production look so easy. Along with his examples of great design solutions, he explains printing requirements and suggests approaches to help you deal with printing limitations.

- **Before & After Graphics for Business**, by John McWade (Peachpit Press, 2005)

- **The Mac Is Not a Typewriter, Second Edition**, by Robin Williams (Peachpit Press, 2003)
  One of the classic guides for desktop publishing, this book helps you learn the rules for creating professional-looking type. Topics range from avoiding amateur mistakes, such as double spaces and straight quotes, to typographic niceties, such as kerning and hanging punctuation.

- **Professional Design Techniques with Adobe Creative Suite 3**, by Scott Citron (Adobe Press, 2007)
  Although the book is written for CS3, the design guidance is not application-specific, and the step-by-step instructions make sense even if you're using a later version of the software.

General Printing

Some of these printing tomes are encyclopedic and can be measured by the pound as well as page count. Some are more instructional in nature. It's difficult to single out any of the books in this list—they're all quite good. But I've earmarked several as being essential guides for designers wanting to deepen their understanding of printing.

- **The Basics of Print Production,** by Mary Hardesty (Graphic Arts Technical Foundation, 2002)

- **The Complete Guide to Digital Color: Creative Use of Color in the Digital Arts**, by Chris Linford (Collins Design, 2004)

- **A Field Guide to Folding**, by Trish Witkowski (Finishing Experts Group, 2007)
  A condensed version of the FOLDRite system, highlighting 85 of the most common folding styles used in the industry today.

- **Fold: The Professional's Guide to Folding (2-Volume Set)**, by Trish Witkowski (Finishing Experts Group, 2002)
  A painstakingly researched and wonderfully detailed (and readable) encyclopedia of folding techniques.

- **Forms, Folds, and Sizes: All the Details Graphic Designers Need to Know But Can Never Find**, by Poppy Evans (Rockport Press, 2004)
  The title says it all: This is a great guide to important printing issues and an essential reference for designers.

- **The GATF Guide to Desktop Publishing**, by Hal Hinderliter and Jim Cavuoto (Graphic Arts Technical Foundation, 2000)

- **Getting It Printed, Fourth Edition**, by Eric Kenly (HOW Design Books, 2004)

- **Getting It Right in Print: Digital Prepress for Graphic Designers,** by Mark Gatter (Harry N. Abrams, 2005)

- **A Guide to Graphic Print Production,** by Kaj Johansson, Peter Lundberg, and Robert Ryberg (John Wiley and Sons, 2002)

- **Handbook of Digital Publishing, Volume I and II**, by Michael L. Kleper (Prentice Hall, 2001)

- **Makeready: A Prepress Resource,** by Dan Margulis (Henry Holt and Company, 1996)
  This book is out of print but is worth searching for on used-book sites.

- **Official Adobe Print Publishing Guide, Second Edition**, by Brian P. Lawler (Adobe Press, 2005)
  This book covers print processes from offset to digital, with excellent examples explaining such concepts as duotones, trapping, and proofing.

- **Pocket Pal, 20th Edition**, by Michael Bruno, Frank Romano, and Michael Riordan (Graphic Arts Technical Foundation, 2007)
  The *Pocket Pal* was first published by International Paper Company, and it is updated every few years. It's small but mighty and includes a glossary and great, short explanations of printing processes. You should have a copy in your backpack at all times.

- **Printing Technology**, by J. Michael Adams and Penny Ann Dolin (Thomson Delmar Learning, 2001)

Typography

Desktop publishing put typesetting into the hands of many eager typists, who often lacked the instincts or training for typographic finesse. But enhancements to design software and the enticing possibilities afforded by OpenType fonts have inspired a return to the art and craft of typography. If you love beautiful typography, or you want to learn more about how typography works as part of designing and printing, here are some books that are part reference, part inspiration.

- **The Complete Manual of Typography**, by James Felici (Adobe Press, 2002)

- **The Elements of Typographic Style**, by Robert Bringhurst (Hartley and Marks Publishers, 2004)

- **Thinking with Type: A Critical Guide for Designers, Writers, Editors, and Students**, by Ellen Lupton (Princeton Arch, 2004)

- **U&lc: Influencing Design and Typography**, by John D. Berry, editor (Mark Batty, 2005)

Software-Specific Books

Somehow, the original software manuals are never enough, are they? They're either arcane or a bit skimpy. And some of them appear to be written by engineers who are proud of the features but may have no idea how their software is used in the real world. The books listed are a great addition to (or replacement for) the original user guides.

Illustrator

- **Illustrator CC: Visual QuickStart Guide**, by Elaine Weinmann, and Peter Lourekas (Peachpit Press, 2013)

InDesign

- **Exploring InDesign CS6**, by Terry Rydberg (Delmar Cengage Learning, 2012)
  A wonderful textbook to teach yourself (or someone else) how to be productive and creative in InDesign. In addition to teaching software techniques, Terry Rydberg weaves in design advice, production knowledge, and subtle hints to do things the right way.
- **InDesign CC for Macintosh and Windows: Visual QuickStart Guide**, by Sandee Cohen (Peachpit Press, 2013)
- **InDesign Type: Professional Typography with Adobe InDesign (2nd Edition)**, by Nigel French (Adobe Press, 2010)
- **Interactive InDesign CC: Bridging the Gap Between Print and Digital Publishing**, by Mira Rubin (Focal Press, 2013)
- **Real World Adobe InDesign CC**, by Olav Martin Kvern, David Blatner, and Bob Bringhurst (Peachpit Press, 2013)

Photoshop

Because Photoshop is important to users across a broad spectrum of industries—from hobbyists and office users to professional photographers, industrial designers, Web designers, video artists, scientists, and medical professionals—there is a tidal wave of books for learning and exploring the application. You could probably add a room to your house constructed solely of Photoshop books (of course, check your local building codes first).

- **The Digital Print: Preparing Images in Lightroom and Photoshop for Printing**, by Jeff Schewe (Peachpit Press, 2013)
- **Photoshop CC: The Missing Manual**, by Lesa Snider (Peachpit Press, 2013) This truly is the missing manual—it's an absolutely indispensible reference for Photoshop.

Photoshop Specialty Topics

There are a few indispensable resources that can greatly improve your mastery of Photoshop in production.

- **Photoshop LAB Color: The Canyon Conundrum and Other Adventures in the Most Powerful Colorspace**, by Dan Margulis (Peachpit Press, 2005)
- **Photoshop Masking & Compositing (2nd Edition)**, by Katrin Eismann, Sean Duggan, and James Porto (New Riders Press, 2012)
- **Photoshop Studio with Bert Monroy: Digital Painting**, by Bert Monroy (New Riders, 2008) Even if you don't aspire to creating digital confections like Bert Monroy's astonishing photorealistic pieces, you can learn valuable techniques for creating something out of nothing when you're called upon to retouch challenging images.
- **Professional Photoshop: The Classic Guide to Color Correction, Fifth Edition**, by Dan Margulis (Peachpit Press, 2006)
- **Real World Color Management, Second Edition**, by Bruce Fraser, Chris Murphy, and Fred Bunting (Peachpit Press, 2004)

Publications

If you agonize over the prospect of killing trees to print magazines, note that some of these publications are available electronically. Highly recommended electronic versions include *Before & After Magazine*, *Design Tools Monthly*, and *InDesign Magazine* (which includes QuickTime movies).

Desktop Publishing

- **Design Tools Monthly**   www.design-tools.com
  Great tips, bug alerts, and industry news condensed into one valuable resource. In addition to the monthly newsletter, you receive shareware and freeware software and fonts. Available in both print and downloadable PDF versions.

- **InDesign Magazine**   www.indesignmag.com
  Despite the name, *InDesign Magazine* is about more than just InDesign. Published six times a year as an electronic magazine (there is no printed version), this engaging publication includes great tips and tricks, information about bug workarounds, and articles about printing issues, plug-ins, and design in general.

Design

- **CMYK Magazine**   www.cmykmag.com
- **Communication Arts**   www.commarts.com
- **HOW Magazine**   www.howdesign.com
- **Print Magazine**   www.printmag.com

Printing Technology

- **American Printer**   www.americanprinter.com
- **Package Design Magazine**   www.packagedesignmag.com
- **Printing Impressions Magazine**   www.piworld.com

Tutorials

- **Before & After Magazine**   www.bamagazine.com
  Succinct and enjoyable, B&A is a combination of tutorials and good design sense.

- **Layers Magazine**   www.layersmagazine.com

Video Training

Don't have time to read? (Darned deadlines...) Videos may be faster, and they're likely to be more current than printed materials.

- The **Learn By Video** series from Adobe Press is always current. http://www.adobepress.com/series/series.asp?ser=2488634

- There's more than one reason why **Lynda.com** is the standard of the video-training industry. In the interest of full disclosure, I should divulge that I'm a Lynda.com author (and subscriber). http://www.lynda.com

Destinations

Maybe I'm the only person who would go to a printing-themed museum on vacation.

Oh, I'm not? Good! I'll see you there!

- **Ben Franklin's Courtyard and Print Shop**
  www.ushistory.org/tour/franklin-court.htm
  318 Market Street
  Philadelphia, PA 19106

- **Center for Book Arts**
  www.centerforbookarts.org
  28 West 27th Street, 3rd Floor
  New York, NY 10001

- **Crane Museum of Papermaking**
  www.crane.com/about/museum
  30 South Street
  Dalton, MA 01226

- **Hamilton Wood Type and Printing Museum**
  www.woodtype.org
  1619 Jefferson Street
  Two Rivers, WI 54241

- **International Printing Museum**
  www.printmuseum.org
  315 Torrance Boulevard
  Carson, CA 90745

- **Museum of Printing**
  www.museumofprinting.org
  800 Massachusetts Avenue
  North Andover, MA 01845

- **Museum of Printing History**
  www.printingmuseum.org
  1324 West Clay Street
  Houston, TX 77019

- **Robert C. Willliams Paper Museum**
  www.ipst.gatech.edu/amp/index.html
  Institute of Paper Science and Technology
  Georgia Institute of Technology
  500 10th Street NW
  Atlanta, GA 30332-0620

Index

CPSIA information can be obtained
at www.ICGtesting.com
Printed in the USA
LVHW011137281119
638735LV00012B/445